AMERICA IN LITERATURE

The West

AMERICA IN LITERATURE

General Editor, Max Bogart

The Northeast, James Lape, editor
The South, Sara Marshall, editor
The West, Peter Monahan, editor
The Midwest, Ronald Szymanski, editor
The Small Town, Flory Jones Schultheiss, editor
The City, Adele Stern, editor

AMERICA IN LITERATURE

The West

EDITED BY

Peter Monahan

Sir Francis Drake High School
San Anselmo, California

CHARLES SCRIBNER'S SONS • NEW YORK

Library of Congress Cataloging in Publication Data
Main entry under title:
America in literature: the West.
  Bibliography: p.
  Includes index.
  1. American literature. 2. The West—Literary
collections. I. Monahan, Peter J.
PS509.W47A5   810'.8'032   78-24512
ISBN 0-684-11087-0

1 3 5 7 9 11 13 15 17 19 V/P 20 18 16 14 12 10 8 6 4 2

Printed in the United States of America

COVER ILLUSTRATION: *Stampeded by Lightning* by Frederick Remington. Courtesy of The Thomas Gilcrease Institute of American History and Art, Tulsa, Oklahoma.

Picture Research: Yvonne Freund

ACKNOWLEDGMENTS

LOREN EISELEY, "The Flow of the River." Copyright 1953 by Loren Eiseley. Reprinted from *The Immense Journey,* by Loren Eiseley, by permission of Random House, Inc.
ROBINSON JEFFERS, "The Beauty of Things." Copyright 1951 by Robinson Jeffers. Reprinted from *Selected Poems,* by Robinson Jeffers, by permission of Random House, Inc.
JOHN MUIR, "The Mono Trail" from *My First Summer in the Sierras* by John Muir. Copyright 1911 by John Muir, renewed 1939 by Wanda Muir Hanna. Reprinted by permission of Houghton Mifflin Company.

Acknowledgments continue on page 307, an extension of the copyright page.

CONTENTS

AMERICA IN LITERATURE

The West

Introduction

Eastward I go only by force;
but westward I go free. —HENRY DAVID THOREAU

Any collection of western literature must initially settle two obvious questions: Where does the West begin? When did the period end? The frontier has been part of the American experience from Colonial times, a two-hundred-year challenge composed in part of wilderness, risk, and the promise of a new, presumably better, life. As the nation has moved across the continent, exploring and settling and developing the virgin lands, geography as much as the will of the people determined the shape of regional character. But most authorities concur that the West begins in the second tier of states beyond the Mississippi, from the Dakotas to Texas. All agree that, although free land disappeared in the early 1900s, the West is still booming.

The American West spans more than half our history and forty percent of the continent. During the first half of the nineteenth century, when boundaries expanded from the Mississippi to the Pacific, it generated ideas that shaped the nation's destiny, and it produced a gallery of figures that became the stuff of legend. In the twentieth century it remains a region where superlatives still apply, where the spectacle of the land still elicits wonder, and where Americans still come in search of a new life. One poet has called it "a country of the mind," a region where imagination is not confined by foreclosed possibilities. Beyond the geographical boundaries and facts of history, something vital to the national experience survives in the West. The region is still growing, still forming. Hope still lives there.

Without exaggeration, elements of epic inhere in the settlement of the western frontier. Tragedy, too, if one remembers the Indians. Much has been written about it all. From the beginning journals were kept, letters went East. Newspapermen and historians chronicled "the winning of the

Introduction

West," and dime novels created melodramatic fables of heroism and adventure, some of them based on fact. Serious writers treated the experiences of men and women whose lives were part of the Westward Movement, or who simply happened to live beyond the hundredth meridian. Eastern writers allowed scale and grandeur to this writing but tended to discount the rest as too new, unformed. From this early critical disdain for local color and regional material grew the first misconception about much western writing: it was quaint, provincial, minor. Even by mid-twentieth century, a considerable body of writing was downgraded, with few exceptions, as local color. Yet besides pulp fiction factories and local colorists, a core of first-rate fiction exists, not "western," though regional.

Another major misconception persists concerning western literature. For many readers a "Western" without horses is unthinkable. The popular story takes place on sage-covered plains or amid mountain wilds where mustangs and bears outnumber humans. These genre "Westerns" (with a capital W) descend from the dime novel and have provided formula entertainment since Owen Wister's Virginian first rode down the trail. Wister was followed by able practitioners like Zane Grey, Luke Short, Max Brand, and Louis L'Amour. One authority has tallied nine dusty plots between sun-up and sundown: "the rustler story, the range war or empire story, the 'good but not worthy' story, the marshal or dedicated lawman story, the revenge story, the outlaw story, the cavalry and Indian story, the ranch story, and the Union Pacific story."* These plots have been virtually ridden into the ground by movies and television, whose commercial dreariness has for the time being almost killed off the genre for all but the most saddle-hardened fans.

For other readers, any fiction beyond the Mississippi represents western literature. Yet the West is made up of many regions and never was as singular as the legends that grew there. Geography and history dictated otherwise. The High Plains, the Southwest, the Rocky Mountains, the Great Basin, the Pacific Northwest, and California—all developed distinctive societies. Gifted writers have grown in and written of each region, moving beyond provincial boundaries; and although all come from the West, their original works address themes larger than mere locality or formula.

The Westward Movement stirred more than writers' imaginations. The

*John R. Milton, "Two Wests," *Antaeus*, Spring/Summer 1977, p. 96.

2

minds of Americans were excited by the prospect of taming a wilderness, discovering El Dorado, claiming virgin land, making a new life, and extending national boundaries all the way to the Pacific. With all the furious, epic activity, four distinct ways of regarding the development of the American West took shape and can be distinguished.

The first of these, which appeared in the early 1800s, was called Manifest Destiny. Actually more a doctrine, it decreed that expansion was part of a natural and inevitable process that compelled the United States to become a continental nation. To the Mexican government in Texas and California, as well as to the English traders in Oregon, this patriotism might seem like imperialism; but never mind. Politicians and poets preached its virtues. War, settlement, and the discovery of gold resolved the matter, and by 1848 the republic stretched from sea to shining sea.

The second of these notions, the Great Wild West Show, began long before Buffalo Bill took his act east. This heroic entertainment featured Pathfinders, El Dorado, the Oregon Trail, the Homestead Act, Railroad Moguls and Cattle Kings and Timber Barons (curious titles for a democracy), Cowpokes and Outlaws and Lawmen, and finally Indian Wars, all portrayed as heroic adventure. When the West was finally won, the reality often proved harsher than the romance—failed hopes, failed farms, failed banks. Still there was always a second chance or another town. So the story went.

A third view transformed this gaudy, sometimes grim, spectacle into theory. In 1893 Frederick Turner proposed a theory of history that has since been known as the Turner Thesis. Actually a hypothesis, it held that the frontier continually renewed the strength of American democracy. By providing free land and fresh opportunity to all "with strong arms and stout hearts," the West guaranteed equality and assured the triumph of the common people. The struggle to bring civilization to the wilderness fostered virtues of individualism, self-reliance, inventiveness, and restless energy. By confirming fundamental beliefs, the Turner Thesis influenced the way we think of our country and ourselves.

A final view, more recent and less optimistic, regarded the West as a plundered province, heedlessly exploited. The genuine achievements of conquest and settlement were accompanied by systematic plunder. The original inhabitants were brutally dispossessed. Natural resources were claimed, staked, extracted, and abandoned: fur, gold, buffalo, minerals, timber, range land were energetically trapped, sluiced, shot, mined, logged, grazed to depletion. What remained was paved, dammed, and developed in grand projects designed without much consideration of consequences. Reckless growth despoiled the land in a pattern described by one Secretary of the Interior as "rape, ruin, and run." Human resources, too, were shamefully exploited: Chinese, Irish, Chicanos, Okies and Blacks knew a darker side of the westward vision. This pattern is also part of western history.

Although twentieth-century urban and industrial growth has changed these ideas, as well as the land and its people, each of the four views retains fierce advocates. Altered notions of Manifest Destiny, Wild West Show, Frontier Theory, and Plundered Province still lure dreamers and developers, still lull and stimulate inhabitants, two-thirds of whom are now gathered in sprawling urban-suburban centers. And these ideas enter literature as they are acted out, argued, and modified in the lives of westerners.

The body of distinguished western writing is not limited to fiction. Some of its finest literature can be discovered in the works of naturalists like John Muir and Loren Eiseley, historians like Bernard De Voto and Francis Parkman, poets like Robinson Jeffers and William Stafford, essayists like Michael Arlen and Joan Didion. Therefore, this collection will extend beyond standard literary selections and established reputations. Obviously the folklore, legends, chronicles, history, and literature of the West cannot be contained in a single volume. A library could hardly contain them all. To give some sense of the whole, chapters deal variously with the land, its people, their history, and finally its present direction. The voices are those of the first explorers like Lewis and Clark, early travelers like Mark Twain, settlers like Elinore Pruitt Stewart, historians like Wallace Stegner, as well as novelists and poets. ("Suggestions for Further Reading" lists other important writers whose works are not included here.)

Literature can help us come to terms with the West of legend and fact. Writers, whether recent travelers like Alistair Cooke or residents like John Steinbeck, by capturing the spirit of the place and its people, contribute to the rich and inexhaustible heritage of the West. Anthologies can sketch themes and represent some writers, but at best they serve as an introduction to a larger field of writing. Like the land, the literature of the West is open and expanding. Great things can be expected of it.

The Land

This place is the noblest thing I have ever seen.
No imaginable
Human presence here could do anything—ROBINSON JEFFERS

The geography of the West is at once magnificent and formidable. Beyond an imaginary line running south from the Dakotas to Texas, the region is vast and marked by extremes: highest and lowest, driest and wettest, hottest and coldest. Its terrain presents imposing barriers: mountain ranges—the Rockies, Sierras, Cascades; canyons—the Colorado, Columbia, and Snake; deserts—the Great Basin, Sonora, Mojave. In all its space and distances east of the Pacific slope, the region is dominated by aridity; little rain falls and the percentage of arable land is small. No one has put it better than Wallace Stegner:

> That is the West's ultimate unity: aridity. In other ways it has a bewildering variety. Its life zones go all the way from arctic to subtropical, from reindeer moss to cactus, from mountain goat to horned toad. Its range of temperature is as wide as its range of precipitation. It runs through twelve degrees of latitude and nearly three miles of altitude. It is short grass plains, alkali flats, creosote bush deserts, irrigated alluvial valleys, sub-arctic fir forests, bare, sun-smitten stone. From the 100th meridian to the Pacific is two-fifths of the United States, by common consent of the local booster clubs the biggest, widest, highest, hopefulest, friendliest region of the footstool.*

*Stegner, "Introduction," *The Sound of Mountain Water* (Garden City, N.Y.: Doubleday, 1969), p. 15.

The Land

Americans have looked upon the western lands alternately as a wilderness to be tamed, a resource to be exploited, a heritage to be preserved, or a dreary, barren passage on the way to El Dorado or Disneyland. When explorers first penetrated the great plains, they called it the Great American Desert. Later reports from the Pacific states promised a New Eden. The Indians who already lived there looked upon the earth as something that belonged to all people and was owned by none. Before it was taken from them, the land was sacred to all tribes, and each found remote and spectacular land forms good places to commune with spirits.

After more than a century of development, the magnificence of the landscape has not been entirely effaced. Some has been saved by the federal government, which administers the National Forests, Bureau of Land Management, and National Park Service. Some has been preserved through the efforts of westerners, who, because they were aware of the way in which land shapes life and had witnessed ruthless development which devastated watersheds and range lands, acted to protect remaining natural wonders.

Earlier writers had been inspired by scenery, interested in natural history, or had imagined themselves as part of the natural world. But until these ways of seeing were fused in the works of Henry David Thoreau, people had looked upon nature as detached observers rather than as participants. Ruled either by artistic impulse, which could appreciate the beautiful and interpret the divine, or directed by a scientific attitude, which could study and classify, or driven by commercial interest, which could attract investment and literally move mountains and rivers, people saw the natural world as something separate from their own being. After Thoreau, a pioneer who never got farther west than the Hudson River, Americans could begin to sense the unity of all living things and perceive the majesty and mystery of the inanimate.

The Flow of the River

LOREN EISELEY

If there is magic on this planet, it is contained in water. Its least stir even, as now in a rain pond on a flat roof opposite my office, is enough to bring me searching to the window. A wind ripple may be translating itself into life. I have a constant feeling that some time I may witness that momentous miracle on a city roof, see life veritably and suddenly boiling out of a heap of rusted pipes and old television aerials. I marvel at how suddenly a water beetle has come and is submarining there in a spatter of green algae. Thin vapors, rust, wet tar and sun are an alembic remarkably like the mind; they throw off odorous shadows that threaten to take real shape when no one is looking.

Once in a lifetime, perhaps, one escapes the actual confines of the flesh. Once in a lifetime, if one is lucky, one so merges with sunlight and air and running water that whole eons, the eons that mountains and deserts know, might pass in a single afternoon without discomfort. The mind has sunk away into its beginnings among old roots and the obscure tricklings and movings that stir inanimate things. Like the charmed fairy circle into which a man once stepped, and upon emergence learned that a whole century had passed in a single night, one can never quite define this secret; but it has something to do, I am sure, with common water. Its substance reaches everywhere; it touches the past and prepares the future; it moves under the poles and wanders thinly in the heights of air. It can assume forms of exquisite perfection in a snowflake, or strip the living to a single shining bone cast up by the sea.

Many years ago, in the course of some scientific investigations in a remote western county, I experienced, by chance, precisely the sort of curious absorption by water—the extension of shape by osmosis—at which I have been hinting. You have probably never experienced in yourself the meandering roots of a whole watershed or felt your outstretched fingers touching, by some kind of clairvoyant extension, the brooks of snow-line glaciers at the same time that you were flowing toward the Gulf over the eroded debris of worndown mountains. A poet, MacKnight Black, has spoken of being "limbed . . . with waters gripping pole and pole." He had the idea, all right, and it is obvious that these sensations are not unique, but they are hard to come by; and the sort of extension of the senses that people will accept when they put their ear against a sea shell, they will smile at in the confessions of a bookish professor. What makes it worse is the fact that because of a traumatic experience in childhood, I am not a swimmer, and am inclined to be timid before any large body of water. Perhaps it was just this, in a way, that contributed to my experience.

As it leaves the Rockies and moves downward over the high plains towards the Missouri, the Platte River is a curious stream. In the spring floods, on occasion, it can be a mile-wide roaring torrent of destruction, gulping farms and bridges. Normally, however, it is a rambling, dispersed series of streamlets flowing erratically over great sand and gravel fans that are, in part, the remnants of a mightier Ice Age stream bed. Quicksands and shifting islands haunt its waters. Over it the prairie suns beat mercilessly throughout the summer. The Platte, "a mile wide and an inch deep," is a refuge for any heat-weary pilgrim along its shores. This is particularly true on the high plains before its long march by the cities begins.

The reason that I came upon it when I did, breaking through a willow thicket and stumbling out through ankle-deep water to a dune in the shade, is of no concern to this narrative. On various purposes of science I have ranged over a good bit of the country on foot, and I know the kinds of bones that come gurgling up through the gravel pumps, and the arrowheads of shining chalcedony that occasionally spill out of water-loosened sand. On that day, however, the sight of sky and willows and the weaving net of water murmuring a little in the shallows on its way to the Gulf stirred me, parched as I was with miles of walking, with a new idea: I was going to float. I was going to undergo a tremendous adventure.

The notion came to me, I suppose, by degrees. I had shed my clothes and was floundering pleasantly in a hole among some reeds when a great desire to stretch out and go with this gently insistent water began to pluck at me. Now to this bronzed, bold, modern generation, the struggle I waged with timidity while standing there in knee-deep water can only seem farcical; yet actually for me it was not so. A near-drowning accident in childhood had scarred my reactions; in addition to the fact that I was a nonswimmer, this "inch-deep river" was treacherous with holes and quicksands. Death was not precisely infrequent along its wandering and illusory channels. Like all broad wastes of this kind, where neither water nor land quite prevails, its thickets were lonely and untraversed. A man in trouble would cry out in vain.

I thought of all this, standing quietly in the water, feeling the sand shifting away under my toes. Then I lay back in the floating position that left my face to the sky, and shoved off. The sky wheeled over me. For an instant, as I bobbed into the main channel, I had the sensation of sliding down the vast tilted face of the continent. It was then that I felt the cold needles of the alpine springs at my fingertips and the warmth of the Gulf pulling me southward. Moving with me, leaving its taste upon my mouth and spouting under me in dancing springs of sand, was the immense body of the continent itself, flowing like the river was flowing, grain by grain, mountain by mountain, down to the sea. I was streaming over ancient sea beds thrust aloft where giant reptiles had once sported; I was wearing down the face of time and trundling cloud-wreathed ranges into oblivion. I touched my margins with the delicacy of a crayfish's antennae, and felt great fishes glide about their work.

I drifted by stranded timber cut by beaver in mountain fastnesses; I slid over shallows that had buried the broken axles of prairie schooners and the mired bones of mammoth. I was streaming alive through the hot and working ferment of the sun, or oozing secretively through shady thickets. I *was* water and the unspeakable alchemies that gestate and take shape in water, the slimy jellies that under the enormous magnification of the sun writhe and whip upward as great barbeled fish mouths, or sink indistinctly back into the murk out of which they arose. Turtle and fish and the pinpoint chirpings of individual frogs are all watery projections, concentrations—as man himself is a concentration—of that indescrible and liquid brew which is compounded in varying proportions of salt and sun and time. It has appearances, but at its heart lies water, and as I was finally edged gently against a sand bar and dropped like any log, I tottered as I rose. I knew once more the body's revolt against emergence into the harsh and unsupporting air, its reluctance to break contact with that mother element which still, at this late point in time, shelters and brings into being nine tenths of everything alive.

As for men, those myriad little detached ponds with their own swarming corpuscular life, what were they but a way that water has of going about beyond the reach of rivers? I, too, was a microcosm of pouring rivulets and floating driftwood gnawed by the mysterious animalcules of my own creation. I was three fourths water, rising and subsiding according to the hollow knocking in my veins: a minute pulse like the eternal pulse that lifts Himalayas and which, in the following systole, will carry them away.

The Beauty of Things

ROBINSON JEFFERS

To feel and speak the astonishing beauty of things—earth,
    stone and water,
Beast, man and woman, sun, moon and stars—
The blood-shot beauty of human nature, its thoughts, frenzies
    and passions,
And unhuman nature its towering reality—
For man's half dream; man, you might say, is nature dreaming,
    but rock
And water and sky are constant—to feel
Greatly, and understand greatly, and express greatly, the
    natural
Beauty, is the sole business of poetry.
The rest's diversion: those holy or noble sentiments, the
    intricate ideas,
The love, lust, longing: reasons, but not the reason.

Valley of the Yosemite, Albert Bierstadt

The Mono Trail

JOHN MUIR

August 7—Early this morning bade good-bye to the bears and blessed silver fir camp, and moved slowly eastward along the Mono Trail. At sundown camped for the night on one of the many small flowery meadows so greatly enjoyed on my excursion to Lake Tenaya. The dusty, noisy flock seems outrageously foreign and out of place in these nature gardens, more so than bears among sheep. The harm they do goes to the heart, but glorious hope lifts above all the dust and din and bids me look forward to a good time coming, when money enough will be earned to enable me to go walking where I like in pure wildness, with what I can carry on my back, and when the breadsack is empty, run down to the nearest point on the breadline for more. Nor will these run-downs be blanks, for, whether up or down, every step and jump on these blessed mountains is full of fine lessons.

August 8—Camp at the west end of Lake Tenaya. Arriving early, I took a walk on the glacier-polished pavements along the north shore, and climbed the magnificent mountain rock at the east end of the lake, now shining in the late afternoon light. Almost every yard of its surface shows the scoring and polishing action of a great glacier that enveloped it and swept heavily over its summit, though it is about two thousand feet high above the lake and ten thousand above sea-level. This majestic, ancient ice-flood came from the eastward, as the scoring and crushing of the surface shows. Even below the waters of the lake the rock in some places is still grooved and polished; the lapping of the waves and their disintegrating action have not as yet obliterated even the superficial marks of glaciation. In climbing the steepest polished places I had to take off shoes and stockings. A fine region this for study of glacial action in mountain-making. . . .

Made sketch of the lake, and sauntered back to camp, my iron-shod shoes clanking on the pavements disturbing the chipmunks and birds. After

13

dark went out to the shore,—not a breath of air astir, the lake a perfect mirror reflecting the sky and mountains with their stars and trees and wonderful sculpture, all their grandeur refined and doubled,—a marvelously impressive picture, that seemed to belong more to heaven than earth.

August 9—I went ahead of the flock, and crossed over the divide between the Merced and Tuolumne Basins. The gap between the east end of the Hoffmann spur and the mass of mountain rocks about Cathedral Peak, though roughened by ridges and waving folds, seems to be one of the channels of a broad ancient glacier that came from the mountains on the summit of the range. In crossing this divide the ice-river made an ascent of about five hundred feet from the Tuolumne meadows. This entire region must have been overswept by ice.

From the top of the divide, and also from the big Tuolumne Meadows, the wonderful mountain called Cathedral Peak is in sight. From every point of view it shows marked individuality. It is a majestic temple of one stone, hewn from the living rock, and adorned with spires and pinnacles in regular cathedral style. The dwarf pines on the roof look like mosses. I hope some time to climb to it to say my prayers and hear the stone sermons.

The big Tuolumne Meadows are flowery lawns, lying along the south fork of the Tuolumne River at a height of about eighty-five hundred to nine thousand feet above the sea, partially separated by forests and bars of glaciated granite. Here the mountains seem to have been cleared away or set back, so that wide-open views may be had in every direction. The upper end of the series lies at the base of Mount Lyell, the lower below the east end of the Hoffmann Range, so the length must be about ten or twelve miles. They vary in width from a quarter of a mile to perhaps three quarters, and a good many branch meadows put out along the banks of the tributary streams. This is the most spacious and delightful high pleasure-ground I have yet seen. The air is keen and bracing, yet warm during the day; and though lying high in the sky, the surrounding mountains are so much higher, one feels protected as if in a grand hall. Mounts Dana and Gibbs, massive red mountains, perhaps thirteen thousand feet high or more, bound the view on the east, the Cathedral and Unicorn Peaks, with many nameless peaks, on the south, the Hoffmann Range on the west, and a number of peaks unnamed, as far as I know, on the north. One of these last is much like the Cathedral. The grass of the meadows is mostly fine and silky, with

14

exceedingly slender leaves, making a close sod, above which the panicles of
minute purple flowers seem to float in airy, misty lightness. . . .

On the return trip I met the flock about three miles east of Lake Tenaya. Here we camped for the night near a small lake lying on top of the
divide in a clump of the two-leaved pine. We are now about nine thousand
feet above the sea. Small lakes abound in all sorts of situations,—on ridges,
along mountain sides, and in piles of moraine boulders, most of them mere
pools. Only in those canyons of the larger streams at the foot of declivities,
where the down thrust of the glaciers was heaviest, do we find lakes of considerable size and depth. How grateful a task it would be to trace them all
and study them! How pure their waters are, clear as crystal in polished
stone basins! None of them, so far as I have seen, have fishes, I suppose on
account of falls making them inaccessible. Yet one would think their eggs
might get into these lakes by some chance or other; on ducks' feet, for example, or in their mouths, or in their crops, as some plant seeds are distrib-
uted. Nature has so many ways of doing such things. How did the frogs,
found in all the bogs and pools and lakes, however high, manage to get up
these mountains? Surely not by jumping. Such excursions through miles of
dry brush and boulders would be very hard on frogs. Perhaps their stringy
gelatinous spawn is occasionally entangled or glued on the feet of water
birds. Anyhow, they are here and in hearty health and voice. I like their
cheery tronk and crink. They take the place of songbirds at a pinch.

August 11—Fine shining weather, with a ten minutes' noon thunderstorm and rain. Rambling all day getting acquainted with the region
north of the river. Found a small lake and many charming glacier meadows
embosomed in an extensive forest of the two-leaved pine. The forest is
growing on broad, almost continuous deposits of moraine material, is remarkably even in its growth, and the trees are much closer together than in
any of the fir or pine woods farther down the range. The evenness of the
growth would seem to indicate that the trees are all of the same age or
nearly so. This regularity has probably been in great part the result of fire. I
saw several large patches and strips of dead bleached spars, the ground beneath them covered with a young even growth. Fire can run in these
woods, not only because the thin bark of the trees is dripping with resin,
but because the growth is close, and the comparatively rich soil produces
good crops of tall broad-leaved grasses on which fire can travel, even when

the weather is calm. Besides these fire-killed patches there are a good many fallen uprooted trees here and there, some with the bark and needles still on, as if they had lately been blown down in some thunderstorm blast. Saw a large black-tailed deer, a buck with antlers like the upturned roots of a fallen pine.

After a long ramble through the dense encumbered woods I emerged upon a smooth meadow full of sunshine like a lake of light, about a mile and a half long, a quarter to half a mile wide, and bounded by tall arrowy pines. The sod, like that of all the glacier meadows hereabouts, is made of silky agrostis and calamagrostis chiefly; their panicles of purple flowers and purple stems, exceedingly light and airy, seem to float above the green plush of leaves like a thin misty cloud, while the sod is brightened by several species of gentian, potentilla, ivesia, orthocarpus, and their corresponding bees and butterflies. All the glacier meadows are beautiful, but few are so perfect as this one. Compared with it the most carefully leveled, licked, snipped artificial lawns of pleasure-grounds are coarse things. . . .

From meadow to meadow, every one beautiful beyond telling, and from lake to lake through groves and belts of arrowy trees, I held my way northward. . . .

Cañon de Chelly—Navaho, Edward S. Curtis

Black Mesa Mine #1

GARY SNYDER

Wind dust yellow cloud swirls
northeast across the fifty-foot
graded bulldozed road,
white cloud puffs,
juniper and pinyon scattered groves
      —firewood for the People
        heaps of wood for all
          at cross-streets in the pueblos,
ancient mother mountain
pools of water
pools of coal
pools of sand
        buried or laid bare

Solitary trucks go slow on grades
smoking sand
writhes around the tires
and on a torn up stony plain
a giant green-and-yellow shovel
whirs and drags
house-size scoops of rock and gravel

Mountain,
be kind,
it will tumble in its hole

18

Five hundred yards   back up the road
a Navajo corral
of stood up dried out poles and logs
all leaned in on an angle,
gleaming in the windy April sun.

Hook

WALTER VAN TILBURG CLARK

I

Hook, the hawks' child, was hatched in a dry spring among the oaks beside the seasonal river, and was struck from the nest early. In the drouth his single-willed parents had to extend their hunting ground by more than twice, for the ground creatures upon which they fed died and dried by the hundreds. The range became too great for them to wish to return and feed Hook, and when they had lost interest in each other they drove Hook down into the sand and brush and went back to solitary courses over the bleaching hills.

Unable to fly yet, Hook crept over the ground, challenging all large movements with recoiled head, erected, rudimentary wings, and the small rasp of his clattering beak. It was during this time of abysmal ignorance and continual fear that his eyes took on the first quality of a hawk, that of being wide, alert and challenging. He dwelt, because of his helplessness, among the rattling brush which grew between the oaks and the river. Even in his thickets and near the water, the white sun was the dominant presence. Except in the dawn, when the land wind stirred, or in the late afternoon, when the sea wind became strong enough to penetrate the half-mile inland to this turn in the river, the sun was the major force, and everything was dry and motionless under it. The brush, small plants and trees alike husbanded the little moisture at their hearts; the moving creatures waited for dark, when sometimes the sea fog came over and made a fine, soundless rain which relieved them.

The two spacious sounds of his life environed Hook at this time. One was the great rustle of the slopes of yellowed wild wheat, with over it the chattering rustle of the leaves of the California oaks, already as harsh and individually tremulous as in autumn. The other was the distant whisper of the foaming edge of the Pacific, punctuated by the hollow shoring of the waves. But these Hook did not yet hear, for he was attuned by fear and hunger to

20

the small, spasmodic rustlings of live things. Dry, shrunken, and nearly starved, and with his plumage delayed, he snatched at beetles, dragging in the sand to catch them. When swifter and stronger birds and animals did not reach them first, which was seldom, he ate the small, silver fish left in the mud by the failing river. He watched, with nearly chattering beak, the quick, thin lizards pause, very alert, and raise and lower themselves, but could not catch them because he had to raise his wings to move rapidly, which startled them.

Only one sight and sound not of his world of microscopic necessity was forced upon Hook. That was the flight of the big gulls from the beaches, which sometimes, in squealing play, came spinning back over the foothills and the river bed. For some inherited reason, the big, ship-bodied birds did not frighten Hook, but angered him. Small and chewed-looking, with his wide, already yellowing eyes glaring up at them, he would stand in an open place on the sand in the sun and spread his shaping wings and clatter his bill like shaken dice. Hook was furious about the swift, easy passage of gulls.

His first opportunity to leave off living like a ground owl came accidentally. He was standing in the late afternoon in the red light under the thicket, his eyes half-filmed with drowse and the stupefaction of starvation, when suddenly something beside him moved, and he struck, and killed a field mouse driven out of the wheat by thirst. It was a poor mouse, shriveled and lice ridden, but in striking, Hook had tasted blood, which raised nest memories and restored his nature. With started neck plumage and shining eyes, he tore and fed. When the mouse was devoured, Hook had entered hoarse adolescence. He began to seek with a conscious appetite, and to move more readily out of shelter. Impelled by the blood appetite, so glorious after his long preservation upon the flaky and bitter stuff of bugs, he ventured even into the wheat in the open sun beyond the oaks, and discovered the small trails and holes among the roots. With his belly often partially filled with flesh, he grew rapidly in strength and will. His eyes were taking on their final change, their yellow growing deeper and more opaque, their stare more constant, their challenge less desperate. Once during this transformation, he surprised a ground squirrel, and although he was ripped and wing-bitten and could not hold his prey, he was not dismayed by the conflict, but exalted. Even while the wing was still drooping and the pinions not grown back, he was excited by other ground squirrels and pursued them

21

futilely, and was angered by their dusty escapes. He realized that his world was a great arena for killing, and felt the magnificence of it.

The two major events of Hook's young life occurred in the same day. A little after dawn he made the customary essay and succeeded in flight. A little before sunset, he made his first sustained flight of over two hundred yards, and at its termination struck and slew a great buck squirrel whose thrashing and terrified gnawing and squealing gave him a wild delight. When he had gorged on the strong meat, Hook stood upright, and in his eyes was the stare of the hawk, never flagging in intensity but never swelling beyond containment. After that the stare had only to grow more deeply challenging and more sternly controlled as his range and deadliness increased. There was no change in kind. Hook had mastered the first of the three hungers which are fused into the single, flaming will of a hawk, and he had experienced the second.

The third and consummating hunger did not awaken in Hook until the following spring, when the exultation of space had grown slow and steady in him, so that he swept freely with the wind over the miles of coastal foothills, circling, and ever in sight of the sea, and used without struggle the warm currents lifting from the slopes, and no longer desired to scream at the range of his vision, but intently sailed above his shadow swiftly climbing to meet him on the hillsides, sinking away and rippling across the brush-grown canyons.

That spring the rains were long, and Hook sat for hours, hunched and angry under their pelting, glaring into the fogs of the river valley, and killed only small, drenched things flooded up from their tunnels. But when the rains had dissipated, and there were sun and sea wind again, the game ran plentiful, the hills were thick and shining green, and the new river flooded about the boulders where battered turtles climbed up to shrink and sleep. Hook then was scorched by the third hunger. Ranging farther, often forgetting to kill and eat, he sailed for days with growing rage, and woke at night clattering on his dead tree limb, and struck and struck and struck at the porous wood of the trunk, tearing it away. After days, in the draft of a coastal canyon miles below his own hills, he came upon the acrid taint he did not know but had expected, and sailing down it, felt his neck plumes rise and his wings quiver so that he swerved unsteadily. He saw the unmated female perched upon the tall and jagged stump of a tree that had been shorn by storm, and he stooped, as if upon game. But she was older

22

than he, and wary of the gripe of his importunity, and banked off screaming, and he screamed also at the intolerable delay.

At the head of the canyon, the screaming pursuit was crossed by another male with a great wing-spread, and the light golden in the fringe of his plumage. But his more skillful opening played him false against the ferocity of the twice-balked Hook. His rising maneuver for position was cut short by Hook's wild, upward swoop, and at the blow he raked desperately and tumbled off to the side. Dropping, Hook struck him again, struggled to clutch, but only raked and could not hold, and, diving, struck once more in passage, and then beat up, yelling triumph, and saw the crippled antagonist side-slip away, half-tumble once, as the ripped wing failed to balance, then steady and glide obliquely into the cover of brush on the canyon side. Beating hard and stationary in the wind above the bush that covered his competitor, Hook waited an instant, but when the bush was still, screamed again, and let himself go off with the current, reseeking, infuriated by the burn of his own wounds, the thin choke-threat of the acrid taint.

On a hilltop projection of stone two miles inland, he struck her down, gripping her rustling body with his talons, beating her wings down with his wings, belting her head when she whimpered or thrashed, and at last clutching her neck with his hook and, when her coy struggles had given way to stillness, succeeded.

In the early summer, Hook drove the three young ones from their nest, and went back to lone circling above his own range. He was complete.

II

Throughout that summer and the cool, growthless weather of the winter, when the gales blew in the river canyon and the ocean piled upon the shore, Hook was master of the sky and the hills of his range. His flight became a lovely and certain thing, so that he played with the treacherous currents of the air with a delicate ease surpassing that of the gulls. He could sail for hours, searching the blanched grasses below him with telescopic eyes, gaining height against the wind, descending in mile-long, gently declining swoops when he curved and rode back, and never beating either wing. At the swift passage of his shadow within their vision, gophers, ground squirrels and rabbits froze, or plunged gibbering into their tunnels beneath matted turf. Now, when he struck, he killed easily in one hard-knuckled blow. Occasionally, in sport, he soared up over the river and drove the heavy and weaponless gulls downstream again, until they would no longer venture inland.

There was nothing which Hook feared now, and his spirit was wholly belligerent, swift and sharp, like his gaze. Only the mixed smells and incomprehensible activities of the people at the Japanese farmer's home, inland of the coastwise highway and south of the bridge across Hook's river, troubled him. The smells were strong, unsatisfactory and never clear, and the people, though they behaved foolishly, constantly running in and out of their built-up holes, were large, and appeared capable, with fearless eyes looking up at him, so that he instinctively swerved aside from them. He cruised over their yard, their gardens, and their bean fields, but he would not alight close to their buildings.

But this one area of doubt did not interfere with his life. He ignored it, save to look upon it curiously as he crossed, his afternoon shadow sliding in an instant over the chicken-and-crate-cluttered yard, up the side of the unpainted barn, and then out again smoothly, just faintly, liquidly rippling over the furrows and then over the stubble of the grazing slopes. When the season was dry, and the dead earth blew on the fields, he extended his range to satisfy his great hunger, and again narrowed it when the fields were once more alive with the minute movements he could not only see but anticipate.

Four times that year he was challenged by other hawks blowing up from behind the coastal hills to scud down his slopes, but two of these he slew in mid-air, and saw hurtle down to thump on the ground and lie still while he circled, and a third, whose wing he tore, he followed closely to earth and beat to death in the grass, making the crimson jet out from its breast and neck into the pale wheat. The fourth was a strong flier and experienced fighter, and theirs was a long, running battle, with brief, rising flurries of striking and screaming, from which down and plumage soared off.

Here, for the first time, Hook felt doubts, and at moments wanted to drop away from the scoring, burning talons and the twisted hammer strokes of the strong beak, drop away shrieking, and take cover and be still. In the end, when Hook, having outmaneuvered his enemy and come above him, wholly in control, and going with the wind, tilted and plunged for the death rap, the other, in desperation, threw over on his back and struck up. Talons locked, beaks raking, they dived earthward. The earth grew and spread under them amazingly, and they were not fifty feet above it when Hook, feeling himself turning toward the underside, tore free and beat up again on heavy, wrenched wings. The other, stroking swiftly, and so close to down that he lost wing plumes to a bush, righted himself and planed up, but flew on lumberingly between the hills and did not return. Hook screamed the triumph, and made a brief pretense of pursuit, but was glad to return, slow and victorious, to his dead tree.

In all these encounters, Hook was injured, but experienced only the fighter's pride and exultation from the sting of wounds received in successful combat. And in each of them he learned new skill. Each time the wounds healed quickly, and left him a more dangerous bird.

In the next spring, when the rains and the night chants of the little frogs were past, the third hunger returned upon Hook with a new violence. In this quest, he came into the taint of a young hen. Others too were drawn by the unnerving perfume, but only one of them, the same with which Hook had fought his great battle, was a worthy competitor. This hunter drove off two, while two others, game but neophytes, were glad enough that Hook's impatience would not permit him to follow and kill. Then the battle between the two champions fled inland, and was a tactical marvel, but Hook lodged the neck-breaking blow, and struck again as they dropped past the treetops. The blood had already begun to pool on the gray, fallen foliage as Hook flapped up between branches, too spent to cry his victory. Yet his hunger would not let him rest until, late in the second day, he drove the female to ground among the laurels of a strange river canyon.

When the two fledglings of this second brood had been driven from the nest, and Hook had returned to his own range, he was not only complete, but supreme. He slept without concealment on his bare limb, and did not open his eyes when, in the night, the heavy-billed cranes coughed in the shallows below him.

III

The turning point of Hook's career came that autumn, when the brush in the canyons rustled dryly and the hills, mowed close by the cattle, smoked under the wind as if burning. One midafternoon, when the black clouds were torn on the rim of the sea and the surf flowered white and high on the rocks, raining in over the low cliffs, Hook rode the wind diagonally across the river mouth. His great eyes, focused for small things stirring in the dust and leaves, overlooked so large and slow a movement as that of the

Japanese farmer rising from the brush and lifting the two black eyes of his shotgun. Too late Hook saw and, startled, swerved, but wrongly. The surf muffled the reports, and nearly without sound, Hook felt the minute whips of the first shot, and the astounding, breath-breaking blow of the second.

Beating his good wing, tasting the blood that quickly swelled into his beak, he tumbled off with the wind and struck into the thickets of the far side of the river mouth. The branches tore him. Wild with rage, he thrust up and clattered his beak, challenging, but when he had fallen over twice, he knew that the trailing wing could not carry, and then heard the boots of the hunter among the stones in the river bed and, seeing him loom at the edge of the bushes, crept back among the thickest brush and was still. When he saw the boots stand before him, he reared back, lifting his good wing and cocking his head for the serpent-like blow, his beak open but soundless, his great eyes hard and very shining. The boots passed on. The Japanese farmer, who believed that he had lost chickens, and who had cunningly observed Hook's flight for many afternoons, until he could plot it, did not greatly want a dead hawk.

When Hook could hear nothing but the surf and the wind in the thicket, he let the sickness and shock overcome him. The fine film of the inner lid dropped over his big eyes. His heart beat frantically, so that it made the plumage of his shot-aching breast throb. His own blood throttled his breathing. But these things were nothing compared to the lightning of pain in his left shoulder, where the shot had bunched, shattering the airy bones so the pinions trailed on the ground and could not be lifted. Yet, when a sparrow lit in the bush over him, Hook's eyes flew open again, hard and challenging, his good wing was lifted and his beak strained open. The startled sparrow darted piping out over the river.

Throughout that night, while the long clouds blew across the stars and the wind shook the bushes about him, and throughout the next day, while the clouds still blew and massed until there was no gleam of sunlight on the sand bar, Hook remained stationary, enduring his sickness. In the second evening, the rains began. First there was a long, running patter of drops upon the beach and over the dry trees and bushes. At dusk there came a heavier squall, which did not die entirely, but slacked off to a continual, spaced splashing of big drops, and then returned with the front of the storm. In long, misty curtains, gust by gust, the rain swept over the sea, beating down its heaving, and coursed up the beach. The little jets of dust

26

ceased to rise about the drops in the fields and the mud began to gleam. Among the boulders of the river bed, darkling pools grew slowly. Still Hook stood behind his tree from the wind, only gentle drops reaching him, falling from the upper branches and then again from the brush. His eyes remained closed, and he could still taste his own blood in his mouth, though it had ceased to come up freshly. Out beyond him, he heard the storm changing. As rain conquered the sea, the heave of the surf became a hushed sound, often lost in the crying of the wind. Then gradually, as the night turned toward morning, the wind also was broken by the rain. The crying became fainter, the rain settled toward steadiness, and the creep of the waves could be heard again, quiet and regular upon the beach.

At dawn there was no wind and no sun, but everywhere the roaring of the vertical, relentless rain. Hook then crept among the rapid drippings of the bushes, dragging his torn sail, seeking better shelter. He stopped often and stood with the shutters of film drawn over his eyes. At midmorning he found a little cave under a ledge at the base of the sea cliff. Here, lost without branches and leaves about him, he settled to await improvement.

When, at midday of the third day, the rain stopped altogether, and the sky opened before a small, fresh wind, letting light through to glitter upon a tremulous sea, Hook was so weak that his good wing trailed also to prop him upright, and his open eyes were lusterless. But his wounds were hardened, and he felt the return of hunger. Beyond his shelter, he heard the gulls flying in great numbers and crying their joy at the cleared air. He could even hear, from the fringe of the river, the ecstatic and unstinted bubblings and chirpings of the small birds. The grassland, he felt, would be full of the stirring anew of the close-bound life, the undrowned insects clicking as they dried out, the snakes slithering down, heads half erect, into the grasses where the mice, gophers and ground squirrels ran and stopped and chewed and licked themselves smoother and drier.

With the aid of this hunger, and on the crutches of his wings, Hook came down to stand in the sun beside his cave, whence he could watch the beach. Before him, in ellipses on tilting planes, the gulls flew. The surf was rearing again, and beginning to shelve and hiss on the sand. Through the white foam-writing it left, the long-billed pipers twinkled in bevies, escaping each wave, then racing down after it to plunge their fine drills into the minute double holes where the sand crabs bubbled. In the third row of breakers two seals lifted sleek, streaming heads and barked, and over them, trailing his spider legs, a great crane flew south. Among the stones at the foot of the cliff, small red and green crabs made a little, continuous rattling and knocking. The cliff swallows glittered and twanged on aerial forays.

The afternoon began auspiciously for Hook also. One of the two gulls which came squabbling above him dropped a freshly caught fish to the sand. Quickly Hook was upon it. Gripping it, he raised his good wing and cocked his head with open beak at the many gulls which had circled and come down at once toward the fall of the fish. The gulls sheered off, cursing raucously. Left alone on the sand, Hook devoured the fish and, after resting in the sun, withdrew again to his shelter.

IV

In the succeeding days, between rains, he foraged on the beach. He learned to kill and crack the small green crabs. Along the edge of the river mouth, he found the drowned bodies of mice and squirrels and even sparrows. Twice he managed to drive feeding gulls from their catch, charging upon them with buffeting wing and clattering beak. He grew stronger slowly, but the shot sail continued to drag. Often, at the choking thought of soaring and striking and the good, hot-blood kill, he strove to take off, but only the one wing came up, winnowing with a hiss, and drove him over onto his side in the sand. After these futile trials, he would rage and clatter. But gradually he learned to believe that he could not fly, that his life must now be that of the discharged nestling again. Denied the joy of space, without which the joy of loneliness was lost, the joy of battle and killing, the blood lust, became his whole concentration. It was his hope, as he charged feeding gulls, that they would turn and offer battle, but they never did. The sandpipers, at his approach, fled peeping, or, like a quiver of arrows shot together, streamed out over the surf in a long curve. Once, pent beyond bearing, he disgraced himself by shrieking challenge at the businesslike heron which flew south every evening at the same time. The heron did not even turn his head, but flapped and glided on.

Hook's shame and anger became such that he stood awake at night. Hunger kept him awake also, for these little leavings of the gulls could not sustain his great body in its renewed violence. He became aware that the gulls slept at night in flocks on the sand, each with one leg tucked under him. He discovered also that the curlews and the pipers, often mingling, likewise slept, on the higher remnant of the bar. A sensation of evil delight filled him in the consideration of protracted striking among them.

There was only half of a sick moon in a sky of running but far-separated clouds on the night when he managed to stalk into the center of the sleeping gulls. This was light enough, but so great was his vengeful pleasure that there broke from him a shrill scream of challenge as he first struck. Without the power of flight behind it, the blow was not murderous, and this newly discovered impotence made Hook crazy, so that he screamed again and again as he struck and tore at the felled gull. He slew the one, but was twice knocked over by its heavy flounderings, and all the others rose above him, weaving and screaming, protesting in the thin moonlight. Wakened by their clamor, the wading birds also took wing, startled and plaintive. When the beach was quiet again, the flocks had settled elsewhere, beyond his pitiful range, and he was left alone beside the single kill. It was a disappointing victory. He fed with lowering spirit.

Thereafter, he stalked silently. At sunset he would watch where the gulls settled along the miles of beach, and after dark he would come like a sharp shadow among them, and drive with his hook on all sides of him, till the beatings of a poorly struck victim sent the flock up. Then he would turn vindictively upon the fallen and finish them. In his best night, he killed five from one flock. But he ate only a little from one, for the vigor resulting from occasional repletion strengthened only his ire, which became so great at such a time that food revolted him. It was not the joyous, swift, controlled hunting anger of a sane hawk, but something quite different, which made him dizzy if it continued too long, and left him unsatisfied with any kill.

Then one day, when he had very nearly struck a gull while driving it from a gasping yellowfin, the gull's wing rapped against him as it broke for its running start, and, the trailing wing failing to support him, he was knocked over. He flurried awkwardly in the sand to regain his feet, but his mastery of the beach was ended. Seeing him, in clear sunlight, struggling after the chance blow, the gulls returned about him in a flashing cloud, circling and pecking on the wing. Hook's plumage showed quick little jets of irregularity here and there. He reared back, clattering and erecting the good wing, spreading the great rusty tail for balance. His eyes shone with a little of the old pleasure. But it died, for he could reach none of them. He was forced to turn and dance awkwardly on the sand, trying to clash bills with each tormentor. They banked up squealing and returned, weaving about him in concentric and overlapping circles. His scream was lost in their clamor, and he appeared merely to be hopping clumsily with his mouth open. Again he fell sideways. Before he could right himself, he was bowled over, and a second time, and lay on his side, twisting his neck to reach them and clappering in blind fury, and was struck three times by three successive gulls, shrieking their flock triumph.

Finally he managed to roll to his breast, and to crouch with his good wing spread wide and the other stretched nearly as far, so that he extended like a gigantic moth, only his snake head, with its now silent scimitar, erect. One great eye blazed under its level brow, but where the other had been was a shallow hole from which thin blood trickled to his russet gap.

In this crouch, by short stages, stopping repeatedly to turn and drive the gulls up, Hook dragged into the river canyon and under the stiff cover of the bitter-leafed laurel. There the gulls left him, soaring up with great clatter of their valor. Till nearly sunset Hook, broken spirited and enduring his hardening eye socket, heard them celebrating over the waves.

When his will was somewhat replenished, and his empty eye socket had stopped the twitching and vague aching which had forced him often to roll ignominiously to rub it in the dust, Hook ventured from the protective lacings of his thicket. He knew fear again, and the challenge of his remaining eye was once more strident, as in adolescence. He dared not return to the beaches, and with a new, weak hunger, the home hunger, enticing him, made his way by short hunting journeys back to the wild wheat slopes and the crisp oaks. There was in Hook an unwonted sensation now, that of the ever-neighboring possibility of death. This sensation was beginning, after his period as a mad bird on the beach, to solidify him into his last stage of life. When, during his slow homeward passage, the gulls wafted inland over him, watching the earth with curious, miserish eyes, he did not cower, but neither did he challenge, either by opened beak or by raised shoulder. He merely watched carefully, learning his first lessons in observing the world with one eye.

At first the familiar surroundings of the bend in the river and the tree with the dead limb to which he could not ascend, aggravated his humiliation, but in time, forced to live cunningly and half-starved, he lost much of his savage pride. At the first flight of a strange hawk over his realm, he was wild at his helplessness, and kept twisting his head like an owl, or spinning in the grass like a small and feathered dervish, to keep the hateful beauty of the windrider in sight. But in the succeeding weeks, as one after another coasted his beat, his resentment declined, and when one of the raiders, a haughty yearling, sighted his upstaring eye, and plunged and struck him dreadfully, and failed to kill him only because he dragged under a thicket in time, the second of his great hungers was gone. He had no longer the true lust to kill, no joy of battle, but only the poor desire to fill his belly.

Then truly he lived in the wheat and the brush like a ground owl, ridden with ground lice, dusty or muddy, ever half-starved, forced to sit for hours by small holes for petty and unsatisfying kills. Only once during the final months before his end did he make a kill where the breath of danger recalled his valor, and then the danger was such as a hawk with wings and eyes would scorn. Waiting beside a gopher hole, surrounded by the high, yellow grass, he saw the head emerge, and struck, and was amazed that there writhed in his clutch the neck and dusty coffin-skull of a rattlesnake. Holding his grip, Hook saw the great, thick body slither up after, the tip an erect, strident blur, and writhe on the dirt of the gopher's mound. The weight of the snake pushed Hook about, and once threw him down, and the rising and falling whine of the rattles made the moment terrible, but the vaulted mouth, gaping from the closeness of Hook's gripe, so that the pale, envenomed sabers stood out free, could not reach him. When Hook replaced the grip of his beak with the grip of his talons, and was free to strike again and again at the base of the head, the struggle was over. Hook tore and fed on the fine, watery flesh, and left the tattered armor and the long, jointed bone for the marching ants.

When the heavy rains returned, he ate well during the period of the first escapes from flooded burrows, and then well enough, in a vulture's way, on the drowned creatures. But as the rains lingered, and the burrows hung full of water, and there were no insects in the grass and no small birds sleeping in the thickets, he was constantly hungry, and finally unbearably hungry. His sodden and ground-broken plumage stood out raggedly about him, so that he looked fat, even bloated, but underneath it his skin clung to his bones. Save for his great talons and clappers, and the rain in his down, he would have been like a handful of air. He often stood for a long time under some bush or ledge, heedless of the drip, his one eye filmed over, his mind neither asleep or awake, but between. The gurgle and swirl of the brimming river, and the sound of chunks of the bank cut away to splash and dissolve in the already muddy flood, became familiar to him, and yet a torment, as if that great, ceaselessly working power of water ridiculed his frailty, within which only the faintest spark of valor still glimmered. The last two nights before the rain ended, he huddled under the floor of the bridge on the coastal highway, and heard the palpitant thunder of motors swell and roar over him. The trucks shook the bridge so that Hook, even in his famished lassitude, would sometimes open his one great eye wide and startled.

v

After the rains, when things became full again, bursting with growth and sound, the trees swelling, the thickets full of song and chatter, the fields, turning green in the sun, alive with rustling passages, and the moonlit nights strained with the song of the peepers all up and down the river and in the pools in the fields, Hook had to bear the return of the one hunger left him. At times this made him so wild that he forgot himself and screamed challenge from the open ground. The fretfulness of it spoiled his hunting, which was now entirely a matter of patience. Once he was in despair, and lashed himself through the grass and thickets, trying to rise when that virgin scent drifted for a few moments above the current of his own river. Then, breathless, his beak agape, he saw the strong suitor ride swiftly down on the wind over him, and heard afar the screaming fuss of the harsh wooing in the alders. For that moment even the battle heart beat in him again. The rim of his good eye was scarlet, and a little bead of new blood stood in the socket of the other. With beak and talon, he ripped at a fallen log, and made loam and leaves fly from about it.

But the season of love passed over to the nesting season, and Hook's love hunger, unused, shriveled in him with the others, and there remained in him only one stern quality befitting a hawk, and that the negative one, the remnant, the will to endure. He resumed his patient, plotted hunting, now along a field of the Japanese farmer, but ever within reach of the river thickets.

Growing tough and dry again as the summer advanced, inured to the family of the farmer, whom he saw daily, stooping and scraping with sticks in the ugly, open rows of their fields, where no lovely grass rustled and no life stirred save the shameless gulls, which walked at the heels of the workers, gobbling the worms and grubs they turned up, Hook became nearly content with his share of life. The only longing or resentment to pierce him was that which he suffered occasionally when forced to hide at the edge of the mile-long bean field from the wafted cruising and the restive, down-bent gaze of his own kind. For the rest, he was without flame, a snappish, dust-colored creature, fading into the grasses he trailed through, and suited to his petty ways.

At the end of that summer, for the second time in his four years, Hook underwent a drouth. The equinoctial period passed without a rain. The laurel and the rabbit-brush dropped dry leaves. The foliage of the oaks shriveled and curled. Even the night fogs in the river canyon failed. The farmer's red cattle on the hillside lowed constantly, and could not feed on the dusty stubble. Grass fires broke out along the highway, and ate fast in the wind, filling the hollows with the smell of smoke, and died in the dirt of the shorn hills. The river made no sound. Scum grew on its vestigial pools, and turtles died and stank among the rocks. The dust rode before the wind, and ascended and flowered to nothing between the hills, and every sunset was red with the dust in the air. The people in the farmer's house quarreled, and even struck one another. Birds were silent, and only the hawks flew much. The animals lay breathing hard for very long spells, and ran and crept jerkily. Their flanks were fallen in, and their eyes were red.

At first Hook gorged at the fringe of the grass fires on the multitudes of tiny things that came running and squeaking. But thereafter there were the blackened strips on the hills, and little more in the thin, crackling grass. He found mice and rats, gophers and ground-squirrels, and even rabbits, dead in the stubble and under the thickets, but so dry and fleshless that only a faint smell rose from them, even on the sunny days. He starved on them. By early December he had wearily stalked the length of the eastern foot-hills, hunting at night to escape the voracity of his own kind, resting often upon his wings. The queer trail of his short steps and great horned toes zig-zagged in the dust and was erased by the wind at dawn. He was nearly dead, and could make no sound through the horn funnels of his clappers.

Then one night the dry wind brought him, with the familiar, lifeless dust, another familiar scent, troublesome, mingled and unclear. In his vision-dominated brain he remembered the swift circle of his flight a year past, crossing in one segment, his shadow beneath him, a yard cluttered with crates and chickens, a gray barn and then again the plowed land and the stubble. Traveling faster than he had for days, impatient of his shrunken sweep, Hook came down to the farm. In the dark wisps of cloud blown

33

among the stars over him, but no moon, he stood outside the wire of the chicken run. The scent of fat and blooded birds reached him from the shelter, and also within the enclosure was water. At the breath of the water, Hook's gorge contracted, and his tongue quivered and clove in its groove of horn. But there was the wire. He stalked its perimeter and found no opening. He beat it with his good wing, and felt it cut but not give. He wrenched at it with his beak in many places, but could not tear it. Finally, in a fury which drove the thin blood through him, he leaped repeatedly against it, beating and clawing. He was thrown back from the last leap as from the first, but in it he had risen so high as to clutch with his beak at the top wire. While he lay on his breast on the ground, the significance of this came upon him.

Again he leapt, clawed up the wire, and, as he would have fallen, made even the dead wing bear a little. He grasped the top and tumbled within. There again he rested flat, searching the dark with quick-turning head. There was no sound or motion but the throb of his own body. First he drank at the chill metal trough hung for the chickens. The water was cold, and loosened his tongue and his tight throat, but it also made him drunk and dizzy, so that he had to rest again, his claws spread wide to brace him. Then he walked stiffly, to stalk down the scent. He trailed it up the runway. Then there was the stuffy, body-warm air, acrid with droppings, full of soft rustlings as his talons clicked on the board floor. The thick, white shapes showed faintly in the darkness. Hook struck quickly, driving a hen to the floor with one blow, its neck broken and stretched out stringily. He leaped the still pulsing body, and tore it. The rich, streaming blood was overpowering to his dried senses, his starved, leathery body. After a few swallows, the flesh choked him. In his rage, he struck down another hen. The urge to kill took him again, as in those nights on the beach. He could let nothing go. Balked of feeding, he was compelled to slaughter. Clattering, he struck again and again. The henhouse was suddenly filled with the squawking and helpless rushing and buffeting of the terrified, brainless fowls.

Hook reveled in mastery. Here was game big enough to offer weight against a strike, and yet unable to soar away from his blows. Turning in the midst of the turmoil, cannily, his fury caught at the perfect pitch, he struck unceasingly. When the hens finally discovered the outlet, and streamed into the yard, to run around the fence, beating and squawking, Hook followed them, scraping down the incline, clumsy and joyous. In the yard, the cock, a bird as large as he, and much heavier, found him out and gave valiant battle. In the dark, and both earthbound, there was little skill, but blow upon blow, and only chance parry. The still squawking hens pressed into one corner of the yard. While the duel went on, a dog, excited by the sustained scuffling, began to bark. He continued to bark, running back and forth along the fence on one side. A light flashed on in an uncurtained window of the farmhouse, and streamed whitely over the crates littering the ground.

Enthralled by his old battle joy, Hook knew only the burly cock before him. Now, in the farthest reach of the window light, they could see each other dimly. The Japanese farmer, with his gun and lantern, was already at the gate when the finish came. The great cock leapt to jab with his spurs and, toppling forward with extended neck as he fell, was struck and extinguished. Blood had loosened Hook's throat. Shrilly he cried his triumph. It was a thin and exhausted cry, but within him as good as when he shrilled in mid-air over the plummeting descent of a fine foe in his best spring.

The light from the lantern partially blinded Hook. He first turned and ran directly from it, into the corner where the hens were huddled. They fled apart before his charge. He essayed the fence, and on the second try, in his desperation, was out. But in the open dust, the dog was on him, circling, dashing in, snapping. The farmer, who at first had not fired because of the chickens, now did not fire because of the dog, and, when he saw that the hawk was unable to fly, relinquished the sport to the dog, holding the lantern up in order to see better. The light showed his own flat, broad, dark face as sunken also, the cheekbones very prominent, and showed the torn-off sleeves of his shirt and the holes in the knees of his overalls. His wife, in a stained wrapper, and barefooted, heavy black hair hanging around a young, passionless face, joined him hesitantly, but watched, fascinated and a little horrified. His son joined them too, encouraging the dog, but quickly grew silent. Courageous and cruel death, however it may afterward sicken the one who has watched it, is impossible to look away from.

In the circle of the light, Hook turned to keep the dog in front of him. His one eye gleamed with malevolence. The dog was an Airedale, and large. Each time he pounced, Hook stood ground, raising his good wing, the pinions newly torn by the fence, opening his beak soundlessly, and, at the closest approach, hissed furiously, and at once struck. Hit and ripped

35

twice by the whetted horn, the dog recoiled more quickly from several subsequent jumps and, infuriated by his own cowardice, began to bark wildly. Hook maneuvered to watch him, keeping his head turned to avoid losing the foe on the blind side. When the dog paused, safely away, Hook watched him quietly, wing partially lowered, beak closed, but at the first move again lifted the wing and gaped. The dog whined, and the man spoke to him encouragingly. The awful sound of his voice made Hook for an instant twist his head to stare up at the immense figures behind the light. The dog again sallied, barking, and Hook's head spun back. His wing was bitten this time, and with a furious side-blow, he caught the dog's nose. The dog dropped him with a yelp, and then, smarting, came on more warily, as Hook propped himself up from the ground again between his wings. Hook's artificial strength was waning, but his heart still stood to the battle, sustained by a fear of such dimension as he had never known before, but only anticipated when the arrogant young hawk had driven him to cover. The dog, unable to find any point at which the merciless, unwinking eye was not watching him, the parted beak waiting, paused and whimpered again.

"Oh, kill the poor thing," the woman begged.

The man, though, encouraged the dog again, saying, "Sick him; sick him."

The dog rushed bodily. Unable to avoid him, Hook was bowled down, snapping and raking. He left long slashes, as from the blade of a knife, on the dog's flank, but before he could right himself and assume guard again, was caught by the good wing and dragged, clattering, and seeking to make a good stroke from his back. The man followed them to keep the light on them, and the boy went with him, wetting his lips with his tongue and keeping his fists closed tightly. The woman remained behind, but could not help watching the diminished conclusion.

In the little, palely shining arena, the dog repeated his successful maneuver three times, growling but not barking, and when Hook thrashed up from the third blow, both wings were trailing, and dark, shining streams crept on his black-fretted breast from the shoulders. The great eye flashed more furiously than it ever had in victorious battle, and the beak still gaped, but there was no more clatter. He faltered when turning to keep front; the broken wings played him false even as props. He could not rise to use his talons.

The man had tired of holding the lantern up, and put it down to rub his arm. In the low, horizontal light, the dog charged again, this time throwing the weight of his forepaws against Hook's shoulder, so that Hook was crushed as he struck. With his talons up, Hook raked at the dog's belly, but the dog conceived the finish, and furiously worried the feathered bulk. Hook's neck went limp, and between his gaping clappers came only a faint chittering, as from some small kill of his own in the grasses.

In this last conflict, however, there had been some minutes of the supreme fire of the hawk whose three hungers are perfectly fused in the one will; enough to burn off a year of shame.

Between the great sails the light body lay caved and perfectly still. The dog, smarting from his cuts, came to the master and was praised. The woman, joining them slowly, looked at the great wingspread, her husband raising the lantern that she might see it better.

"Oh, the brave bird," she said.

Indians

I claim a right to live on my land, and accord you the privilege to live on yours. —CHIEF JOSEPH

The winning of the West was in one respect a tragic defeat. The conquest of the American Indians, bitterly concluded at the Wounded Knee Massacre in 1890, followed a one-hundred-year war, undeclared and waged along the advancing frontier. The native peoples, estimated to number three hundred thousand, were deceived, defeated, and dispossessed. Those who survived epidemic, warfare, and starvation were confined to reservations where the remnants of their culture were destroyed. Americans could find no room for the Indian in the Land of the Free.

Before westward expansion, the Indians were not one people but many. Different languages and dialects, customs and values marked each tribe which thought of itself as a separate nation, a superior people. Often tribal names translated simply as "The People" to distinguish them from all the other upstart peoples on the prairies or mountains or European newcomers advancing from the East. The plains tribes (Blackfeet, Crow, Dakota, Cheyenne, Arapahoe, Kiowa, Commanche), the mountain tribes (Nez Percé, Flathead, Shoshoni, Ute) the desert tribes (Apache, Navaho, Paiute), the coastal tribes of California and the Northwest (Pomo, Yakima, Modoc), were no more red brothers than all citizens of the republic were enlightened Christians. Cultural diversity, rivalry, oppression, and warfare were established ways of life before Americans ventured West.

In the nineteenth century the history of the Indians was largely written by their enemies. Their fate was not much kinder in most fiction. Portrayed as a noble or vicious savage, the Indian often appeared as one of several stock figures. Warrior chiefs, cruel braves, stoic squaws, and bloodthirsty primitives decorated the pages of western fiction. There they posed as obstacles to manifest destiny or menaces to pioneers or a threat—finally defeated—to the cavalry. Conquered and demoralized, the final caricature of the drunken Indian became a painful social reality.

Often misrepresented in literature and denied respect in life, the Indian has been treated with more understanding in history and biography, as well as in twentieth-century fiction. In addition, a rich literature of song, oratory, and legend, carefully collected by anthropologists, has found a growing audience. In recent years an increasing number of Indian poets, novelists, and historians have been published. At last the Indian voice—dignified, grave, angry, reverent, sad—which was almost lost in the despair of reservations, has found eloquent expression.

The Way to Rainy Mountain

N. SCOTT MOMADAY

A single knoll rises out of the plain in Oklahoma, north and west of the Wichita Range. For my people, the Kiowas, it is an old landmark, and they gave it the name Rainy Mountain. The hardest weather in the world is there. Winter brings blizzards, hot tornadic winds arise in the spring, and in summer the prairie is an anvil's edge. The grass turns brittle and brown, and it cracks beneath your feet. There are green belts along the rivers and creeks, linear groves of hickory and pecan, willow and witch hazel. At a distance in July or August the steaming foliage seems almost to writhe in fire. Great green and yellow grasshoppers are everywhere in the tall grass, popping up like corn to sting the flesh, and tortoises crawl about on the red earth, going nowhere in the plenty of time. Loneliness is an aspect of the land. All things in the plain are isolate; there is no confusion of objects in the eye, but *one* hill or *one* tree or *one* man. To look upon that landscape in the early morning, with the sun at your back, is to lose the sense of proportion. Your imagination comes to life, and this, you think, is where Creation was begun.

I returned to Rainy Mountain in July. My grandmother had died in the spring, and I wanted to be at her grave. She had lived to be very old and at last infirm. Her only living daughter was with her when she died, and I was told that in death her face was that of a child.

I like to think of her as a child. When she was born, the Kiowas were living that last great moment of their history. For more than a hundred years they had controlled the open range from the Smoky Hill River to the Red, from the headwaters of the Canadian to the fork of the Arkansas and Cimarron. In alliance with the Comanches, they had ruled the whole of the southern Plains. War was their sacred business, and they were among the finest horsemen the world has ever known. But warfare for the Kiowas was preeminently a matter of disposition rather than of survival, and they never understood the grim, unrelenting advance of the U.S. Cavalry. When at

41

last, divided and ill-provisioned, they were driven onto the Staked Plains in the cold rains of autumn, they fell into panic. In Palo Duro Canyon they abandoned their crucial stores to pillage and had nothing then but their lives. In order to save themselves, they surrendered to the soldiers at Fort Sill and were imprisoned in the old stone corral that now stands as a military museum. My grandmother was spared the humiliation of those high gray walls by eight or ten years, but she must have known from birth the affliction of defeat, the dark brooding of old warriors.

Her name was Aho, and she belonged to the last culture to evolve in North America. Her forebears came down from the high country in western Montana nearly three centuries ago. They were a mountain people, a mysterious tribe of hunters whose language has never been positively classified in any major group. In the late seventeenth century they began a long migration to the south and east. It was a journey toward the dawn, and it led to a golden age. Along the way the Kiowas were befriended by the Crows, who gave them the culture and religion of the Plains. They acquired horses, and their ancient nomadic spirit was suddenly free of the ground. They acquired Tai-me, the sacred Sun Dance doll, from that moment the object and symbol of their worship, and so shared in the divinity of the sun. Not least, they acquired the sense of destiny, therefore courage and pride. When they entered upon the southern Plains they had been transformed. No longer were they slaves to the simple necessity of survival; they were a lordly and dangerous society of fighters and thieves, hunters and priests of the sun. According to their origin myth, they entered the world through a hollow log. From one point of view, their migration was the fruit of an old prophecy, for indeed they emerged from a sunless world.

Although my grandmother lived out her long life in the shadow of Rainy Mountain, the immense landscape of the continental interior lay like memory in her blood. She could tell of the Crows, whom she had never seen, and of the Black Hills, where she had never been. I wanted to see in reality what she had seen more perfectly in the mind's eye, and travelled fifteen hundred miles to begin my pilgrimage.

Yellowstone, it seemed to me, was the top of the world, a region of deep lakes and dark timber, canyons and waterfalls. But, beautiful as it is, one might have the sense of confinement there. The skyline in all directions is close at hand, the high wall of the woods and deep cleavages of shade. There is a perfect freedom in the mountains, but it belongs to the eagle and the elk, the badger and the bear. The Kiowas reckoned their stature by the distance they could see, and they were bent and blind in the wilderness.

Descending eastward, the highland meadows are a stairway to the plain. In July the inland slope of the Rockies is luxuriant with flax and buckwheat, stonecrop and larkspur. The earth unfolds and the limit of the land recedes. Clusters of trees, and animals grazing far in the distance, cause the vision to reach away and wonder to build upon the mind. The sun follows a longer course in the day, and the sky is immense beyond all comparison. The great billowing clouds that sail upon it are shadows that move upon the grain like water, dividing light. Farther down, in the land of the Crows and Blackfeet, the plain is yellow. Sweet clover takes hold of the hills and bends upon itself to cover and seal the soil. There the Kiowas paused on their way; they had come to the place where they must change their lives. The sun is at home on the plains. Precisely there does it have the certain character of a god. When the Kiowas came to the land of the Crows, they could see the dark lees of the hills at dawn across the Bighorn River, the profusion of light on the grain shelves, the oldest deity ranging after the solstices. Not yet would they veer southward to the caldron of the land that lay below; they must wean their blood from the northern winter and hold the mountains a while longer in their view. They bore Tai-me in procession to the east.

A dark mist lay over the Black Hills, and the land was like iron. At the top of a ridge I caught sight of Devil's Tower upthrust against the gray sky as if in the birth of time the core of the earth had broken through its crust and the motion of the world was begun. There are things in nature that engender an awful quiet in the heart of man; Devil's Tower is one of them. Two centuries ago, because they could not do otherwise, the Kiowas made a legend at the base of the rock. My grandmother said:

> Eight children were there at play, seven sisters and their brother. Suddenly the boy was struck dumb; he trembled and began to run upon his hands and feet. His fingers became claws, and his body was covered with fur. Directly there was a bear where the boy had been. The sisters were terrified; they ran, and the bear after them. They came to the stump of a great tree, and the tree spoke to them. It bade them climb upon it, and as they did so it began to rise into the air. The bear came to kill them, but they were just beyond its reach. It reared against the tree and scored the bark all around with its claws. The seven sisters were borne into the sky, and they became the stars of the Big Dipper.

43

From that moment, and so long as the legend lives, the Kiowas have kinsmen in the night sky. Whatever they were in the mountains, they could be no more. However tenuous their well-being, however much they had suffered and would suffer again, they had found a way out of the wilderness.

My grandmother had a reverence for the sun, a holy regard that now is all but gone out of mankind. There was a wariness in her, and an ancient awe. She was a Christian in her later years, but she had come a long way about, and she never forgot her birthright. As a child she had been to the Sun Dances; she had taken part in those annual rites, and by them she had learned the restoration of her people in the presence of Tai-me. She was about seven when the last Kiowa Sun Dance was held in 1887 on the Washita River above Rainy Mountain Creek. The buffalo were gone. In order to consummate the ancient sacrifice—to impale the head of a buffalo bull upon the medicine tree—a delegation of old men journeyed into Texas, there to beg and barter for an animal from the Goodnight herd. She was ten when the Kiowas came together for the last time as a living Sun Dance culture. They could find no buffalo, they had to hang an old hide from the sacred tree. Before the dance could begin, a company of soldiers rode out from Fort Sill under orders to disperse the tribe. Forbidden without cause the essential act of their faith, having seen the wild herds slaughtered and left to rot upon the ground, the Kiowas backed away forever from the medicine tree. That was July 20, 1890, at the great bend of the Washita. My grandmother was there. Without bitterness, and for as long as she lived, she bore a vision of deicide.

Now that I can have her only in memory, I see my grandmother in the several postures that were peculiar to her: standing at the wood stove on a winter morning and turning meat in a great iron skillet; sitting at the south window, bent above her beadwork, and afterwards, when her vision failed, looking down for a long time into the fold of her hands; going out upon a cane, very slowly as she did when the weight of age came upon her; praying. I remember her most often at prayer. She made long, rambling prayers out of suffering and hope, having seen many things. I was never sure that I had the right to hear, so exclusive were they of all mere custom and company. The last time I saw her she prayed standing by the side of her bed at night, naked to the waist, the light of a kerosene lamp moving upon her dark skin. Her long, black hair, always drawn and braided in the day, lay upon her shoulders and against her breasts like a shawl. I do not speak

Kiowa, and I never understood her prayers, but there was something inherently sad in the sound, some merest hesitation upon the syllables of sorrow. She began in a high and descending pitch, exhausting her breath to silence; then again and again—and always the same intensity of effort, of something that is, and is not, like urgency in the human voice. Transported so in the dancing light among the shadows of her room, she seemed beyond the reach of time. But that was illusion; I think I knew then that I should not see her again.

Houses are like sentinels in the plain, old keepers of the weather watch. There, in a very little while, wood takes on the appearance of great age. All colors wear soon away in the wind and rain, and then the wood is burned gray and the grain appears and the nails turn red with rust. The windowpanes are black and opaque; you imagine there is nothing within, and indeed there are many ghosts, bones given up to the land. They stand here and there against the sky, and you approach them for a longer time than you expect. They belong in the distance; it is their domain.

Once there was a lot of sound in my grandmother's house, a lot of coming and going, feasting and talk. The summers there were full of excitement and reunion. The Kiowas are a summer people; they abide the cold and keep to themselves, but when the season turns and the land becomes warm and vital they cannot hold still; an old love of going returns upon them. The aged visitors who came to my grandmother's house when I was a child were made of lean and leather, and they bore themselves upright. They wore great black hats and bright ample shirts that shook in the wind. They rubbed fat upon their hair and wound their braids with strips of colored cloth. Some of them painted their faces and carried the scars of old and cherished enmities. They were an old council of warlords, come to remind and be reminded of who they were. Their wives and daughters served them well. The women might indulge themselves; gossip was at once the mark and compensation of their servitude. They made loud and elaborate talk among themselves, full of jest and gesture, fright and false alarm. They went abroad in fringed and flowered shawls, bright beadwork and German silver. They were at home in the kitchen, and they prepared meals that were banquets.

There were frequent prayer meetings, and great nocturnal feasts. When I was a child I played with my cousins outside, where the lamplight fell upon the ground and the singing of the old people rose up around us and carried away into the darkness. There were a lot of good things to eat, a lot of laughter and surprise. And afterwards, when the quiet returned, I lay down with my grandmother and could hear the frogs away by the river and feel the motion of the air.

Now there is a funeral silence in the rooms, the endless wake of some final word. The walls have closed in upon my grandmother's house. When I returned to it in mourning, I saw for the first time in my life how small it was. It was late at night, and there was a white moon, nearly full. I sat for a long time on the stone steps by the kitchen door. From there I could see out across the land; I could see the long row of trees by the creek, the low light upon the rolling plains, and the stars of the Big Dipper. Once I looked at the moon and caught sight of a strange thing. A cricket had perched upon the handrail, only a few inches away from me. My line of vision was such that the creature filled the moon like a fossil. It had gone there, I thought, to live and die, for there, of all places, was its small definition made whole and eternal. A warm wind rose up and purled like the longing within me.

The next morning I awoke at dawn and went out on the dirt road to Rainy Mountain. It was already hot, and the grasshoppers began to fill the air. Still, it was early in the morning, and the birds sang out of the shadows. The long yellow grass on the mountain shone in the bright light, and a scissortail hied above the land. There, where it ought to be, at the end of a long and legendary way, was my grandmother's grave. Here and there on the dark stones were ancestral names. Looking back once, I saw the mountain and came away.

Death Valley—Zabriskie Point

Sitting Bull, photo by D. T. Barry

On Treaties

SITTING BULL

What treaty that the whites have kept has the red man broken? Not one. What treaty that the white man ever made with us have they kept? Not one. When I was a boy the Sioux owned the world; the sun rose and set on their land; they sent ten thousand men to battle. Where are the warriors today? Who slew them? Where are our lands? Who owns them? What white man can say I ever stole his land or a penny of his money? Yet, they say I am a thief. What white woman, however lonely, was ever captive or insulted by me? Yet they say I am a bad Indian. What white man has ever seen me drunk? Who has ever come to me hungry and unfed? Who has ever seen me beat my wives or abuse my children? What law have I broken? Is it wrong for me to love my own? Is it wicked for me because my skin is red? Because I am a Sioux; because I was born where my father lived; because I would die for my people and my country?

A Prayer
of the Night Chant

NAVAJO PRAYER

Tségihi.
House made of dawn.
House made of evening light.
House made of the dark cloud.
House made of male rain.
House made of dark mist.
House made of female rain.
House made of pollen.
House made of grasshoppers.
Dark cloud is at the door.
The trail out of it is dark cloud.
The zigzag lightning stands high upon it.
Male diety!
Your offering I make.
I have prepared a smoke for you.
Restore my feet for me.
Restore my legs for me.
Restore my body for me.
Restore my mind for me.
This very day take out your spell for me.
Your spell remove for me.
You have taken it away for me.
Far off it has gone.
Happily I recover.
Happily my interior becomes cool.
Happily I go forth.
My interior feeling cool, may I walk.

No longer sore, may I walk.
Impervious to pain, may I walk.
With lively feelings may I walk.
As it used to be long ago, may I walk.
Happily may I walk.
Happily, with abundant dark clouds, may I walk.
Happily, with abundant showers, may I walk.
Happily, with abundant plants, may I walk.
Happily, on a trail of pollen, may I walk.
Happily may I walk.
Being as it used to be long ago, may I walk.
May it be beautiful before me.
May it be beautiful behind me.
May it be beautiful below me.
May it be beautiful above me.
May it be beautiful all around me.
In beauty it is finished.

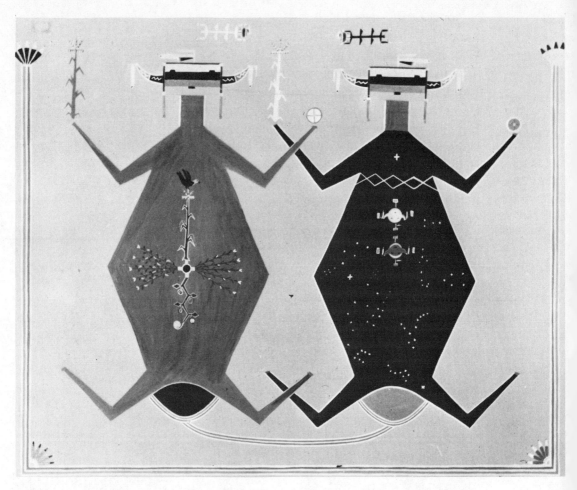

Blue Mother Earth and Sky Father, Navaho Sand Painting

All the Young Men

OLIVER LA FARGE

Old Singer was one of those Indians the trader would point out to strangers whenever he came into the store.

"See that old buck there? That's the real thing, a medicine man, too. You'd never think he was eighty, would you?" The trader would nod, and then add the fact which is a special badge of distinction among Navajos: "He was one of Haskinini's men; you know, the band that never was caught when Kit Carson rounded up the tribe and took them into exile."

He dressed well, in the later Navajo style of velveteen, calico, and silver; he carried himself with easy pride, his strong, dark face was stamped with the kindness and control of a religious man. His word carried weight in council.

As a young man, in the long past warlike days, he had been called "Hasty Arrow." Whatever the hastiness was, it disappeared after he became a medicine man, governed by the precepts of the Navajo religion. He was known as "Mountain Singer," and latterly "Old Singer."

When his wife died he began to go to pieces. From being a tall, straight old man he became bent and aged and frail. Not even the trader had realized how completely his wife had managed their business, Old Singer being wrapped up in the mysteries of his chants and dances. Now he made little or no effort to collect his fees, pawned his jewelry thoughtlessly, seemed to have become oblivious of material things.

He talked a great deal about old times, when the Navajos were true to themselves; and occasionally to men he knew well, like the trader, he would tell about the terror of that day when artillery opened on them, when they thought they had the Americans trapped and beaten, and they broke and fled under the shrapnel at Segi Chinlin.

His wife's clan divided her sheep. He let them all go, saying, "Take them. She herded them. I don't want them." With the flocks gone, and his carelessness, and a habit he developed of buying real turquoise and mother-

53

of-pearl for his ceremonial offerings, he became poor quickly. It meant nothing to him that his clothes were ragged, that he had no jewelry, that he lived in a leaky hogahn, sometimes cooking for himself, more often eating with the Indians roundabout.

The trader urged him to change his ways. Old Singer made a cigarette and smoked nearly half of it before he answered.

"As a man full of needs and wants, I am finished," he said. "I know so many songs and prayers, and the stories that stand behind them, that it would take me from the first frost to the first thunderstorm just to think them all over to myself.

"Behind all those stories, in turn, is a greater truth than they have on their faces. I am thinking about that. It is all that really matters. I am thinking about the faces that are behind the masks of the gods. I am reaching behind Nayeinezgani's mask to the one great thing."

The trader sighed. Since he was a young man Old Singer had been especially concerned with Nayeinezgani. The name means "Slayer of Enemy Gods." He is the great war god.

The trader said: "I have better than five hundred dollars' worth of your jewelry in pawn. I won't sell it, but it stands for so much goods which I bought, and I have to pay for them."

The next time Old Singer held a mountain chant he collected his full fee, and paid the trader fifty sheep on account, which released almost all his pawn. He didn't want to embarrass his friend, so when he borrowed on his goods again, he did it at other trading posts, with men he did not know so well.

He looked so poor and unworldly that the Indians stopped listening to his counsel, but as a singer—a medicine man—his reputation remained great. When he was not holding ceremonies, he meditated, or discussed with other old men like himself, who had worked on the philosophy of their religion so long, and penetrated so deep into its mysteries, that no ordinary Indian would have understood what they were saying.

His granddaughter heard how poor and ragged he was, and finally she sent for him to live with her and her husband, Homer Wesley. They were a smart pair of educated Indians who dressed well and spoke good English, and affected to despise Navajo ways. Sometimes they professed Christianity, but really they had no religion save, in the secret part of their hearts, a little longing for and a real fear of the old gods.

Wesley might have made a warrior once—he had strength and brains— but, like so many school Indians, he wanted chiefly to be slicker than white men in their manner, and he was pretty slick. It was trying to be up to the minute, and wanting a new car, that got him started running liquor into the reservation. That was dangerous work, but he did it well, drank little himself, and made big money.

They lived south of the reservation, in one of those sections where Indian allotments and white homesteads and public domain are all mixed together, the breeding grounds of continual trouble. Old Singer did not care. It was right that his granddaughter should house him. He wouldn't have to go visiting for his meals any more; he would have more time for his religion. That was enough.

But he was seriously disturbed when he found out what Wesley was doing. He'd tried liquor when he was young, knew it was fun, and a bad thing when it got going the way it had among the Navajos in recent years. He had seen the spread of drinking, and was worried about it. He hated to see bootlegging right in his family, and tried to persuade them to stop.

Even down in that section there was reputation to be gained from a famous medicine man, and Wesley was careful to collect the fees, so they bore with his talk. When Old Singer would hammer at them about being Navajos, and being true to themselves, and how completeness inside a man or a woman was all that mattered, the young man would grow sullen.

He minded being lectured by an old back number, and minded doubly because fragments of belief, and his voiceless blood, responded to what was said. In anger he conceived the idea of getting Old Singer to drink, and he finally managed it. He had known a Kiowa once, who belonged to the peyote cult, and, borrowing the idea from that man's talk, claimed that his liquor would bring beautiful, mystic experiences and religious communions, and thus persuaded the medicine man to try it.

Old Singer did have an extraordinary experience. For an hour or two he recaptured the full flavour of the old days, and later thought he was talking almost directly with Nayeinezgani. Wesley kept at it, building up the habit, aided by a nasty, raw, wet autumn. By midwinter Old Singer was drinking regularly.

His granddaughter objected at first, but Wesley convinced her. He said he was afraid of the old man's telling on them, but his taking to drink would keep his mouth shut. Besides, they could chalk off the value of the liquor

55

against his fees if he ever tried to claim what they had collected. So she let things slide until it was too late, and her grandfather was a drunkard.

Early the next winter he got drunk in the course of conducting a hail chant, and messed things up so that another singer had to be called in to do it all over again. After that no one sent for him. Leading the prayers and chants was the breath of his nostrils. He felt more and more empty and lonely as the months went by without a call. He attended many ceremonies, watching how the younger medicine men were careless and cut things short.

He was utterly apart from his granddaughter and Wesley, who began to let him see that he was a nuisance to them. The liquor did not bring him such happy experiences now. He would catch the glorious feeling, but it was confused, and then he would fall to thinking of the old days, and the decay of his nation, and at last would have a kind of horrors, talking disconnectedly about the boom of the fieldpieces at Segi Chinlin and the white man's lightning, which destroyed the lightning of Slayer of Enemy Gods.

They built him a small hogahn at some distance from the house, and fed him what was convenient when he came round. Wesley let him have liquor, hoping he would drink himself to death. As he grew decrepit, he lived further and further into the past until he was surrounded by the shades of his youth, against which the miserable present was thrown in sharp relief.

That winter and summer went by. The first frosts of autumn came, bringing again the longing for the ceremonies, his mind full of the sacred names which could not be spoken in the thunder months. He fingered his medicine bundle sadly. It contained sacred jewels, real turquoise, mother-of-pearl, red shell, and black stone. It contained the strongest kinds of medicine, and was wrapped in a perfect buckskin, which is the hide of the animal killed without wounding, absolutely unblemished.

Wesley, feeling cheerful over a big profit he had made, brought the old man two bottles of whiskey. He hadn't had a drink for nearly a week, and he needed it badly. Now he took a big pull, and sat back, looking at his bundle. It was the time for ceremonies. He took another drink and began softly singing a song for Nayeinezgani.

> Now, Slayer of Enemy Gods, I come
> Striding the mountain tops . . .

This was a bad country. These people here might be Navajos, but they were lost. Living with them, he, too, had lost his way. In Zhil Tlizhini, on the slopes of Chiz Lan-Hozhoni, were still Navajos who were men, he knew. There he could find himself; he could give them the message, to keep the gods, the power of the gods, the strength of Nayeinezgani. He started reciting the names in a half chant:

> Slayer of Enemy Gods, Child of the Waters, White Shell Woman, House God, Dawn Boy, Thunders All Around—their names fall down; the great power of their names falls down. Here the people turn them back, here the air turns them back, here the earth turns them back, here the water turns them back, their great names, the great power of their names.

He took a long drink. Quite steady and not apparently drunk, he went to the house. Standing to his full height, so that he filled the door, he said to Wesley:

"I am going away for good. Give me a horse."

Wesley stared at him. He said, "Take the pinto mare in the corral."

By the time he had his rickety saddle on the mare he was stooped again; his hands were uncertain. On the saddle he tied his blanket, with the untouched bottle in it, and his medicine bundle. That was all he owned. He took another drink and mounted.

He was dressed in cast-off overall trousers and a grotesquely ragged coat. Of his ancient style remained only the long hair, knotted behind and wrapped in a dirty, red turban, and his moccasins. The toes of one foot came through, and, having long ago sold his silver buttons, the footgear was tied on with bits of rag around the ankle.

The mare followed a cart track leading from Wesley's house to the road, then turned south. Old Singer took no heed of her direction. Whenever the liquor began to die in him he took a drink, so that by mid-afternoon he had emptied the first bottle. Everything he saw made him feel worse—badly dressed Indians, automobiles, men on horseback in the clothes of white labourers, usually pretty ragged.

Always he saw short hair and the stupid-smart expression of the young men. They wore clothes over clothes. No one stood up clean and straight in breechclout and moccasins; no one let the sun strike on strong chest and shoulders; no one wore the dignity of the old, strong blankets.

These shapes moved in and out through his dream of the past, so that he rode in a nightmare. The Navajos were dead; these were the children of dead people. He and a few others had been condemned to go on moving around after the big guns on wheels had killed them all. The lucky ones were the ones who stopped right there.

With that he remembered Hurries-to-War, who had been his friend. He remembered with longing how they had hunted and gone on the warpath together, and the warrior's figure as he stood ready for battle. He remembered this, and looked at a boy going by in an old flivver. He groaned, and started on the second bottle.

About sunset he reached a town. At first the houses had no reality to him, then he realized he was entering a white settlement, and drew rein by the roadside. The houses were strange to him. Raising his eyes, he saw cliffs to the eastward, very bold in the level sunlight with their banding of dull, greenish-white and orange strata. He recognized the cliffs. This was Tseina-chigi. They passed this way when they raided Zuñi, two hundred men, when he and Hurries-to-War were just beginning to be warriors.

This was country over which the Navajos swept at will, their raiding ground and their plaything. Now here was a big town, and the railroad. He began to be dismayed, realizing how far he had ridden in the wrong direction, regaining at this sight his urgent intention to head north for country that was still Navajo.

He dismounted and sat down wearily, cradling his medicine bundle. He needed to think. He took a little more whiskey, having reached the stage of weary intoxication where each drink braced and confused him, then quickly died away. He decided he must not sleep yet, drunk as he was, and knowing in what condition he would wake.

White men spoke just behind him; he turned to see two coming toward him. They had badges on their shirts, and one carried a gun. They spoke to him in English, then in Spanish, out of which he understood something about liquor and being drunk. He told them in Spanish that he was a good Indian, the Americans' friend.

They laughed, and took away his bottle. He let it go. Then they reached for his bundle, but he clutched it to him. They laughed again. Each took one of his elbows and hustled him along to a house, into which they took him. There was a desk, at which sat a big Mexican, also wearing a badge.

58

He and the Americans talked together, and he wrote something in a book. Old Singer stood all hunched up, hugging his bundle. Now they went seriously about taking it away from him.

After they got it, one of them had to hold him. He went on struggling and protesting in mixed Navajo and Spanish. When they opened the bundle and saw its contents, they seemed to find it funny. They poked around with their fingers among the sacred objects and made jokes. Old Singer was frantic. One of them said something. The Mexican nodded, wrapped the bundle carelessly, and gave it back. Old Singer held it tight and mumbled over it. They took him along a corridor, opened a door, shoved him into a room, slammed and locked the door.

He sat down with his bundle in his lap. For several minutes his mind was blank. Then he looked around. The room was narrow and quite bare. The door was of metal. There was one small, high, barred window. This was jail, then; they were going to keep him in jail. With the Navajos' horror of being enclosed, he went into a panic. At last, wearily, he set his bundle on the dirt floor.

This was his end; he might at least pray. This was his great need. He might at least meet his end talking with the gods, if they would hear him, if he had not cut himself off from them forever. He had everything here—prayer sticks, breath plumes, sacred jewels.

As his hands performed the familiar acts of arrangement, he gained a little courage. Life pollen, sacred cigarettes, Nayeinezgani's cigarette, clear stones, blue feathers, yellow feathers and a perfect buckskin.

That was the keystone of his power, to pray sitting before the unwounded skin. Having taken everything out of it, he began smoothing it out, his hands moving slowly. Then his hands stopped; his heart jumped downward, and his eyes ceased seeing. It was torn, ripped wide across near the head.

After sunset the cell grew dark and chilly in a short time. In the complete blackness, with the fumes of liquor and great fatigue, his fear reached fantastic depths and grew into a kind of exaltation. His right hand began to move forward with a slight downstroke, and back, as though he were shaking a rattle. His lips formed a prayer to Slayer of Enemy Gods. By the second verse his voice had risen to a soft whisper. His eyes were closed and his ears were stopped.

59

The cold slid in along his skin; he might as well have had no clothes on. As though in opposition to the reality, he began the prayer, "Dawn Boy, little chief." It was very chilly.

He would have done well to have brought a blanket, but then one would not want to seem soft. It had been long and slow, lying out on the mesa, watching just that one line of pass against the night sky for a movement, a quiver of the horizon, that would mean the Americans were coming. Now when he rose and stretched he was stiff. He reached his arms out to the white line in the east, intoning his prayer softly.

Day seeped into the sky overhead, but had not yet touched the cañon below him. The east was brilliant. He looked to the south again, and his blood leaped. A column of smoke rose from Tletsosenili—broke, rose, broke, rose. He read the code, twanged his bowstring, and ran down the gully to where his pony was tethered.

In the cañon he met Hurries-to-War on his blue roan.

"Come along," his friend said; "it is time."

They rode together. Hasty Arrow was surprised to see how handsome the man was. Everything was familiar, but he seemed to have new eyes, a new perception. He felt a sharp pleasure at the sight of a warrior stripped for battle, at the long hair on his brown shoulders, his muscles, his lance. The rich, strong colours of his blanket almost sang.

He saw Segi Cañon, too, as though it had just been made, the wide valley and high, red cliffs with spruce trees on the upper ledges; the brilliant, gold sunlight touching the highest places. They loped, feeling the morning air tingle against their chests.

More and more men joined them until they led an army. Hasty Arrow looked back at the tossing, feathered spears, the bright headbands, the brown torsos and strong blankets and lively horses. He felt the vigour of his people. We cannot be beaten, he thought.

Hurries-to-War said, "Over here."

They turned into a narrow side cañon and mounted a precipitous trail where their ponies climbed like goats, now at a fast walk, now at a scrambling trot. They came out on a high, small mesa where a clump of spruce trees stood by a clear spring. Halting, the two friends looked about them.

From here one could see all around to the blue, distant boundary mountains at the extreme ends of the four directions. Mesa and cañon and plain, the immensity of the Navajo country was under their hands. From Tlet-sosenili the smoke of the signal fire still rose.

"Make a prayer for us," said Hurries-to-War. "You have everything."

Hasty Arrow put his hand behind his saddle and felt the bundle. Dismounting, he spread the objects around his buckskin, just as though he were an initiated singer. The young men gathered behind and on each side of him, save Hurries-to-War, who sat his horse just in front. Hasty Arrow looked around, half smiling, at the familiar, brave faces, thinking about their true names, concentrating himself.

He offered the cigarettes and threw the life pollen, then he began to sing. He did not follow a prescribed ceremony. Songs came to his lips in an order which seemed to be dictated to them.

> Now Slayer of Enemy Gods, alone I see him coming;
> Down from the skies, alone I see him coming.
> His voice sounds all about,
> His voice sounds divine!

He went on through the four verses, calling the warrior gods. Looking up at his friend, he was disturbed by his beauty. It was almost intolerable.

> Now with a god I walk,
> Striding over mountains . . .

It was not just his friend, not just a man. The blue pony stood on the ground, but it was high above them. Hasty Arrow swung into another song.

> Now, Nayeinezgani, on my
> turquoise horse I ride . . .

He sat above them on his horse, standing on the end of a bent rainbow; not the masked impersonation of the dances, but the great, young war god himself in majesty. The turquoise horse struck lightning with his hoofs. His mane and tail were rain; lightning rustled as it played around the arrows in the god's quiver; sunbeams were gathered above his head. He looked down, smiling.

Hasty Arrow was rent with joy and exalted fear. His heart was high above him.

61

> Lightnings flash out from me; they zigzag
> > Four times.
> Striking and returning, they zigzag
> > Four times.

He began the final song.

> I am thinking about the enemy gods . . .

An alien voice sounded somewhere, and heavy footsteps. A cold fear without meaning rose in him. Behind what he saw was something trying to be seen. He sang louder. The heavy voice spoke again, and there was pounding. The big guns began to boom, the white men's lightning flashed in the air, and Nayeinezgani's arrows stayed in his quiver.

He was two things at once; he was fighting down a knowledge in his mind. All the young men were dead long ago; they faded before his eyes, and the war god was high upon his rainbow. He clung desperately to his song, singing with all his voice and all his being. The young men, the beauty of the Navajos, were riding off into the sky. He was alone, making a prayer with a torn buckskin.

> The enemy gods, the enemy gods,
> I wander among their weapons . . .

He sang, trying to keep that vision, to keep away the cell walls. He was an old man praying in agony. White men were opening the door to do something to him. Over Nayeinezgani came a mask of a ragged, drunken Indian with a bottle in his hand. Old Singer's voice rose frantically:

> Now on the old-age trail, now on the path of beauty walking,
> The enemy gods, the enemy gods . . .

Slayer of Enemy Gods leaned down, smiling, and picked him up as one might pick up a child. He placed Old Singer behind the saddle on his turquoise horse, wheeled on the rainbow, and galloped up after the warriors, beyond the reach of white men.

María Concepción

KATHERINE ANNE PORTER

María Concepción walked carefully, keeping to the middle of the white dusty road, where the maguey thorns and the treacherous curved spines of organ cactus had not gathered so profusely. She would have enjoyed resting for a moment in the dark shade by the roadside, but she had no time to waste drawing cactus needles from her feet. Juan and his chief would be waiting for their food in the damp trenches of the buried city.

She carried about a dozen living fowls slung over her right shoulder, their feet fastened together. Half of them fell upon the flat of her back, the balance dangled uneasily over her breast. They wriggled their benumbed and swollen legs against her neck, they twisted their stupefied eyes and peered into her face inquiringly. She did not see them or think of them. Her left arm was tired with the weight of the food basket, and she was hungry after her long morning's work.

Her straight back outlined itself strongly under her clean bright blue cotton rebozo. Instinctive serenity softened her black eyes, shaped like almonds, set far apart, and tilted a bit endwise. She walked with the free, natural, guarded ease of the primitive woman carrying an unborn child. The shape of her body was easy, the swelling life was not a distortion, but the right inevitable proportions of a woman. She was entirely contented. Her husband was at work and she was on her way to market to sell her fowls.

Her small house sat half-way up a shallow hill, under a clump of pepper-trees, a wall of organ cactus enclosing it on the side nearest to the road. Now she came down into the valley, divided by the narrow spring, and crossed a bridge of loose stones near the hut where María Rosa the bee-keeper lived with her old godmother, Lupe the medicine woman. María Concepción had no faith in the charred owl bones, the singed rabbit fur, the cat entrails, the messes and ointments sold by Lupe to the ailing of the village. She was a good Christian, and drank simple herb teas for headache and stomachache, or bought her remedies bottled, with printed directions

63

that she could not read, at the drugstore near the city market, where she went almost daily. But she often bought a jar of honey from young María Rosa, a pretty, shy child only fifteen years old.

María Concepción and her husband, Juan Villegas, were each a little past their eighteenth year. She had a good reputation with the neighbors as an energetic religious woman who could drive a bargain to the end. It was commonly known that if she wished to buy a new rebozo for herself or a shirt for Juan, she could bring out a sack of hard silver coins for the purpose.

She had paid for the license, nearly a year ago, the potent bit of stamped paper which permits people to be married in the church. She had given money to the priest before she and Juan walked together up to the altar the Monday after Holy Week. It had been the adventure of the villagers to go, three Sundays one after another, to hear the banns called by the priest for Juan de Dios Villegas and María Concepción Manríquez, who were actually getting married in the church, instead of behind it, which was the usual custom, less expensive, and as binding as any other ceremony. But María Concepción was always as proud as if she owned a hacienda.

She paused on the bridge and dabbled her feet in the water, her eyes resting themselves from the sun-rays in a fixed gaze to the far-off mountains, deeply blue under their hanging drift of clouds. It came to her that she would like a fresh crust of honey. The delicious aroma of bees, their slow thrilling hum, awakened a pleasant desire for a flake of sweetness in her mouth.

"If I do not eat it now, I shall mark my child," she thought, peering through the crevices in the thick hedge of cactus that sheered up nakedly, like bared knife blades set protectingly around the small clearing. The place was so silent she doubted if María Rosa and Lupe were at home.

The leaning jacal of dried rush-withes and corn sheaves, bound to tall saplings thrust into the earth, roofed with yellowed maguey leaves flattened and overlapping like shingles, hunched drowsy and fragrant in the warmth of noonday. The hives, similarly made, were scattered towards the back of the clearing, like small mounds of clean vegetable refuse. Over each mound there hung a dusty golden shimmer of bees.

A light gay scream of laughter rose from behind the hut; a man's short laugh joined in. "Ah, hahahaha!" went the voices together high and low, like a song.

64

"So María Rosa has a man!" María Concepción stopped short, smiling, shifted her burden slightly, and bent forward shading her eyes to see more clearly through the spaces of the hedge.

María Rosa ran, dodging between beehives, parting two stunted jasmine bushes as she came, lifting her knees in swift leaps, looking over her shoulder and laughing in a quivering, excited way. A heavy jar, swung to her wrist by the handle, knocked against her thighs as she ran. Her toes pushed up sudden spurts of dust, her half-raveled braids showered around her shoulders in long crinkled wisps.

Juan Villegas ran after her, also laughing strangely, his teeth set, both rows gleaming behind the small soft black beard growing sparsely on his lips, his chin, leaving his brown cheeks girl-smooth. When he seized her, he clenched so hard her chemise gave way and ripped from her shoulder. She stopped laughing at this, pushed him away and stood silent, trying to pull up the torn sleeve with one hand. Her pointed chin and dark red mouth moved in an uncertain way, as if she wished to laugh again; her long black lashes flickered with the quick-moving lights in her hidden eyes.

María Concepción did not stir nor breathe for some seconds. Her forehead was cold, and yet boiling water seemed to be pouring slowly along her spine. An unaccountable pain was in her knees, as if they were broken. She was afraid Juan and María Rosa would feel her eyes fixed upon them and would find her there, unable to move, spying upon them. But they did not pass beyond the enclosure, nor even glance towards the gap in the wall opening upon the road.

Juan lifted one of María Rosa's loosened braids and slapped her neck with it playfully. She smiled softly, consentingly. Together they moved back through the hives of honey-comb. María Rosa balanced her jar on one hip and swung her long full petticoats with every step. Juan flourished his wide hat back and forth, walking proudly as a game-cock.

María Concepción came out of the heavy cloud which enwrapped her head and bound her throat, and found herself walking onward, keeping the road without knowing it, feeling her way delicately, her ears strumming as if all María Rosa's bees had hived in them. Her careful sense of duty kept her moving toward the buried city where Juan's chief, the American archeologist, was taking his midday rest, waiting for his food.

Juan and María Rosa! She burned all over now, as if a layer of tiny fig-cactus bristles, as cruel as spun glass, had crawled under her skin. She wished to sit down quietly and wait for her death, but not until she had cut the throats of her man and that girl who were laughing and kissing under the cornstalks. Once when she was a young girl she had come back from market to find her jacal burned to a pile of ash and her few silver coins gone. A dark empty feeling had filled her; she kept moving about the place, not believing her eyes, expecting it all to take shape again before her. But it was gone, and though she knew an enemy had done it, she could not find out who it was, and could only curse and threaten the air. Now here was a worse thing, but she knew her enemy. María Rosa, that sinful girl, shameless! She heard herself saying a harsh, true word about María Rosa, saying it aloud as if she expected someone to agree with her: "Yes, she is a whore! She has no right to live."

At this moment the gray untidy head of Givens appeared over the edges of the newest trench he had caused to be dug in his field of excavations. The long deep crevasses, in which a man might stand without being seen, lay crisscrossed like orderly gashes of a giant scalpel. Nearly all of the men of the community worked for Givens, helping him to uncover the lost city of their ancestors. They worked all the year through and prospered, digging every day for those small clay heads and bits of pottery and fragments of painted walls for which there was no good use on earth, being all broken and encrusted with clay. They themselves could make better ones, perfectly stout and new, which they took to town and peddled to foreigners for real money. But the unearthly delight of the chief in finding these wornout things was an endless puzzle. He would fairly roar for joy at times, waving a shattered pot or a human skull above his head, shouting for his photographer to come and make a picture of this!

Now he emerged, and his young enthusiast's eyes welcomed María Concepción from his old-man face, covered with hard wrinkles and burned to the color of red earth. "I hope you've brought me a nice fat one." He selected a fowl from the bunch dangling nearest him as María Concepción, wordless, leaned over the trench. "Dress it for me, there's a good girl. I'll broil it."

María Concepción took the fowl by the head, and silently, swiftly drew her knife across its throat, twisting the head off with the casual firmness she might use with the top of a beet.

"Good God, woman, you do have nerve," said Givens, watching her. "I can't do that. It gives me the creeps."

66

"My home country is Guadalajara," explained María Concepción, without bravado, as she picked and gutted the fowl.

She stood and regarded Givens condescendingly, that diverting white man who had no woman of his own to cook for him, and moreover appeared not to feel any loss of dignity in preparing his own food. He squatted now, eyes squinted, nose wrinkled to avoid the smoke, turning the roasting fowl busily on a stick. A mysterious man, undoubtedly rich, and Juan's chief, therefore to be respected, to be placated.

"The tortillas are fresh and hot, señor," she murmured gently. "With your permission I will now go to market."

"Yes, yes, run along; bring me another of these tomorrow." Givens turned his head to look at her again. Her grand manner sometimes reminded him of royalty in exile. He noticed her unnatural paleness. "The sun is too hot, eh?" he asked.

"Yes, sir. Pardon me, but Juan will be here soon?"

"He ought to be here now. Leave his food. The others will eat it."

She moved away; the blue of her rebozo became a dancing spot in the heat waves that rose from the gray-red soil. Givens liked his Indians best when he could feel a fatherly indulgence for their primitive childish ways. He told comic stories of Juan's escapades, of how often he had saved him, in the past five years, from going to jail, and even from being shot, for his varied and always unexpected misdeeds.

"I am never a minute too soon to get him out of one pickle or another," he would say. "Well, he's a good worker, and I know how to manage him."

After Juan was married, he used to twit him, with exactly the right shade of condescension, on his many infidelities to María Concepción. "She'll catch you yet, and God help you!" he was fond of saying, and Juan would laugh with immense pleasure.

It did not occur to María Concepción to tell Juan she had found him out. During the day her anger against him died, and her anger against María Rosa grew. She kept saying to herself, "When I was a young girl like María Rosa, if a man had caught hold of me so, I would have broken my jar over his head." She forgot completely that she had not resisted even so much as María Rosa, on the day that Juan had first taken hold of her. Besides she had married him afterwards in the church, and that was a very different thing.

Juan did not come home that night, but went away to war and María Rosa went with him. Juan had a rifle at his shoulder and two pistols at his belt. María Rosa wore a rifle also, slung on her back along with the blankets and the cooking pots. They joined the nearest detachment of troops in the field, and María Rosa marched ahead with the battalion of experienced women at war, which went over the crops like locusts, gathering provisions for the army. She cooked with them, and ate with them what was left after the men had eaten. After battles she went out on the field with the others to salvage clothing and ammunition and guns from the slain before they should begin to swell in the heat. Sometimes they would encounter the women from the other army, and a second battle as grim as the first would take place.

There was no particular scandal in the village. People shrugged, grinned. It was far better that they were gone. The neighbors went around saying that María Rosa was safer in the army than she would be in the same village with María Concepción.

María Concepción did not weep when Juan left her; and when the baby was born, and died within four days, she did not weep. "She is mere stone," said old Lupe, who went over and offered charms to preserve the baby.

"May you rot in hell with your charms," said María Concepción.

If she had not gone so regularly to church, lighting candles before the saints, kneeling with her arms spread in the form of a cross for hours at a time, and receiving holy communion every month, there might have been talk of her being devil-possessed, her face was so changed and blind-looking. But this was impossible when, after all, she had been married by the priest. It must be, they reasoned, that she was being punished for her pride. They decided that this was the true cause for everything: she was altogether too proud. So they pitied her.

During the year that Juan and María Rosa were gone María Concepción sold her fowls and looked after her garden and her sack of hard coins grew. Lupe had no talent for bees, and the hives did not prosper. She began to blame María Rosa for running away, and to praise María Concepción for her behavior. She used to see María Concepción at the market or at church, and she always said that no one could tell by looking at her now that she was a woman who had such a heavy grief.

"I pray God everything goes well with María Concepción from this out," she would say, "for she has had her share of trouble."

When some idle person repeated this to the deserted woman, she went down to Lupe's house and stood within the clearing and called to the medicine woman, who sat in her doorway stirring a mess of her infallible cure for sores: "Keep your prayers to yourself, Lupe, or offer them for others who need them. I will ask God for what I want in this world."

"And will you get it, you think, María Concepción?" asked Lupe, tittering cruelly and smelling the wooden mixing spoon. "Did you pray for what you have now?"

Afterward everyone noticed that María Concepción went oftener to church, and even seldomer to the village to talk with the other women as they sat along the curb, nursing their babies and eating fruit, at the end of the market-day.

"She is wrong to take us for enemies," said old Soledad, who was a thinker and a peace-maker. "All women have these troubles. Well, we should suffer together."

But María Concepción lived alone. She was gaunt, as if something were gnawing her away inside, her eyes were sunken, and she would not speak a word if she could help it. She worked harder than ever, and her butchering knife was scarcely ever out of her hand.

Juan and María Rosa, disgusted with military life, came home one day without asking permission of anyone. The field of war had unrolled itself, a long scroll of vexations, until the end had frayed out within twenty miles of Juan's village. So he and María Rosa, now lean as a wolf, burdened with a child daily expected, set out with no farewells to the regiment and walked home.

They arrived one morning about daybreak. Juan was picked up on sight by a group of military police from the small barracks on the edge of town, and taken to prison, where the officer in charge told him with impersonal cheerfulness that he would add one to a catch of ten waiting to be shot as deserters the next morning.

María Rosa, screaming and falling on her face in the road, was taken under the armpits by two guards and helped briskly to her jacal, now sadly run down. She was received with professional importance by Lupe, who helped the baby to be born at once.

Limping with foot soreness, a layer of dust concealing his fine new clothes got mysteriously from somewhere, Juan appeared before the captain at the barracks. The captain recognized him as head digger for his good friend Givens, and dispatched a note to Givens saying: "I am holding the person of Juan Villegas awaiting your further disposition."

When Givens showed up Juan was delivered to him with the urgent request that nothing be made public about so humane and sensible an operation on the part of military authority.

Juan walked out of the rather stifling atmosphere of the drumhead court, a definite air of swagger about him. His hat, of unreasonable dimensions and embroidered with silver thread, hung over one eyebrow, secured at the back by a cord of silver dripping with bright blue tassels. His shirt was of a checkerboard pattern in green and black, his white cotton trousers were bound by a belt of yellow leather tooled in red. His feet were bare, full of stone bruises, and sadly ragged as to toenails. He removed his cigarette from the center of his full-lipped wide mouth. He removed the splendid hat. His black dusty hair, pressed moistly to his forehead, sprang up suddenly in a cloudy thatch on his crown. He bowed to the officer, who appeared to be gazing at a vacuum. He swung his arm wide in a free circle upsoaring towards the prison window, where forlorn heads poked over the window sill, hot eyes following after the lucky departing one. Two or three of the heads nodded, and a half dozen hands were flipped at him in an effort to imitate his own casual and heady manner.

Juan kept up this insufferable pantomime until they rounded the first clump of fig-cactus. Then he seized Givens' hand and burst into oratory. "Blessed be the day your servant Juan Villegas first came under your eyes. From this day my life is yours without condition, ten thousand thanks with all my heart!"

"For God's sake stop playing the fool," said Givens irritably. "Some day I'm going to be five minutes too late."

"Well, it is nothing much to be shot, my chief—certainly you know I was not afraid—but to be shot in a drove of deserters, against a cold wall, just in the moment of my home-coming, by order of that . . ."

Glittering epithets tumbled over one another like explosions of a rocket. All the scandalous analogies from the animal and vegetable worlds were applied in a vivid, unique and personal way of life, loves, and family history of the officer who had just set him free. When he had quite cursed himself dry, and his nerves were soothed, he added: "With your permission, my chief!"

"What will María Concepción say to all this?" asked Givens. "You are very informal, Juan, for a man who was married in the church."

Juan put on his hat.

"Oh, María Concepción! That's nothing. Look, my chief, to be married in the church is a great misfortune for a man. After that he is not himself any more. How can that woman complain when I do not drink even at fiestas enough to be really drunk? I do not beat her; never, never. We were always at peace. I say to her, Come here, and she comes straight. I say, Go there, and she goes quickly. Yet sometimes I looked at her and thought, Now I am married to that woman in the church, and I felt a sinking inside, as if something were lying heavy on my stomach. With María Rosa it is all different. She is not silent; she talks. When she talks too much, I slap her and say, Silence, thou simpleton! and she weeps. She is just a girl with whom I do as I please. You know how she used to keep those clean little bees in their hives? She is like their honey to me. I swear it. I would not harm María Concepción because I am married to her in the church; but also, my chief, I will not leave María Rosa, because she pleases me more than any other woman."

"Let me tell you, Juan, things haven't been going as well as you think. You be careful. Some day María Concepción will just take your head off with that carving knife of hers. You keep that in mind."

Juan's expression was the proper blend of masculine triumph and sentimental melancholy. It was pleasant to see himself in the role of hero to two such desirable women. He had just escaped from the threat of a disagreeable end. His clothes were new and handsome, and they had cost him just nothing. María Rosa had collected them for him here and there after battles. He was walking in the early sunshine, smelling the good smells of ripening cactus-figs, peaches, and melons, of pungent berries dangling from the pepper-trees, and the smoke of his cigarette under his nose. He was on his way to civilian life with his patient chief. His situation was ineffably perfect, and he swallowed it whole.

"My chief," he addressed Givens handsomely, as one man of the world to another, "women are good things, but not at this moment. With your permission, I will now go to the village and eat. My God, *how* I shall eat! Tomorrow morning very early I will come to the buried city and work like seven men. Let us forget María Concepción and María Rosa. Each one in her place. I will manage them when the time comes."

News of Juan's adventure soon got abroad, and Juan found many friends about him during the morning. They frankly commended his way of leaving the army. It was in itself the act of a hero. The new hero ate a great deal and drank somewhat, the occasion being better than a feast-day. It was almost noon before he returned to visit María Rosa.

He found her sitting on a clean straw mat, rubbing fat on her three-hour-old son. Before this felicitous vision Juan's emotions so twisted him that he returned to the village and invited every man in the "Death and Resurrection" pulque ship to drink with him.

Having thus taken leave of his balance, he started back to María Rosa, and found himself unaccountably in his own house, attempting to beat María Concepción by way of reestablishing himself in his legal household.

María Concepción, knowing all the events of that unhappy day, was not in a yielding mood, and refused to be beaten. She did not scream nor implore; she stood her ground and resisted; she even struck at him. Juan, amazed, hardly knowing what he did, stepped back and gazed at her inquiringly through a leisurely whirling film which seemed to have lodged behind his eyes. Certainly he had not even thought of touching her. Oh, well, no harm done. He gave up, turned away, half-asleep on his feet. He dropped amiably in a shadowed corner and began to snore.

María Concepción, seeing that he was quiet, began to bind the legs of her fowls. It was market-day and she was late. She fumbled and tangled the bits of cord in her haste, and set off across the plowed fields instead of taking the accustomed road. She ran with a crazy panic in her head, her stumbling legs. Now and then she would stop and look about her, trying to place herself, then go on a few steps, until she realized that she was not going towards the market.

At once she came to her senses completely, recognized the thing that troubled her so terribly, was certain of what she wanted. She sat down quietly under a sheltering thorny bush and gave herself over to her long devouring sorrow. The thing which had for so long squeezed her whole body into a tight dumb knot of suffering suddenly broke with shocking violence. She jerked with the involuntary recoil of one who receives a blow, and the sweat poured from her skin as if the wounds of her whole life were shedding their salt ichor. Drawing her rebozo over her head, she bowed her forehead on her updrawn knees, and sat there in deadly silence and immobility. From time to time she lifted her head where the sweat formed steadily and poured down her face, drenching the front of her chemise, and her mouth had the shape of crying, but there were no tears and no sound. All her being was a dark confused memory of grief burning in her at night, of deadly baffled anger eating at her by day, until her very tongue tasted bitter, and her feet were as heavy as if she were mired in the muddy roads during the time of rains.

After a great while she stood up and threw the rebozo off her face, and set out walking again.

Juan awakened slowly, with long yawns and grumblings, alternated with short relapses into sleep full of visions and clamors. A blur of orange light seared his eyeballs when he tried to unseal his lids. There came from somewhere a low voice weeping without tears, saying meaningless phrases over and over. He began to listen. He tugged at the leash of his stupor, he strained to grasp those words which terrified him even though he could not quite hear them. Then he came awake with frightening suddenness, sitting up and staring at the long sharpened streak of light piercing the corn-husk walls from the level disappearing sun.

María Concepción stood in the doorway, looming colossally tall to his betrayed eyes. She was talking quickly, and calling his name. Then he saw her clearly.

"God's name!" said Juan, frozen to the marrow, "here I am facing my death!" for the long knife she wore habitually at her belt was in her hand. But instead, she threw it away, clear from her, and got down on her knees, crawling toward him as he had seen her crawl many times toward the shrine at Guadalupe Villa. He watched her approach with such horror that the hair of his head seemed to be lifting itself away from him. Falling forward upon her face, she huddled over him, lips moving in a ghostly whisper. Her words became clear, and Juan understood them all.

For a second he could not move nor speak. Then he took her head between both his hands, and supported her in this way, saying swiftly, anxiously reassuring, almost in a babble:

"Oh, thou poor creature! Oh, madwoman! Oh, my María Concepción, unfortunate! Listen. . . . Don't be afraid. Listen to me! I will hide thee away, I thy own man will protect thee! Quiet! Not a sound!"

Trying to collect himself, he held her and cursed under his breath for a few moments in the gathering darkness. María Concepción bent over, face almost on the ground, her feet folded under her, as if she would hide behind him. For the first time in his life Juan was aware of danger. This was danger. María Concepción would be dragged away between two gendarmes, with him following helpless and unarmed, to spend the rest of her days in Belén Prison, maybe. Danger! The night swarmed with threats. He stood up and dragged her up with him. She was silent and perfectly rigid, holding to him with resistless strength, her hands stiffened on his arms.

"Get me the knife," he told her in a whisper. She obeyed, her feet slipping along the hard earth floor, her shoulders straight, her arms close to her side. He lighted a candle. María Concepción held the knife out to him. It was stained and dark even to the handle with drying blood.

He frowned at her harshly, noting the same stains on her chemise and hands.

"Take off thy clothes and wash thy hands," he ordered. He washed the knife carefully, and threw the water wide of the doorway. She watched him and did likewise with the bowl in which she had bathed.

"Light the brasero and cook food for me," he told her in the same peremptory tone. He took her garments and went out. When he returned, she was wearing an old soiled dress, and was fanning the fire in the charcoal burner. Seating himself cross-legged near her, he stared at her as a creature unknown to him, who bewildered him utterly, for whom there was no possible explanation. She did not turn her head, but kept silent and still, except for the movements of her strong hands fanning the blaze which cast sparks and small jets of white smoke, flaring and dying rhythmically with the motion of the fan, lighting her face and darkening it by turns.

Juan's voice barely disturbed the silence: "Listen to me carefully, and tell me the truth, and when the gendarmes come here for us, thou shalt have nothing to fear. But there will be something for us to settle between us afterward."

The light from the charcoal burner shone in her eyes; a yellow phosphorescence glimmered behind the dark iris.

"For me everything is settled now," she answered, in a tone so tender, so grave, so heavy with suffering, that Juan felt his vitals contract. He wished to repent openly, not as a man, but as a very small child. He could not fathom her, nor himself, nor the mysterious fortunes of life grown so instantly confused where all had seemed so gay and simple. He felt too that she had become invaluable, a woman without equal among a million women, and he could not tell why. He drew an enormous sigh that rattled in his chest.

"Yes, yes, it is all settled. I shall not go away again. We must stay here together."

Whispering, he questioned her and she answered whispering, and he instructed her over and over until she had her lesson by heart. The hostile darkness of the night encroached upon them, flowing over the narrow threshold, invading their hearts. It brought with it sighs and murmurs, the pad of secretive feet in the near-by road, the sharp staccato whimper of wind through the cactus leaves. All these familiar, once friendly cadences were now invested with sinister terrors; a dread, formless and uncontrollable, took hold of them both.

"Light another candle," said Juan, loudly, in too resolute, too sharp a tone. "Let us eat now."

They sat facing each other and ate from the same dish, after their old habit. Neither tasted what they ate. With food halfway to his mouth, Juan listened. The sound of voices rose, spread, widened at the turn of the road along the cactus wall. A spray of lantern light shot through the hedge, a single voice slashed the blackness, ripped the fragile layer of silence suspended above the hut.

"Juan Villegas!"

"Pass, friends!" Juan roared back cheerfully.

They stood in the doorway, simple cautious gendarmes from the village, mixed-bloods themselves with Indian sympathies, well known to all the community. They flashed their lanterns almost apologetically upon the pleasant, harmless scene of a man eating supper with his wife.

"Pardon, brother," said the leader. "Someone has killed the woman María Rosa, and we must question her neighbors and friends." He paused, and added with an attempt at severity, "Naturally!"

"Naturally," agreed Juan. "You know that I was a good friend of María Rosa. This is bad news."

They all went away together, the men walking in a group, María Concepción following a few steps in the rear, near Juan. No one spoke.

The two points of candlelight at María Rosa's head fluttered uneasily; the shadows shifted and dodged on the stained darkened walls. To

María Concepción everything in the smothering enclosing room shared an evil restlessness. The watchful faces of those called as witnesses, the faces of old friends, were made alien by the look of speculation in their eyes. The ridges of the rose-colored rebozo thrown over the body varied continually, as though the thing it covered was not perfectly in repose. Her eyes swerved over the body in the open painted coffin, from the candle tips at the head to the feet, jutting up thinly, the small scarred soles protruding, freshly washed, a mass of crooked, half-healed wounds, thorn-pricks and cuts of sharp stones. Her gaze went back to the candle flame, to Juan's eyes warning her, to the gendarmes talking among themselves. Her eyes would not be controlled.

With a leap that shook her, her gaze settled upon the face of María Rosa. Instantly her blood ran smoothly again: there was nothing to fear. Even the restless light could not give a look of life to that fixed countenance. She was dead. María Concepción felt her muscles give way softly; her heart began beating steadily without effort. She knew no more rancor against that pitiable thing, lying indifferently in its blue coffin under the fine silk rebozo. The mouth drooped sharply at the corners in a grimace of weeping arrested half-way. The brows were distressed; the dead flesh could not cast off the shape of its last terror. It was all finished. María Rosa had eaten too much honey and had had too much love. Now she must sit in hell, crying over her sins and her hard death forever and ever.

Old Lupe's cackling voice arose. She had spent the morning helping María Rosa, and it had been hard work. The child had spat blood the moment it was born, a bad sign. She thought then that bad luck would come to the house. Well, about sunset she was in the yard at the back of the house grinding tomatoes and peppers. She had left mother and babe asleep. She heard a strange noise in the house, a choking and smothered calling, like someone wailing in sleep. Well, such a thing is only natural. But there followed a light, quick, thudding sound—

"Like the blows of a fist?" interrupted an officer.

"No, not at all like such a thing."

"How do you know?"

"I am well acquainted with that sound, friends," retorted Lupe. "This was something else."

She was at a loss to describe it exactly. A moment later, there came the sound of pebbles rolling and slipping under feet; then she knew someone had been there and was running away.

"Why did you wait so long before going to see?"

"I am old and hard in the joints," said Lupe. "I cannot run after people. I walked as fast as I could to the cactus hedge, for it is only by this way that anyone can enter. There was no one in the road, sir, no one. Three cows, with a dog driving them; nothing else. When I got to María Rosa, she was lying all tangled up, and from her neck to her middle she was full of knifeholes. It was a sight to move the Blessed Image Himself! Her eyes were—"

"Never mind. Who came oftenest to her house before she went away? Did you know her enemies?"

Lupe's face congealed, closed. Her spongy skin drew into a network of secretive wrinkles. She turned withdrawn and expressionless eyes upon the gendarmes.

"I am an old woman. I do not see well. I cannot hurry on my feet. I know no enemy of María Rosa. I did not see anyone leave the clearing."

"You did not hear splashing in the spring near the bridge?"

"No, sir."

"Why, then, do our dogs follow a scent there and lose it?"

"God only knows, my friend. I am an old wom—"

"Yes. How did the footfalls sound?"

"Like the tread of an evil spirit!" Lupe broke forth in a swelling oracular tone that startled them. The Indians stirred uneasily, glanced at the dead, then at Lupe. They half expected her to produce the evil spirit among them at once.

The gendarme began to lose his temper.

"No, poor unfortunate; I mean, were they heavy or light? The footsteps of a man or of a woman? Was the person shod or barefoot?"

A glance at the listening circle assured Lupe of their thrilled attention. She enjoyed the dangerous importance of her situation. She could have ruined that María Concepción with a word, but it was even sweeter to make fools of these gendarmes who went about spying on honest people. She raised her voice again. What she had not seen she could not describe, thank God! No one could harm her because her knees were stiff and she could not run even to seize a murderer. As for knowing the difference between footfalls, shod or bare, man or woman, nay, between devil and human, who ever heard of such madness?

"My eyes are not ears, gentlemen," she ended grandly, "but upon my heart I swear those footsteps fell as the tread of the spirit of evil!"

"Imbecile!" yapped the leader in a shrill voice. "Take her away, one of you! Now, Juan Villegas, tell me—"

Juan told his story patiently, several times over. He had returned to his wife that day. She had gone to market as usual. He had helped her prepare her fowls. She had returned about mid-afternoon, they had talked, she had cooked, they had eaten, nothing was amiss. Then the gendarmes came with the news about María Rosa. That was all. Yes, María Rosa had run away with him, but there had been no bad blood between his wife and María Rosa. Everybody knew that his wife was a quiet woman.

María Concepción heard her own voice answering without a break. It was true at first she was troubled when her husband went away, but after that she had not worried about him. It was the way of men, she believed. She was a church-married woman and knew her place. Well, he had come home at last. She had gone to market, but had come back early, because now she had her man to cook for. That was all.

Other voices broke in. A toothless old man said: "She is a woman of good reputation among us, and María Rosa was not." A smiling young mother, Anita, baby at breast, said: "If no one thinks so, how can you accuse her? It was the loss of her child, and not of her husband that changed her so." Another: "María Rosa had a strange life, apart from us. How do we know who might have come from another place to do her evil?" And old Soledad spoke up boldly: "When I saw María Concepción in the market today, I said, 'Good luck to you, María Concepción, this is a happy day for you!'" and she gave María Concepción a long easy stare, and the smile of a born wise-woman.

María Concepción suddenly felt herself guarded, surrounded, upborne by her faithful friends. They were around her, speaking for her, defending her, the forces of life were ranged invincibly with her against the beaten dead. María Rosa had thrown away her share of strength in them, she lay forfeited among them. María Concepción looked from one to the other of the circling, intent faces. Their eyes gave back reassurance, understanding, a secret and mighty sympathy.

The gendarmes were at a loss. They, too, felt that sheltering wall cast impenetrably around her. They were certain she had done it, and yet they could not accuse her. Nobody could be accused; there was not a shred of true evidence. They shrugged their shoulders and snapped their fingers and shuffled their feet. Well, then, good night to everybody. Many pardons for having intruded. Good health!

A small bundle lying against the wall at the head of the coffin squirmed like an eel. A wail, a mere sliver of sound, issued. María Concepción took the son of María Rosa in her arms.

"He is mine," she said clearly, "I will take him with me."

No one assented in words, but an approving nod, a bare breath of complete agreement, stirred among them as they made way for her.

María Concepción, carrying the child, followed Juan from the clearing. The hut was left with its lighted candles and a crowd of old women who would sit up all night, drinking coffee and smoking and telling ghost stories.

Juan's exaltation had burned out. There was not an ember of excitement left in him. He was tired. The perilous adventure was over. María Rosa had vanished, to come no more forever. Their days of marching, of eating, of quarreling and making love between battles, were all over. Tomorrow he would go back to dull and endless labor, he must descend into the trenches of the buried city as María Rosa must go into her grave. He felt his veins fill up with bitterness, with black unendurable melancholy. Oh, Jesus! what bad luck overtakes a man!

Well, there was no way out of it now. For the moment he craved only to sleep. He was so drowsy he could scarcely guide his feet. The occasional light touch of the woman at his elbow was as unreal, as ghostly as the brushing of a leaf against his face. He did not know why he had fought to save her, and now he forgot her. There was nothing in him except a vast blind hurt like a covered wound.

He entered the jacal, and without waiting to light a candle, threw off his clothing, sitting just within the door. He moved with lagging, half-awake hands, to strip his body of its heavy finery. With a long groaning sigh of relief he fell straight back on the floor, almost instantly asleep, his arms flung up and outward.

María Concepción, a small clay jar in her hand, approached the gentle little mother goat tethered to a sapling, which gave and yielded as she pulled at the rope's end after the farthest reaches of grass about her. The kid, tied up a few feet away, rose bleating, its feathery fleece shivering in the fresh wind. Sitting on her heels, holding his tether, she allowed him to suckle a few moments. Afterward—all her movements very deliberate and even—she drew a supply of milk for the child.

She sat against the wall of her house, near the doorway. The child, fed and asleep, was cradled in the hollow of her crossed legs. The silence over-filled the world, the skies flowed down evenly to the rim of the valley, the stealthy moon crept slantwise to the shelter of the mountains. She felt soft and warm all over; she dreamed that the newly born child was her own, and she was resting deliciously.

María Concepción could hear Juan's breathing. The sound vapored from the low doorway, calmly; the house seemed to be resting after a burdensome day. She breathed, too, very slowly and quietly, each inspiration saturating her with repose. The child's light, faint breath was a mere shadowy moth of sound in the silver air. The night, the earth under her, seemed to swell and recede together with a limitless, unhurried, benign breathing. She drooped and closed her eyes, feeling the slow rise and fall within her own body. She did not know what it was, but it eased her all through. Even as she was falling asleep, head bowed over the child, she was still aware of a strange, wakeful happiness.

Explorers and Mountain Men

*The wilderness and the idea of wilderness is one of the perma-
nent homes of the human spirit.* —JOSEPH WOOD KRUTCH

Maps of the western United States at the time of the Louisiana Purchase (1803) unfurl a rich mix of mystery and fantasy. Between the Mississippi and the Pacific lay a largely blank space,
shaped by rumor and wish. Cartographers imagined navigable rivers, the Missouri ascending to a height of land from which descended the River of the West, called Buenaventura. Mountains arranged themselves conveniently in a single north-south chain and
the land was fertile beyond belief. Lewis and Clark's great recon-
naissance went in search of the legendary water route and put that
myth to rest.

Military expeditions by Pike in 1806 and Long in 1820 penetrated the Southern Rockies, leaving the unfinished riddles of western geography to be solved by the mountain men. Their pursuit of
beaver sent them up all the tributaries of the Missouri, down the
Green and Colorado and Rio Grande, down the Snake and the Columbia, into the Great Basin and across the Sierras to California. By
the end of the 1820s, these resolute men, led by Jedediah Smith and
Jim Bridger and Tom Fitzpatrick, would know the entire region
firsthand. When in 1842 John Fremont, who wished to be known as
The Pathfinder, was guided around the mountains by Kit Carson,
the information he later published had been known to some trappers
for more than a generation.

Nothing less than heroic, the task of the early explorers and
mountain men involved coming to terms with wilderness, dealing

81

with Indians, adapting to extremes of climate and terrain. Intense hardship, strain, fatigue, pain, hunger, hazard were part of their days. Wonder and exhilaration, too, for they encountered marvels and lived, for a brief period, almost pure adventure.

By 1840 beaver had been trapped out, and mountain men turned to other pursuits on the frontier—scouting, guiding, trading, hunting buffalo, fighting Indians. By 1869 the last official government exploration under Major Powell had run the Grand Canyon of the Colorado, ending the major mysteries of the continent. But even with the maps completed, wonder remained, both at the vast and majestic land and at the exploits of those first Americans who ventured into the unknown.

Toward the Shining Mountains

FROM *THE JOURNALS OF LEWIS AND CLARK*

LEWIS / *Sunday, May 26th 1805*

In the after part of the day I also walked out and ascended the river hills which I found sufficiently fortiegueing. on arriving to the summit [of] one of the highest points in the neighbourhood I thought myself well repaid for my labour; as from this point I beheld the Rocky Mountains for the first time, I could only discover a few of the most elivated points above the horizon, the most remarkable of which by my pocket compass I found bore N. 65° W. being a little to the N. of the N.W. extremity of the range of broken mountains seen this morning by Capt. C. these points of the Rocky Mountains were covered with snow and the sun shone on it in such manner as to give me the most plain and satisfactory view. while I viewed these mountains I felt a secret pleasure in finding myself so near the head of the heretofore conceived boundless Missouri; but when I reflected on the difficulties which this snowey barrier would most probably throw in my way to the Pacific, and the sufferings and hardships of myself and party in thim, it in some measure counterballanced the joy I had felt in the first moments in which I gazed on them; but as I have always held it a crime to anticipate evils I will believe it a good comfortable road untill I am compelled to believe differently.

LEWIS / *Wednesday, May 29th 1805*

Last night we were all allarmed by a large buffaloe Bull, which swam over from the opposite shore and coming along side of the white perogue, climbed over it to land, he then allarmed ran up the bank in full speed directly towards the fires, and was within 18 inches of the heads of some of the men who lay sleeping before the centinel could allarm him or make him change his course, still more alarmed, he now took his direction immediately towards our lodge, passing between 4 fires and within a few inches of the heads of one range of the men as they yet lay sleeping, when he came near the tent, my dog saved us by causing him to change his course a second time, which he did by turning a little to the right, and was quickly out of sight, leaving us by this time all in an uproar with our guns in o[u]r hands, enquiring of each other the ca[u]se of the alarm, which after a few moments was explained by the centinel: we were happy to find no one hirt.

LEWIS / *Friday, May 31st 1805*

The hills and river Clifts which we passed today exhibit a most romantic appearance. The bluffs of the river rise to the hight of from 2 to 300 feet and in most places nearly perpendicular; they are formed of remarkable white sandstone which is sufficiently soft to give way readily to the impression of water; . . . The water in the course of time in decending from those hills and plains on either side of the river has trickled down the soft sand clifts and woarn it into a thousand grotesque figures, which with the help of a little immagination and an oblique view, at a distance are made to represent eligant ranges of lofty freestone buildings, having their parapets well stocked with statuary; collumns of various sculpture both grooved and plain, are also seen supporting long galleries in front of those buildings; in other places on a much nearer approach and with the help of less immagination we see the remains or ruins of eligant buildings; some collumns standing and almost entire with their pedestals and capitals; others retaining their pedestals but deprived by time or accident of their capitals, some lying prostrate an broken othe[r]s in the form of vast pryamids of connic structure bearing a serees of other pyramids on their tops becoming less as they ascend and finally terminating in a sharp point. nitches and alcoves of various forms and sizes are seen at different hights as we pass. the thin stratas of hard freestone intermixed with the soft sandstone seems to have aided the water in forming this curious scenery. As we passed on it seemed as if those seens of visionary inchantment would never have and [an] end; for here it is too that nature presents to the view of the traveler vast ranges of walls of tolerable workmanship,   so perfect indeed are those walls that I should have thought that nature had attempted here to rival the human art of masonry had I not recollected that she had first began her work.

LEWIS / *Thursday, June 13th 1805*

I had proceded on this course about two miles with Goodrich at some distance behind me whin my ears were saluted with the agreeable

*Passage through Stone Walls, Not Far Below
the Mouth of the Marias River on the Missouri*, Karl Bodmer

sound of a fall of water and advancing a little further I saw the spray arrise above the plain like a collumn of smoke which would frequently dispear again in an instant caused I presume by the wind which blew pretty hard from the S.W. I did not however loose my direction to this point which soon began to make a roaring too tremendious to be mistaken for any cause short of the great falls of the Missouri. here I arrived about 12 OClock having traveled by estimate about 15. Miles. . . . immediately at the cascade the river is about 300 yds. wide; about ninty or a hundred yards of this next the Lard. bluff is a smoth even sheet of water falling over a precipice of at least eighty feet,   the remaining part of about 200 yards on my right formes the grandest sight I ever beheld,   the hight of the fall is the same of the other but the irregular and somewhat projecting rocks below receives the water in it's passage down and brakes it into a perfect white foam which assumes a thousand forms in a moment sometimes flying up in jets of sparkling foam to the hight of fifteen or twenty feet and are scarcely formed before large roling bodies of the same beaten and foaming water is thrown over and conceals them. in short the rocks seem to be most happily fixed to present a sheet of the whitest beaten froath for 200 yards in length and about 80 feet perpendicular. the water after decending strikes against the butment before mentioned or that on which I stand and seems to reverberate and being met by the more impetuous courant they roll and swell into half formed billows of great hight which rise and again disappear in an instant. . . .

LEWIS / *Sunday, June 16th 1805*

. . . about 2 P.M. I reached the camp found the Indian woman extreemly ill and much reduced by her indisposition. this gave me some concern as well for the poor object herself, then with a young child in her arms, as from the consideration of her being our only dependence for a friendly negociation with the Snake Indians on whom we depend for horses to assist us in our portage from the Missouri to the columbia river. . . . I found that two dozes of barks and opium which I had given her [Sacajawea] since my arrival had produced an alteration in her pulse for the better; they were now much fuller and more regular. I caused her to drink the mineral water altogether. she complains principally of the lower region of the abdomen, I therefore continued the cataplasms of barks and laudnumn which had been previously used by my friend Capt. Clark. . . .

LEWIS / *Wednesday, June 19th 1805*

. . . the Indian woman was much better this morning she walked out and gathered a considerable quantity of the white apples of which she eat so heartily in their raw state, together with a considerable quantity of dryed fish without my knowledge that she complained very much and her fever again returned. I rebuked Sharbono severely for suffering her to indulge herself with such food. . . . I now gave her broken dozes of diluted nitre untill it produced perspiration and at 10 P.M. 30 drops of laudnum which gave her a tolerable nights rest. . . .

LEWIS / *Sunday, June 23rd 1905*

. . . this evening the men repaired their mockersons, and put on double souls to protect their feet from the prickley pears. . . . they are obliged to halt and rest frequently for a few minutes, at every halt these poor fellows tumble down and are so much fortiegued that many of them are asleep in an instant; in short their fatiegues are incredible; some are limping from the soreness of their feet, others faint and unable to stand for a few minutes, with heat and fatigue, yet no one complains, all go with cheerfullness. . . .

CLARK / *Saturday, June 29th 1805*

. . . the first shower was moderate accompanied with a violent wind, the effects of which we did not feel,   soon after a torrent of rain and hail fell more violent than ever I saw before,   the rain fell like one voley of water falling from the heavens and gave us time only to get out of the way of a torrent of water which was Poreing down the hill in the River with emence force tareing everything before it takeing with it large rocks & mud,

I took my gun & shot pouch in my left hand, and with the right scrambled up the hill pushing the Interpreters wife (who had her child in her arms) before me, the Interpreter himself makeing attempts to pull up his wife by the hand much scared and nearly without motion,   we at length reached the top of the hill safe where I found my servent in serch of us greatly agitated, for our wellfar. before I got out of the bottom of the reveen which was a flat dry rock when I entered it, the water was up to my waste & wet my watch,   I scercely got out before it raised 10 feet deep with a torrent which [was] turrouble to behold, and by the time I reached the top of the hill, at least 15 feet water,

87

LEWIS / *Thursday, July 4th 1805*

. . . have concluded not to dispatch a canoe with a part of our men to St Louis as we had intended early in the spring. we fear also that such a measure might possibly discourage those who would in such case remain, and might possibly hazzard the fate of the expedition. we have never once hinted to any one of the party that we had such a scheme in contemplation, and all appear perfectly to have made up their minds to suceed in the expedition or purish in the attempt. we all believe that we are now about to enter on the most perilous and difficult part of our voyage, yet I see no one repining; all appear ready to me[e]t those difficulties which await us with resolution and becoming fortitude. . . .

LEWIS / *Saturday, July 13th 1805*

. . . from the head of the white bear Islands I passed in a S.W. direction and struck the Missouri at 3 Miles and continued up it to Capt. Clark's camp where I arrived about 9 A.M. and found them busily engaged with their canoes Meal &c. . . .
. . . the hunters killed three buffaloe today which were in good order. the flesh was brought in dryed the skins wer also streached for covering our baggage. we eat an emensity of meat; it requires 4 deer, an Elk and a deer, or one buffaloe, to supply us plentifully 24 hours. meat now forms our food prinsipally as we reserve our flour parched meal and corn as much as possible for the rocky mountains which we are shortly to enter. . . . The Musquetoes and knats are more troublesome here if possible. . . .

LEWIS / *Thursday, July 18th 1805*

as we were anxious now to meet with the Sosonees or snake Indians as soon as possible in order to obtain information relative to the geography of the country and also if necessary, some horses we thought it better for one of us either Capt. C. or myself to take a small party & proceed on up the river some distance before the canoes, in order to discover them, should they be on the river before the daily discharge of our guns, which was necessary in procuring subsistence for the party, should allarm and cause them to retreat to the mountains and conceal themselves, supposing us to be their enemies who visit them usually by the way of this river.

Mountain Skills

BERNARD DE VOTO

In the Indian bestiary all animals were wise and had supernatural powers but the beaver was always among the most sagacious. The religious rituals for taking him were very complicated. The wilderness mind of the white trappers might also call on magic to assist the hunt when it was going badly, and not a few regularly invoked amulets or incantations when they set their traps. They too knew that the beaver was very wise—and their job was to outthink him.

Part of the trapper's skill was to know the habits of beaver, to recognize likely sign, and to decide the right places to set his traps. A brigade making a hunt broke up into small parties which normally worked by themselves for several days at a time, splitting further into twos and threes for the actual trapping. They worked the streams and we must think of them mostly in mountain meadows or similar flats where the streams were slow enough to be dammed. Late in the afternoon, 'between sunset and dark' was the usual time to set traps. In some secrecy. For, says Osborne Russell, one of our best annalists, 'it was not good policy for a trapper to let too many know where he intended to set his traps'—plews were valuable. Normally they worked upstream, because sign of other trappers or of Indians might come downstream and because the country grew safer as you moved higher. With the incessant cognition of electronics, the trapper's mind was receiving and recording impressions all the time. He hunted beaver, read the country, recorded his route, watched for hostiles, and planned for all eventualities—in a simultaneous sentience. . . .

It is hardly too much to say that a mountain man's life was skill. He not only worked in the wilderness, he also lived there and he did so from sun to sun by the exercise of total skill. It was probably as intricate a skill as any ever developed by any way of working or living anywhere. Certainly it was the most complex of the wilderness crafts practiced on this continent. The mountains, the aridity, the distances, and the climates imposed severities

89

Beadle's Dime New York Library

COPYRIGHTED IN 1878, BY BEADLE & ADAMS.

Vol. I. Complete In One Number. Beadle & Adams, Publishers, No. 98 WILLIAM STREET, NEW YORK. Price, Ten Cents. No. 3.

Kit Carson, Jr., the Crack Shot of the West.

A WILD LIFE ROMANCE, BY "BUCKSKIN SAM."

KIT CARSON, JR.

far greater than those laid on forest-runners, rivermen, or any other of our symbolic pioneers. Mountain craft developed out of the crafts which earlier pioneers had acquired and, like its predecessors, incorporated Indian crafts, but it had a unique integration of its own. It had specific crafts, technologies, theorems and rationales and rules of thumb, codes of operating procedure—but it was a pattern of total behavior.

Treatises could be written on the specific details; we lack space even for generalizations. Why do you follow the ridges into or out of unfamiliar country? What do you do for a companion who has collapsed from want of water while crossing a desert? How do you get meat when you find yourself without gunpowder in a country barren of game? What tribe of Indians made this trail, how many were in the band, what errand were they on, were they going to or coming back from it, how far from home were they, were their horses laden, how many horses did they have and why, how many squaws accompanied them, what mood were they in? Also, how old is the trail, where are those Indians now, and what does the product of these answers require of you? Prodigies of such sign-reading are recorded by impressed greenhorns, travelers, and army men, and the exercise of critical reference and deduction which they exhibit would seem prodigious if it were not routine. But reading formal sign, however, impressive to Doctor Watson or Captain Frémont, is less impressive than the interpretation of observed circumstances too minute to be called sign. A branch floats down a stream—is this natural, or the work of animals, or of Indians or trappers? Another branch or a bush or even a pebble is out of place—why? On the limits of the plain, blurred by heat mirage, or against the gloom of distant cottonwoods, or across an angle of sky between branches or where hill and mountain meet, there is a tenth of a second of what may have been movement—did men or animals make it, and, if animals, why? Buffalo are moving downwind, an elk is in an unlikely place or posture, too many magpies are hollering, a wolf's howl is off key—what does it mean?

Such minutiae could be extended indefinitely. As the trapper's mind is dealing with them, it is simultaneously performing a still more complex judgment on the countryside, the route across it, and the weather. It is recording the immediate details in relation to the remembered and the forecast. A ten-mile traverse is in relation to a goal a hundred miles, or five hundred miles, away: there are economies of time, effort, comfort, and horseflesh on any of which success or even survival may depend. Modify the reading further, in relation to season, to Indians, to what has happened. Modify it again in relation to stream flow, storms past, storms indicated. Again in relation to the meat supply. To the state of the grass. To the equipment on hand. . . . You are two thousand miles from depots of supply and from help in time of trouble.

All this (with much more) is a continuous reference and checking along the margin or in the background of the trapper's consciousness while he practices his crafts as hunter, wrangler, furrier, freighter, tanner, cordwainer, smith, gunmaker, dowser, merchant. The result is a high-level integration of faculties. The mountain man had mastered his conditions—how well is apparent as soon as soldiers, goldseekers, or emigrants come into his country and suffer where he has lived comfortably and die where he has been in no danger. He had no faculties or intelligence that the soldier or the goldseeker lacked; he had none that you and I lack. He had only skill. A skill so effective that, living in an Indian country, he made a more successful adaptation to it than the Indian—and this without reference to his superior material equipment. There was no craft and no skill at which the mountain man did not come to excel the Indian. He saw, smelled, and heard just as far and no farther. But there is something after all in the laborious accretion that convolutes the forebrain and increases the cultural heritage, for he made more of it.

Trapper's Report

ADRIEN STOUTENBERG

They are domestic, faithful to their families,
    often work by moonlight,
    clerks and engineers in brisk overcoats,
    wearing keen incisors between wind-puffed cheeks,
    comedians of poplars and ponds,
    lovers of calculus
    and the long blue sums of water,
    subject, by nature, to seasons
    of lightning and frost
    but pitching always above muddy foundations
    their precise households
    with porches as round
    as the white hearts of birches.

They are captured easily in winter
    in their domed cities.
    When the light comes in with the hunter's axe,
    and the bedroom floor—draped for darkness—
    dazzles and blinks,
    they run on their shoeless feet
    to the sudden window,
    confused by so early an April
    and by the steep noose slung
    around a low throat.

Explorers and Mountain Men

Hauled into day
    (out of the dusky, two-story chamber
    mattressed with summer and sleep,
    clean as dead wheat,
    and mumbling with babies),
    their whiskers sweat,
    beaded like a red abacus.
        They are full of blood
        when slit down the belly
        from neck to crotch
        and also on the inside of each leg
        to the center cut,
            the outer garment then peeled off
            both ways toward the spine
            and stretched on an oval frame,
            the guard hairs plucked
            to leave, brown-rayed and warm,
            a breathless velvet hung
            against the white and ever-naked wind.

Setting Traps for Beaver, Alfred Jacob Miller

Mountain Medicine

A. B. GUTHRIE, JR.

The mist along the creek shone in the morning sun, which was coming up lazy and half-hearted, as if of a mind to turn back and let the spring season wait. The cottonwoods and quaking aspens were still bare and the needles of the pines old and dark with winter, but beaver were prime and beaver were plenty. John Clell made a lift and took the drowned animal quietly from the trap and stretched it in the dugout with three others.

Bill Potter said, "If 'tweren't for the Injuns! Or if 'tweren't for you and your notions!" For all his bluster, he still spoke soft, as if on the chance that there were other ears to hear.

Clell didn't answer. He reset the trap and pulled from the mud the twig that slanted over it and unstoppered his goat-horn medicine bottle, dipped the twig in it and poked it back into the mud.

"Damn if I don't think sometimes you're scary," Potter went on, studying Clell out of eyes that were small and set close. "What kind of medicine is it makes you smell Injuns with nary one about?"

"Time you see as many of them as I have, you'll be scary too," Clell answered, slipping his paddle into the stream. He had a notion to get this greenhorn told off, but he let it slide. What was the use? You couldn't put into a greenhorn's head what it was you felt. You couldn't give him the feel of distances and sky-high mountains and lonely winds and ideas spoken out of nowhere, ideas spoken into the head by medicines a man couldn't put a name to. Like now. Like here. Like this idea that there was brown skin about, and Blackfoot skin at that.

"I seen Blackfeet enough for both of us," he added. His mind ran back to Lewis and Clark and a time that seemed long ago because so much had come between; to days and nights and seasons of watching out, with just himself and the long silence for company; to last year and a hole that lay across the mountains to the south, where the Blackfeet and the Crows had fought, and he had sided with the Crows and got a wound in the leg that

96

hurt sometimes yet. He could still see some of the Blackfeet faces. He would know them, and they would know him, being long-remembering.

He knew Blackfeet all right, but he couldn't tell Bill Potter why he thought some of them were close by. There wasn't any sign he could point to; the creek sang along and the breeze played in the trees, and overhead a big eagle was gliding low, and nowhere was there a footprint or a movement or a whiff of smoke. It was just a feeling he had, and Potter wouldn't understand it, but would only look at him and maybe smile with one side of his mouth.

"Ain't anybody I knows of carries a two-shoot gun but you," Potter said, still talking as if Clell was scared over nothing.

Clell looked down at it, where he had it angled to his hand. It had two barrels, fixed on a swivel. When the top one was fired, you slipped a catch and turned the other up. One barrel was rifled, the other bigger and smooth-bored, and sometimes he loaded the big one with shot, for birds, and sometimes with a heavy ball, for bear or buffalo, or maybe with ball and buck both, just for what-the-hell. There was shot in it this morning, for he had thought maybe to take ducks or geese, and so refresh his taste for buffalo meat. The rifle shone in the morning sun. It was a nice piece, with a patch box a man wouldn't know to open until someone showed him the place to press his thumb. For no reason at all, Clell called his rifle Mule Ear.

He said, "You're a fool, Potter, more ways than one. Injuns'll raise your hair for sure, if it don't so happen I do it myself. As for this here two-shooter, I like it, and that's that."

Bill Potter always took low when a man dared him like that. Now all he said was "It's heavy as all hell."

Slipping along the stream, with the banks rising steep on both sides, Clell thought about beaver and Indians and all the country he had seen— high country, pretty as paint, wild as any animal and lonesome as time, and rivers unseen but by him, and holes and creeks without a name, and one place where water spouted hot and steaming and sometimes stinking from the earth, and another where a big spring flowed with pure tar; and no one believed him when he told of them, but called him the biggest liar yet. It was all right, though. He knew what he knew, and kept it to himself now, being tired of queer looks and smiles and words that made out he was half crazy.

Sometimes, remembering things, he didn't see what people did or hear what they said or think to speak when spoken to. It was all right. It didn't matter what was said about his sayings or his doings or his ways of thinking. A man long alone where no other white foot ever had stepped got different. He came to know what the Indians meant by medicine. He got to feeling like one with the mountains and the great sky and the lonesome winds and the animals and Indians, too, and it was a little as if he knew what they knew, a little as if there couldn't be a secret but was whispered to him, like the secret he kept hearing now.

"Let's cache," he said to Potter. The mist was gone from the river and the sun well up and decided on its course. It was time, and past time, to slide back to their hidden camp.

"Just got one more trap to lift," Potter argued.

"All right, then."

Overhead the eagle still soared close. Clell heard its long, high cry.

He heard something else, too, a muffled pounding of feet on the banks above. "Injuns!" he said, and bent the canoe into the cover of an overhanging bush. "I told you."

Potter listened. "Buffalo is all. Buffalo trampin' around."

Clell couldn't be sure, except for the feeling in him. Down in this little canyon a man couldn't see to the banks above. It could be buffalo, all right, but something kept warning, "Injuns! Injuns!"

Potter said, "Let's git on. Can't be cachin' from every little noise. Even sparrers make noise."

"Wait a spell."

"Scary." Potter said just the one word, and he said it under his breath, but it was enough. Clell dipped his paddle. One day he would whip Potter, but right now he reckoned he had to go on.

It wasn't fear that came on him a shake later, but just the quick knowing he had been right all along, just the holding still, the waiting, the watching what to do, for the banks had broken out with Indians—Indians with feathers in their hair, and bows and war clubs and spears in their hands; Indians yelling and motioning and scrambling down to the shores on both sides and fitting arrows to their bow strings.

Potter's face had gone white and tight like rawhide drying. He grabbed at his rifle.

Clell said, "Steady!" and got the pipe that hung from around his neck and held it up, meaning he meant peace.

These were the Blackfeet sure enough. These were the meanest Indians living. He would know them from the Rees and Crows and Pierced Noses and any other. He would know them by their round heads and bent noses and their red-and-green leather shields and the moccasins mismatched in color, and their bows and robes not fancy, and no man naked in the bunch.

The Indians waved them in. Clell let go his pipe and stroked with his paddle. Potter's voice was shrill. "You fool! You gonna let 'em torment us to death?"

That was the way with a mouthy greenhorn—full of himself at first, and then wild and shaken. "Steady!" Clell said again. "I aim to pull to shore. Don't point that there rifle 'less you want a skinful of arrows."

There wasn't a gun among the Indians, not a decent gun, but only a few rusty trade muskets. They had battle axes, and bows taken from their cases, ready for business, and some had spears, and all looked itching for a white man's hair. They waited, their eyes bright as buttons, their faces and bare forearms and right shoulders shining brown in the sun. Only men were at the shore line, but Clell could see the faces of squaws and young ones looking down from the bank above.

An Indian splashed out and got hold of the prow of the canoe and pulled it in. Clell stepped ashore, holding up his pipe. He had to watch Potter. Potter stumbled out, his little eyes wide and his face white, and fear showing even for an Indian to see. When he stepped on the bank, one of the Indians grabbed his rifle and wrenched it from him, and Potter just stood like a scared rabbit, looking as if he might jump back in the dugout any minute.

Clell reached out and took a quick hold on the rifle and jerked it away and handed it back to Potter. There was a way to treat Indians. Act like a squaw and they treated you bad; act like a brave man and you might have a chance.

Potter snatched the gun and spun around and leaped. The force of the jump carried the canoe out. He made a splash with the paddle. An arrow whispered in the air and made a little thump when it hit. Clell saw the end of it, shaking from high in Potter's back.

Potter cried out, "I'm hit! I'm hit, Clell!"

"Come back! Easy! Can't get away!"

99

Instead, Potter swung around with the rifle. There were two sounds, the crack of the powder and the gunshot plunk of a ball. Clell caught a glimpse of an Indian going down, and then the air was full of the twang of bowstrings and the whispered flight of arrows, and Potter slumped slowly back in the canoe, his body stuck like a pincushion. An Indian splashed out to take the scalp. Two others carried the shot warrior up the bank. Already a squaw was beginning to keen.

Clell stood quiet as a stump, letting only his eyes move. It was so close now that his life was as good as gone. He could see it in the eyes around him, in the hungry faces, in the hands moving and the spears and the bows being raised. He stood straight, looking their eyes down, thinking the first arrow would come any time now, from anyplace, and then he heard the eagle scream. Its shadow lazed along the ground. His thumb slipped the barrel catch, his wrist twisted under side up. He shot without knowing he aimed. Two feathers puffed out of the bird. It went into a steep climb and faltered and turned head down and spun to the ground, making a thump when it hit.

The Indians' eyes switched back to him. Their mouths fell open, and slowly their hands came over the mouth holes in the sign of surprise. It was as he figured in that flash between life and death. They thought all guns fired a single ball. They thought he was big medicine as a marksman. One of them stepped out and laid his hand on Mule Ear, as if to draw some of its greatness into himself. A murmur started up, growing into an argument. They ordered Clell up the bank. When he got there, he saw one Indian high-tailing it for the eagle, and others following, so's to have plumes for their war bonnets, maybe, or to eat the raw flesh for the medicine it would give them.

There was a passel of Indians on the bank, three or four hundred, and more coming across from the other side. The man Clell took for the chief had mixed red earth with spit and dabbed it on his face. He carried a bird-wing fan in one hand and wore a half-sleeved hunting shirt made of bighorn skin and decorated with colored porcupine quills. His hair was a wild bush over his eyes and ears. At the back of it he had a tuft of owl feathers hanging. He yelled something and motioned with his hands, and the others began drifting back from the bank, except for a couple of dozen that Clell figured were head men. Mostly, they wore leggings and moccasins, and leather shirts or robes slung over the left shoulder. A few had scarlet trade blankets, which had come from God knew where. One didn't wear anything under his robe.

The squaws and the little squaws in their leather sacks of dresses, the naked boys with their potbellies and swollen navels, and the untried and middling warriors were all back now. The chief and the rest squatted down in a half circle, with Clell standing in front of them. They passed a pipe around. After a while they began to talk. He had some of the hang of Blackfoot, and he knew, even without their words, they were arguing what to do with him. One of them got up and came over and brought his face close to Clell's. His eyes picked at Clell's head and eyes and nose and mouth. Clell could smell grease on him and wood smoke and old sweat, but what came to his mind above all was that here was a man he had fought last season while siding with the Crows. He looked steadily into the black eyes and saw the knowing come into them, too, and watched the man turn back and take his place in the half circle and heard him telling what he knew.

They grunted like hogs, the Blackfeet did, like hogs about to be fed, while the one talked and pointed, arguing that here was a friend of their old enemies, the Crows. The man rubbed one palm over the other, saying in sign that Clell had to be rubbed out. Let them stand him up and use him for a target, the man said. The others said yes to that, not nodding their heads as white men would, but bowing forward and back from the waist.

Clell had just one trick left. He stepped over and showed his gun and pointed to the patch box and, waving one hand to catch their eyes, he sprang the cover with the other thumb. He closed the cover and handed the gun to the chief.

The chief's hands were red with the paint he had smeared on his face. Clell watched the long thumbnail, hooked like a bird claw, digging at the cover, watched the red fingers feeling for a latch or spring. While the others stretched their necks to see, the chief turned Mule Ear over, prying at it with his eyes. It wasn't any use. Unless he knew the hidden spot to press, he couldn't spring the lid. Clell took the piece back, opened the patch box again, closed it and sat down.

He couldn't make more medicine. He didn't have a glass to bring the sun down, and so to light a pipe, or even a trader's paper-backed mirror for the chief to see how pretty he was. All he had was the shot at the eagle and the patch box on Mule Ear, and he had used them both and had to take what came.

101

Maybe it was the eagle that did it, or the hidden cover, or maybe it was just the crazy way of Indians. The chief got up, and with his hands and with his tongue asked if the white hunter was a good runner.

Clell took his time answering, as a man did when making high palaver. He lighted his pipe. He said, "The white hunter is a bad runner. The other Long Knives think he runs fast. Their legs are round from sitting on a horse. They cannot run."

The chief grunted, letting the sign talk and the slow words sink into him. "The Long Knife will run." He pointed to the south, away from the creek. "He will run for the trading house that the whiteface keeps among the Crows. He will go as far as three arrows will shoot, and then he will run. My brothers will run. If my brothers run faster—" The chief brought his hand to his scalp lock.

The other Indians had gathered around, even the squaws and the young ones. They were grunting with excitement. The chief took Mule Ear. Other hands stripped off Clell's hunting shirt, the red-checked woolen shirt underneath, his leggings, his moccasins, his small-clothes, until he stood white and naked in the sun, and the squaws and young ones came up close to see what white flesh looked like. The squaws made little noises in their throats. They poked at his bare hide. One of them grabbed the red-checked shirt from the hands of a man and ran off with it. The chief made the sign for "Go!"

Clell walked straight, quartering into the sun. He walked slow and solemn, like going to church. If he hurried, they would start the chase right off. If he lazed along, making out they could be damned for all he cared, they might give him more of a start.

He was two hundred yards away when the first whoop sounded, the first single whoop, and then all the voices yelling and making one great whoop. From the corner of his eye he saw their legs driving, saw the uncovered brown skins, the feathered hair, the bows and spears, and then he was running himself, seeing ahead of him the far tumble and roll of high plains and hills, with buffalo dotting the distances and a herd of prairie goats sliding like summer mist, and everywhere, so that not always could his feet miss them, the angry knobs of cactus. South and east, many a long camp away where the Bighorn joined the Roche Jaune, lay Lisa's Fort, the trading house among the Crows.

He ran so as to save himself for running, striding long and loose through the new-sprouting buffalo grass, around the cactus, around the pieces of sandstone where snakes were likely to lie. He made himself breathe easy, breathe deep, breathe full in his belly. Far off in his feelings he felt the cactus sting him and the spines pull off to sting again. The sun looked him in the face. It lay long and warm on the world. At the sky line the heat sent up a little shimmer. There wasn't a noise anywhere except the thump of his feet and his heart working in his chest and his breath sucking in and out and, behind him, a cry now and then from the Indians, seeming not closer or farther away than at first. He couldn't slow himself with a look. He began to sweat.

A man could run a mile, or two or three, and then his breath wheezed in him. It grew into a hard snore in the throat. The air came in, weak and dry, and burned his pipes and went out in one spent rush while his lungs sucked for more. He felt as if he had been running on forever. He felt strange and out of the world, a man running in a dream, except that the ache in his throat was real and the fire of cactus in his feet. The earth spread away forever, and he was lost in it and friendless, and not a proper part of it any more; and it served him right. When a man didn't pay any mind to his medicine, but went ahead regardless, as he had done, his medicine played out on him.

Clell looked back. He had gained, fifty yards, seventy-five, half a musket shot; he had gained on all the Indians except one, and that one ran as swift and high-headed as a prairie goat. He was close and coming closer.

Clell had a quick notion to stop and fight. He had an idea he might dodge the spear the Indian carried and come to grips with him. But the rest would be on him before he finished. It took time to kill a man just with the hands alone. Now was the time for the running he had saved himself for. There was strength in his legs yet. He made them reach out, farther, faster, faster, farther. The pound of them came to be a sick jolting inside his skull. His whole chest fought for air through the hot, closed tunnel of his throat. His legs weren't a part of him; they were something to think about, but not to feel, something to watch and to wonder at. He saw them come out and go under him and come out again. He saw them weakening, the knees bending in a little as the weight came on them. He felt wetness on his face, and reached up and found his nose was streaming blood.

He looked over his shoulder again. The main body of Indians had fallen farther back, but the prairie goat had gained. Through a fog he saw the

103

man's face, the chin set high and hard, the black eyes gleaming. He heard the moccasins slapping in the grass.

Of a sudden, Clell made up his mind. Keep on running and he'd get a spear in the back. Let it come from the front. Let it come through the chest. Let him face up to death like a natural man and to hell with it. His feet jolted him to a halt. He swung around and threw up his hands as if to stop a brute.

The Indian wasn't ready for that. He tried to pull up quick. He made to lift his spear. And then he stumbled and fell ahead. The spear handle broke as the point dug in the ground. Clell grabbed at the shaft, wrenched the point from the earth and drove it through the man. The Indian bucked to his hands and knees and strained and sank back. It was as easy as that.

Bending over him, Clell let his chest drink, let his numb legs rest, until he heard the yells of the Indians and, looking up, saw them strung out in a long file, with the closest of them so close he could see the set of their faces. He turned and ran again, hearing a sudden, louder howling as the Indians came on the dead one, and then the howling dying again to single cries as they picked up the chase. They were too many for him, and too close. He didn't have a chance. He couldn't fort up and try to stand them off, not with his hands bare. There wasn't any place to hide. He should have listened to his medicine when it was talking to him back there on the creek.

Down the slope ahead of him a river ran—the Jefferson Fork of the Missouri, he thought, while he made his legs drive him through a screen of brush. A beaver swam in the river, its moving head making a quiet V in the still water above a dam. As he pounded closer, its flat tail slapped the water like a pistol shot, the point of the V sank from sight, and the ripples spread out and lost themselves. He could still see the beaver, though, swimming under water, its legs moving and the black tail plain, like something to follow. It was a big beaver, and it was making for a beaver lodge at Clell's right.

Clell dived, came up gasping from the chill of mountain water, and started stroking for the other shore. Beaver lodge! Beaver lodge! It was as if something spoke to him, as if someone nudged him, as if the black tail pulled him around. It was a fool thing, swimming under water and feeling for the tunnel that led up into the lodge. A fool thing. A man got so winded and weak that he didn't know medicine from craziness. A fool thing. A man couldn't force his shoulders through a beaver hole. The point of his shoulder pushed into mud. A snag ripped his side. He clawed ahead, his lungs bursting. And then his head was out of water, in the dark, and his lungs pumped air.

He heard movement in the lodge and a soft churring, but his eyes couldn't see anything. He pulled himself up, still hearing the churring, expecting the quick slice of teeth in his flesh. There was a scramble. Something slid along his leg and made a splash in the water of the tunnel, and slid again and made another splash.

His hands felt sticks and smooth, dry mud and the softness of shed hair. He sat up. The roof of the lodge just cleared his head if he sat slouched. It was a big lodge, farther across than the span of his arms. And it was as dark, almost, as the inside of a plugged barrel. His hand crossing before his eyes was just a shapeless movement.

He sat still and listened. The voices of the Indians sounded far off. He heard their feet in the stream, heard the moccasins walking softly around the lodge, heard the crunch of dried grass under their steps. It was like something dreamed, this hiding and being able to listen and to move. It was like being a breath of air, and no one able to put a hand on it.

After a while the footsteps trailed off and the voices faded. Now Clell's eyes were used to blackness, the lodge was a dark dapple. From the shades he would know it was day, but that was all. He felt for the cactus spines in his feet. He had been cold and wet at first, but the wetness dried and the lodge warmed a little to his body. Shivering, he lay down, feeling the dried mud under his skin, and the soft fur. When he closed his eyes he could see the sweep of distances and the high climb of mountains, and himself all alone in all the world, and, closer up, he could see the beaver swimming under water and its flat tail beckoning. He could hear voices, the silent voices speaking to a lonesome man out of nowhere and out of everywhere, and the beaver speaking, too, the smack of its tail speaking.

He woke up later, quick with alarm, digging at his dream and the noise that had got mixed with it. It was night outside. Not even the dark dapple showed inside the lodge, but only such a blackness as made a man feel himself to make sure he was real. Then he heard a snuffling of the air, and the sound of little waves lapping in the tunnel, and he knew that a beaver had nosed up and smelled him and drawn back into the water.

When he figured it was day, he sat up slowly, easing his muscles into action. He knew, without seeing, that his feet were puffed with the poison of

105

the cactus. He crawled to the tunnel and filled his lungs and squirmed into it. He came up easy, just letting his eyes and nose rise above the water. The sun had cleared the eastern sky line. Not a breath of air stirred; the earth lay still, flowing into spring. He could see where the Indians had flattened the grass and trampled an edging of rushes, but there were no Indians about, not on one side or the other, not from shore line to sky line. He struck out for the far shore.

Seven days later a hunter at Fort Lisa spotted a figure far off. He watched it for a long spell, until a mist came over his eyes, and then he called to the men inside the stockade. A half dozen came through the big gate, their rifles in the crooks of their arms, and stood outside and studied the figure too.

"Man, all right. Somep'n ails him. Look how he goes."

"Injun, I say. A Crow, maybe, with a Blackfoot arrer in him."

"Git the glass."

One of them went inside and came back and put the glass to his eye. "Naked as a damn jay bird."

"Injun, ain't it?"

"Got a crop of whiskers. Never seed a Injun with whiskers yet."

"Skin's black."

"Ain't a Injun, though."

They waited.

"It ain't! Yes, I do believe it's John Clell! It's John Clell or I'm a Blackfoot!"

They brought him in and put his great, raw swellings of feet in hot water and gave him brandy and doled out roast liver, and bit by bit, that day and the next, he told them what had happened.

They knew why he wouldn't eat prairie turnips afterward, seeing as he lived on raw ones all that time, but what they didn't understand, because he didn't try to tell them, was why he never would hunt beaver again.

Buffalo Chase

FRANCIS PARKMAN

The country before us was now thronged with buffalo and a sketch of the manner of hunting them will not be out of place. There are two methods commonly practiced, "running" and "approaching." The chase on horseback, which goes by the name of "running," is the more violent and dashing mode of the two, that is to say, when the buffalo are in one of their wild moods; for otherwise it is tame enough. A practiced and skillful hunter, well mounted, will sometimes kill five or six cows in a single chase, loading his gun again and again as his horse rushes through the tumult. In attacking a small band of buffalo, or in separating a single animal from the herd and assailing it apart from the rest, there is less excitement and less danger. In fact, the animals are at times so stupid and lethargic that there is little sport in killing them. With a bold and well-trained horse the hunter may ride so close to the buffalo that as they gallop side by side he may touch him with his hand; nor is there much danger in this as long as the buffalo's strength and breath continue unabated; but when he becomes tired and can no longer run with ease, when his tongue lolls out and the foam flies from his jaws, then the hunter had better keep a more respectful distance; the distressed brute may turn upon him at any instant; and especially at the moment when he fires his gun. The horse then leaps aside, and the hunter has need of a tenacious seat in the saddle, for if he is thrown to the ground there is no hope for him. When he sees his attack defeated, the buffalo resumes his flight, but if the shot is well directed he soon stops; for a few moments he stands still, then totters and falls heavily upon the prairie.

The chief difficulty in running buffalo, as it seems to me, is that of loading the gun or pistol at full gallop. Many hunters for convenience' sake carry three or four bullets in the mouth; the powder is poured down the muzzle of the piece, the bullet dropped in after it, the stock struck hard upon the pommel of the saddle, and the work is done. The danger of this is obvious. Should the blow on the pommel fail to send the bullet home, or should the

107

bullet, in the act of aiming, start from its place and roll towards the muzzle, the gun would probably burst in discharging. Many a shattered hand and worse casualties besides have been the result of such an accident. To obviate it, some hunters make use of a ramrod, usually hung by a string from the neck, but this materially increases the difficulty of loading. The bows and arrows which the Indians use in running buffalo have many advantages over firearms, and even white men occasionally employ them.

The danger of the chase arises not so much from the onset of the wounded animal as from the nature of the ground which the hunter must ride over. The prairie does not always present a smooth, level, and uniform surface; very often it is broken with hills and hollows, intersected by ravines, and in the remoter parts studded by the stiff wild sage bushes. The most formidable obstructions, however, are the burrows of wild animals, wolves, badgers, and particularly prairie dogs, with whose holes the ground for a very great extent is frequently honeycombed. In the blindness of the chase the hunter rushes over it unconscious of danger; his horse, at full career, thrusts his leg deep into one of the burrows; the bone snaps, the rider is hurled forward to the ground and probably killed. Yet accidents in buffalo running happen less frequently than one would suppose; in the recklessness of the chase, the hunter enjoys all the impunity of a drunken man, and may ride in safety over gullies and declivities, where, should he attempt to pass in his sober senses, he would infallibly break his neck.

The method of "approaching," being practiced on foot, has many advantages over that of "running"; in the former, one neither breaks down his horse nor endangers his own life; he must be cool, collected, and watchful; must understand the buffalo, observe the features of the country and the course of the wind, and be well skilled in using the rifle. The buffalo are strange animals; sometimes they are so stupid and infatuated that a man may walk up to them in full sight on the open prairie, and even shoot several of their number before the rest will think it necessary to retreat. At another moment they will be so shy and wary that in order to approach them the utmost skill, experience, and judgment are necessary. Kit Carson, I believe, stands preëminent in running buffalo; in approaching, no man living can bear away the palm from Henry Chatillon.

After Tête Rouge had alarmed the camp, no further disturbance occurred during the night. The Arapahoes did not attempt mischief, or if they did the wakefulness of the party deterred them from effecting their purpose. The next day was one of activity and excitement, for about ten o'clock the man in advance shouted the gladdening cry of *buffalo, buffalo!* and in the hollow of the prairie just below us, a band of bulls were grazing. The temptation was irresistible, and Shaw and I rode down upon them. We were badly mounted on our traveling horses, but by hard lashing we over-took them, and Shaw, running alongside a bull, shot into him both balls of his double-barreled gun. Looking around as I galloped by, I saw the bull in his mortal fury rushing again and again upon his antagonist, whose horse constantly leaped aside, and avoided the onset. My chase was more pro-tracted, but at length I ran close to the bull and killed him with my pistols. Cutting off the tails of our victims by way of trophy, we rejoined the party in about a quarter of an hour after we had left it. Again and again that morn-ing rang out the same welcome cry of *buffalo, buffalo!* Every few moments, in the broad meadows along the river, we saw bands of bulls, who, raising their shaggy heads, would gaze in stupid amazement at the approaching horsemen, and then break into a clumsy gallop, file off in a long line across the trail in front, towards the rising prairie on the left. At noon, the plain before us was alive with thousands of buffalo,—bulls, cows, and calves,—all moving rapidly as we drew near; and far off beyond the river the swelling prairie was darkened with them to the very horizon. The party was in gayer spirits than ever. We stopped for a nooning near a grove of trees by the river.

"Tongues and hump-ribs to-morrow," said Shaw, looking with contempt at the venison steaks which Deslauriers placed before us. Our meal fin-ished, we lay down to sleep. A shout from Henry Chatillon aroused us, and we saw him standing on the cartwheel, stretching his tall figure to its full height, while he looked towards the prairie beyond the river. Following the direction of his eyes, we could clearly distinguish a large, dark object, like the black shadow of a cloud, passing rapidly over swell after swell of the dis-tant plain; behind it followed another of similar appearance, though smaller, moving more rapidly, and drawing closer and closer to the first. It was the hunters of the Arapahoe camp chasing a band of buffalo. Shaw and I caught and saddled our best horses, and went plunging through sand and water to the farther bank. We were too late. The hunters had already mingled with the herd, and the work of slaughter was nearly over. When we reached the ground we found it strewn far and near with numberless carcasses, while the remnants of the herd, scattered in all directions, were flying away in terror, and the Indians still rushing in pursuit. Many of the hunters, however, remained upon the spot, and among the rest was our yesterday's acquaintance, the chief of the village. He had alighted by the side of a cow, into which he had shot five or six arrows, and his squaw, who had followed him on horseback to the hunt, was giving him a draft of water from a canteen, purchased or plundered from some volunteer soldier. Recrossing the river, we overtook the party, who were already on their way.

We had gone scarcely a mile when we saw an imposing spectacle. From the river bank on the right, away over the swelling prairie on the left, and in front as far as the eye could reach, was one vast host of buffalo. The outskirts of the herd were within a quarter of a mile. In many parts they were crowded so densely together that in the distance their rounded backs presented a surface of uniform blackness; but elsewhere they were more scattered, and from amid the multitude rose little columns of dust where some of them were rolling on the ground. Here and there a battle was going forward among the bulls. We could distinctly see them rushing against each other, and hear the clattering of their horns and their hoarse bellowing. Shaw was riding at some distance in advance, with Henry Chatillon; I saw him stop and draw the leather covering from his gun. With such a sight before us, but one thing could be thought of. That morning I had used pistols in the chase. I had now a mind to try the virtue of a gun. Deslauriers had one, and I rode up to the side of the cart; there he sat under the white covering, biting his pipe between his teeth and grinning with excitement.

"Lend me your gun, Deslauriers."

"Oui, Monsieur, oui," said Deslauriers, tugging with might and main to stop the mule, which seemed obstinately bent on going forward. Then everything but his moccasins disappeared as he crawled into the cart and pulled at the gun to extricate it.

"Is it loaded?" I asked.

"Oui, bien chargé; you'll kill, mon bourgeois; yes, you'll kill—c'est un bon fusil."

I handed him my rifle and rode forward to Shaw.

"Are you ready?" he asked.

"Come on," said I.

"Keep down that hollow," said Henry, "and then they won't see you till you get close to them."

The hollow was a kind of wide ravine; it ran obliquely towards the buffalo, and we rode at a canter along the bottom until it became too shallow; then we bent close to our horses' necks, and, at last, finding that it could no longer conceal us, came out of it and rode directly toward the herd. It was within gunshot; before its outskirts, numerous grizzly old bulls were scattered, holding guard over their females. They glared at us in anger and astonishment, walked towards us a few yards, and then turning slowly round, retreated at a trot which afterwards broke into a clumsy gallop. In an instant the main body caught the alarm. The buffalo began to crowd away from the point towards which we were approaching, and a gap was opened in the side of the herd. We entered it, still restraining our excited horses. Every instant the tumult was thickening. The buffalo, pressing together in large bodies, crowded away from us on every hand. In front and on either side we could see dark columns and masses, half hidden by clouds of dust, rushing along in terror and confusion, and hear the tramp and clattering of ten thousand hoofs. That countless multitude of powerful brutes, ignorant of their own strength, were flying in a a panic from the approach of two feeble horsemen. To remain quiet longer was impossible.

"Take that band on the left," said Shaw; "I'll take these in front."

He sprang off, and I saw no more of him. A heavy Indian whip was fastened by a band to my wrist; I swung it into the air and lashed my horse's flank with all the strength of my arm. Away she darted, stretching close to the ground. I could see nothing but a cloud of dust before me, but I knew that it concealed a band of many hundreds of buffalo. In a moment I was in the midst of the cloud, half suffocated by the dust and stunned by the trampling of the flying herd; but I was drunk with the chase and cared for nothing but the buffalo. Very soon a long dark mass became visible, looming through the dust; then I could distinguish each bulky carcass, the hoofs flying out beneath, the short tails held rigidly erect. In a moment I was so close that I could have touched them with my gun. Suddenly, to my amazement, the hoofs were jerked upwards, the tails flourished in the air, and amid a cloud of dust the buffalo seemed to sink into the earth before me. One vivid impression of that instant remains upon my mind. I remember looking down upon the backs of several buffalo dimly visible through the dust. We had run unawares upon a ravine. At that moment I was not the most accurate judge of depth and width, but when I passed it on my return, I found it about twelve feet deep and not quite twice as wide at the bottom. It was impossible to stop; I would have done so gladly if I could; so, half

111

sliding, half plunging, down went the little mare. She came down on her knees in the loose sand at the bottom; I was pitched forward against her neck and nearly thrown over her head among the buffalo, who amid dust and confusion came tumbling in all around. The mare was on her feet in an instant and scrambling like a cat up the opposite side. I thought for a moment that she would have fallen back and crushed me, but with a violent effort she clambered out and gained the hard prairie above. Glancing back, I saw the huge head of a bull clinging as it were by the forefeet at the edge of the dusty gulf. At length I was fairly among the buffalo. They were less densely crowded than before, and I could see nothing but bulls, who always run at the rear of a herd to protect their females. As I passed among them they would lower their heads, and turning as they ran, try to gore my horse; but as they were already at full speed there was no force in their onset, and as Pauline ran faster than they, they were always thrown behind her in the effort. I soon began to distinguish cows amid the throng. One just in front of me seemed to my liking, and I pushed close to her side. Dropping the reins, I fired, holding the muzzle of the gun within a foot of her shoulder. Quick as lightning she sprang at Pauline; the little mare dodged the attack, and I lost sight of the wounded animal amid the tumult. Immediately after, I selected another, and urging forward Pauline, shot into her both pistols in succession. For a while I kept her in view, but in attempting to load my gun, lost sight of her also in the confusion. Believing her to be mortally wounded and unable to keep up with the herd, I checked my horse. The crowd rushed onwards. The dust and tumult passed away, and on the prairie, far behind the rest, I saw a solitary buffalo galloping heavily. In a moment I and my victim were running side by side. My firearms were all empty, and I had in my pouch nothing but rifle bullets, too large for the pistols and too small for the gun. I loaded the gun, however, but as often as I leveled it to fire, the bullets would roll out of the muzzle and the gun returned only a report like a squib, as the powder harmlessly exploded. I rode in front of the buffalo and tried to turn her back; but her eyes glared, her mane bristled, and, lowering her head, she rushed at me with the utmost fierceness and activity. Again and again I rode before her, and again and again she repeated her furious charge. But little Pauline was in her element. She dodged her enemy at every rush, until at length the buffalo stood still, exhausted with her own efforts, her tongue lolling from her jaws.

Riding to a little distance, I dismounted, thinking to gather a handful of dry grass to serve the purpose of wadding, and load the gun at my leisure. No sooner were my feet on the ground than the buffalo came bounding in such a rage towards me that I jumped back again into the saddle with all possible dispatch. After waiting a few minutes more, I made an attempt to ride up and stab her with my knife; but Pauline was near being gored in the attempt. At length, bethinking me of the fringes at the seams of my buckskin trousers, I jerked off a few of them, and, reloading the gun, forced them down the barrel to keep the bullet in its place; then approaching, I shot the wounded buffalo through the heart. Sinking to her knees, she rolled over lifeless on the prairie. To my astonishment, I found that, instead of a cow, I had been slaughtering a stout yearling bull. No longer wondering at his fierceness I opened his throat, and cutting out his tongue, tied it at the back of my saddle. My mistake was one which a more experienced eye than mine might easily make in the dust and confusion of such a chase.

Then for the first time I had leisure to look at the scene around me. The prairie in front was darkened with the retreating multitude, and on either hand the buffalo came filing up in endless columns from the low plains upon the river. The Arkansas was three or four miles distant. I turned and moved slowly towards it. A long time passed before, far in the distance, I distinguished the white covering of the cart and the little black specks of horsemen before and behind it. Drawing near, I recognized Shaw's elegant tunic, the red flannel shirt, conspicuous far off. I overtook the party, and asked him what success he had had. He had assailed a fat cow, shot her with two bullets, and mortally wounded her. But neither of us was prepared for the case that afternoon, and Shaw, like myself, had no spare bullets in his pouch; so he abandoned the disabled animal to Henry Chatillon, who followed, dispatched her with his rifle, and loaded his horse with the meat.

We encamped close to the river. The night was dark, and as we lay down we could hear, mingled with the howlings of wolves, the hoarse bellowing of the buffalo, like the ocean beating upon a distant coast.

Pioneers and Settlers

All of the past we leave behind,
We debouch upon a newer mightier world, varied world,
Fresh and strong the world we seize, world of labor
    and the march,
       Pioneers! O pioneers!—WALT WHITMAN

The promise of new opportunity, new land, and a better life drew many people "across the wide Missouri." While few thought of themselves as adventurers, survivors realized that what they had done was part of a stern and splendid experience.

The first wave of emigrants began in the 1840s, heading out for Oregon and California. Trains of Conestoga wagons rattled overland, across prairie and mountain and desert, a journey of about two thousand miles in five months if all went well. With their bonneted wives and children, possessions and provisions, plows and livestock, settlers dreamed of farms and towns flowering in the wilderness. The first ones, too, marched in behalf of Manifest Destiny, for Oregon was still under British control and until 1848 Mexico included California, Nevada, Arizona, and Utah. The Mormons in 1847 were in fact fleeing savage persecution in the United States when they established what they hoped would be the independent state of Deseret. But war with Mexico and the discovery of gold altered Mormon dreams of autonomy.

The subsequent rush of Forty-Niners to California in search of gold changed the pattern of migration and settlement. Prospectors formed makeshift, predominantly male boom towns, then rushed on to new El Dorados as the mining frontier moved to the next watershed, or Nevada, Idaho, Colorado, and Montana. The whole spec-

115

tacle moved James Clyman, who had been a trapper, emigrant guide, Forty-Niner, and California settler, to observe on the Oregon Trail in 1847:

> It is remarkable . . . and strange that so many of all kinds and classes of People should sell out comfortable homes in Missouri and Elsewhere pack up and start across such an emmence Barren waste to settle in some new Place of which they have at most so uncertain information but such is the character of my countrymen.*

Many of those who set out for the promised land never got there. Plains Indians menaced the covered wagons, and disease and exhaustion claimed about one of every nine emigrants. And when bad judgment combined with bad luck, entire trains met bleak disaster, as happened to the Donner Party.

The Homestead Act of 1862, which promised land to anyone who could "prove up" one hundred and sixty acres, moved farmers onto the western plains. The Homesteaders made a raw livelihood on the treeless prairie in homes made of dried sod and fueled by buffalo dung; they were harassed by cattlemen, who regarded sod busters as one cut above a dead Indian and one notch below a sheep herder. European immigrants, their passage paid by railroad corporations so both could get free government land, also moved onto the plains after the completion of the transcontinental railroad in 1869. All were scorched by summers, nearly frozen in winter, and in lean seasons watched the wind blow their soil into the next county. The harshness was captured by one of Kansas' leading optimists in a ballad titled "Starving to Death on a Government Claim." One refrain extended this invitation to all would-be sod busters:

> Then come to Lane County. Here is a home for you all
> Where the winds never cease and the rains never fall,

---

*Camp, Charles, *James Clyman: American Frontiersman* (San Francisco: San Francisco Historical Society, 1928), p. 73.

116

And the sun never sets but will always remain
Till it burns you all up on a Government claim.*

The decision to make a new life in the West, a recurring theme from the beginning of the republic, required tremendous courage. The real pioneers were not gold seekers or cowmen but the families determined to find good soil in Oregon or on the plains. In contrast to the melodramatics of the Wild West Show, but not without its own drama, settlers, by making homes in the new land, made the land livable.

Some of the land, however, was occupied before the pioneers and settlers arrived. And while perhaps not consciously racist, their concept of what was American turned out to be exclusively white. Thus emerging western communities fostered a pervasive discrimination that was brutal, violent, and often murderous. Mexican-Americans who for generations had lived in the Southwest were "legally" dispossessed of their lands and denied all but the lowest forms of labor. Chinese emigrants whose industry and willingness to work enraged unemployed whites were periodically harried and terrorized. And if the black American found that he was not the only despised minority in the promised land, conditions were not much improved for him either. Western society was dominantly, at times defiantly, white. Yet minority groups, who were part of the history but were omitted from the legends, helped shape the regional heritage.

*Lingerfelter and Dwyer, *Songs of the American West* (Berkeley: University of California Press, 1968), p. 458.

This is the Place

WALLACE STEGNER

Their camp that night was at the head of Echo Canyon, near the cave that they named for Jackson Redding, who was the first into it. But the Lion of the Lord was not with them. At noon he had come down with a violent attack of mountain fever, and in doing so had demonstrated not only the virulence of the disease but the prerogatives of command. Any of the rest of them who had been stricken must jolt on over the boulders no matter how their joints and backs ached and no matter how they raved. When Brother Brigham was similarly taken they dared not risk for him what they accepted for themselves: his wagons and Heber Kimball's stopped and let the company go on. Next morning Kimball and Howard Egan rode ahead to suggest that an advance company be sent on into Weber Canyon to search out "Mr. Reid's route." So twenty-two wagons, mostly with ox teams, started on under the command of Orson Pratt. From that point on, thanks to sickness, uncertainty about the road, and difficult terrain, the pioneer company that had started out so stiffly organized from the Elkhorn straggled in two or three groups separated by a good many miles. Fortunately the grass was good, their water was from bright mountain streams or cold springs, the scenery was increasingly romantic and grand, and there was plenty of game. And they had no fear of Indians. Except for a few lodges of Sioux at Fort Laramie and a few of Shoshones at Fort Bridger, they had seen none since the end of May, back on the North Platte. For weeks now the night guard had consisted of only two or three men.

It is a kind of awkwardness in the strenuously encouraged Mormon myth that on the last leg of their long journey, just when they seemed about to break through the final barriers into the promised land, the Moses of this people—and not for any fault that had incurred the Lord's displeasure—should have been held back sick and raving in the rear. Wanting to be led into Canaan, the Saints had to lead themselves; wanting to focus upon the leader, the chroniclers have to shuffle unhappily between his rear-guard wagons and the advance party of Orson Pratt.

While the main company dawdled and waited for Brigham to improve, and amused itself shouting or shooting or tooting its band instruments against the cliffs, this advance group went down Echo Canyon to where it empties into the broad valley of the Weber, and down the Weber until it pinched in to become a narrow slot filled wall-to-wall by the river. The Harlan-Young wagons the year before had gone ten miles down that river-bed, floundering and crashing among the boulders in the swift water, and made it through; the Donner party had turned aside and hunted another way through the mountains. It was the Donner trail, "Reed's Cutoff," that Pratt was searching for. On July 15 Port Rockwell found it, a dim trace that crossed the Weber and crawled south into the relatively welcoming gateway of what would some day be called Main Canyon, at the modern village of Henefer, Utah. Sending Rockwell back to report to Heber, Pratt put up a sign to mark the turnoff, and went on.

By the testimony of every diarist, the thirty-six last miles, from the Weber to the Salt Lake Valley, were worse than anything on the whole road. It was as if sanctuary withheld itself, as if safety could be had only by intensifying ordeal. The road had already been broken, if that was the word, by the Donner-Reed wagoners, but Orson Pratt's forty-two men, slaving with ax and shovel and pry-pole to make a few miles a day, fell into camp every night with a respect approaching awe for the quarrelsome Gentiles who had first taken wagons through those canyons. They had uphill, down-hill, sidehill, boulders, creek-crossings, willows—above all willows, thick as a porcupine's quills and hardly less troublesome to get through. Growing, they screened rocks and holes and dropoffs that could break a wheel; chopped off, they left stumps sharp as spears, and ruinous to the feet of men and animals. When they had to travel, as they did much of the way, with one wheel in the creek and one blundering along a steep bank sown with these stubs, they could literally count their progress one wheel's turn at a time.

From the Weber there were five miles of stiff *up* over Hogsback Summit, then seven miles of equally stiff *down* along the sidehill into what is now called Dixie Hollow. On July 17 Pratt's company cut their way up what Pratt called Canyon Creek (now East Canyon Creek) for six exhausting miles. On the eighteenth, Sunday, they rested—for cause. That day, back near the mouth of Echo Canyon, the pioneers agreed to leave several wagons behind with Brother Brigham, who had rallied and joined them only to relapse again, while the rest followed Pratt as fast as possible, to hurry seeds into the ground. On Monday, July 19, Pratt's axmen attacked the willows again, while the main company, making better time because of the advance party's labors, but not such good time that they failed to abominate the road, turned out of Weber Canyon and made it over the Hogsback to Dixie Hollow. And out ahead Orson Pratt, advance man for Zion and regent for Zion's Moses, rode on with John Brown to reconnoiter the trail, which had finally left the creek and started off to the right, up a ravine folded among high, confusing ridges. Four miles up that difficult trace the two tied their horses and climbed on foot to the crest.

They were on a very high place (7,245 feet) in the very midst of wild mountains. Before them the land fell away, sagebrush-covered on the southward-facing slopes, timbered with aspen and spruce on the slopes that leaned north. Right, left, before, behind, the mountains tossed up their granite and snow. Straight ahead, jutting up like a front gunsight into the notch of the ravine that began at their feet and deepened swiftly into a canyon aimed west, was a dark isolated mountain, and many miles beyond that stretched the towering, hazy crest of another range. They had no way of identifying the far range, for it so far had no status in geography; it would turn out to be the Oquirrhs, on the west side of the Salt Lake Valley. But reaching to its feet, and visible on both sides past the dark gunsight mountain, they could see a broad plain, treeless, shimmering pale gold and paler amethyst, and that they thought they could identify.

Pratt and Brown hurried to their horses and rode down through the dense brush of the ravine, expecting to come out of the baffling mountains within a few miles. Instead, the apparently open canyon closed in to become a slot as impassable as the lower canyon of the Weber. They were on the spot that many years later would be the site of the Mountain Dell reservoir, at the head of the canyon that would be named Parley's for Orson Pratt's brother. In 1850 Parley would open the Golden Pass road through the slot, and it would ultimately become the route of the main highway into the valley, U.S. 30S. But in 1847 it was no place to risk a wagon. The Donners had so decided: their frustrated trail kinked back on itself and climbed again, clear over the ridge to the north. Instead of following them further, Pratt and Brown rode back over the high pass of Big Mountain until they met the advance party, which by killing labor had cut another six and a half miles of willows and dug nine crossings of Canyon Creek during the day.

According to Port Rockwell, who came up from the rear, the middle division was only nine miles back. Brigham was still sick in Weber Canyon.

The trail of July 20 up the side of Big Mountain impressed Levi Jackman, one of Pratt's road gang, as profoundly gloomy, "as though we were Shut up in a gulph," and it was so laborious that the company behind them temporarily abandoned there the cannon they had hauled 1,000 miles. Going down the other side was little if any easier, and the next day's hot switchback climb out of Mountain Dell and over Little Mountain into what Pratt called Last Creek (Emigration) Canyon, was as bad as anything yet. But from the Little Mountain ridge, before they started their wheel-locked slide down to the stream, they caught another glimpse: as Jackman said, "like Moses from Pisgay's top" they saw their "long antisipated home."

Whether indeed this valley was to be their long-anticipated home was not quite so plain to the leaders as to Jackman, but it was pretty sure to be their temporary stopping place. For now came Erastus Snow up from the main company with a letter from Willard Richards and George A. Smith containing the instructions of Brother Brigham, a leader who led even from the rear. He directed Pratt to steer away from Utah Valley, which had had the best billing from Bridger but which was inhabited in force by the Utes. "We had better keep further north towards the Salt Lake, which is more a warlike or neutral ground, and by so doing we should be less likely to be disturbed and also have a chance to form an acquaintance with the Utes, and having done our planting shall select a site for our location at our leisure."

Riding and tying one horse, Pratt and Snow went down Emigration Canyon to see what lay ahead. Four miles below the foot of the Little Mountain grade they found where the Donner-Reed party had pulled over an impossibly steep, narrow, dangerous hill to get out of the tree-and-boulder-choked V of the canyon. It has occurred to historians since that by that stage the Donner party would have climbed a vertical wall rather than cut any more willows. At Donner Hill the wall was as near vertical as wagons have ever managed. According to the diary of Virginia Reed Murphy, "almost every yoke in the train" of twenty-three wagons—which would have meant fifty or sixty animals—had to be hitched onto each one to get it over. That was where the Donner party took the heart out of their animals. If they had cut and dug instead of pulling Donner Hill, they might have saved the extra strength and the extra day or two of time that would have meant safety later.

Stephen Markham's road crew would dig around that hill in four hours the next day. For now, Pratt and Snow followed the gouges of the Donner wheels to the top. And abruptly there it was, the whole great valley shimmering in summer heat, one of the great views of the continent. From where they stood above the alluvial fan of Emigration Creek, the Wasatch ran in an abrupt wall southward, but on the north it swung an arm around to half enclose the valley. Beginning nearly straight west of them, perhaps twenty-five airline miles away, the high smooth crestline of the Oquirrhs also ran southward until it all but met the Wasatch at a low notch on the southern sky. And northward and westward from the northernmost foot of the Oquirrhs, fabulous, dark blue, floating its pale islands, lapping the world's rim, went the Great Salt Lake.

"We could not refrain from a shout of joy," Orson Pratt wrote. The developed legend says they swung their hats and cried three times, "Hosannah! Hosannah! Hosannah!" The twelve-mile circuit they made of the valley that day was amplified the day following by a more extensive tour taken by a larger group. They found hardly a whisker of timber, many rattlesnakes, many great black crickets; but the alluvial soil looked good, and the slopes were threaded by a half dozen good mountain streams. At the foot of the northwest corner of the mountains, below a hill that Brigham would shortly name Ensign Peak, were hot mineral springs.

Whether it was promised land or only temporary stopping place, they had no time to waste. On July 23, with the promptness and efficiency that had marked them as a community ever since Missouri, they moved their camp north onto City Creek and broke three acres of ground and several plows. By the day following they had completed a dam across City Creek and brought water in ditches to their fields. When Brigham was driven out of the mouth of Emigration Canyon on July 24, and Woodruff's carriage paused to let him take his first look at the valley, he looked down upon a camp that had already half committed itself by putting seeds and potatoes in the ground.

The spot where Woodruff's carriage paused is now marked by Mahonri Young's fine monument, erected in the centennial year; the highest achievement of Mormon art commemorates the high moment of the Mormon hegira. It is popularly called the "This Is the Place" monument, because Brother Brigham is supposed to have said, after remaining a moment lost in a vision, "It is enough. This is the right place, drive on." It is a great statement, one that gathers up in a phrase history and hope and fulfillment, and it is now an ineradicable part of the Mormon myth. But as Dale Morgan has pointed out, the phrase was not part of the original record. It does not seem to have been coined until the fiftieth anniversary of the Church, thirty-three years after the Mormon leader was brought to the brink of the valley. Woodruff's journal, written at the time of the arrival, reports that Brigham "expressed his full satisfaction in the appearance of the valley as a resting-place for the Saints, and was amply repaid for his journey"; and Brigham's own journal for that day says only that they had to cross Emigration Creek eighteen times before emerging from the canyon and joining the main camp at 2:00 P.M.

Nevertheless one is glad that Woodruff either resurrected or happily misremembered Brigham's words. If Brother Brigham didn't make that reverberating phrase, he should have; and once the decision had been made to stay there where the Donners' trail had led them, it could appropriately be put in his mouth.

North from Berthold Pass, photograph by William Henry Jackson

All Gold Canyon

JACK LONDON

It was the green heart of the canyon, where the walls swerved back from the rigid plan and relieved their harshness of line by making a little sheltered nook and filling it to the brim with sweetness and roundness and softness. Here all things rested. Even the narrow stream ceased its turbulent down-rush long enough to form a quiet pool. Knee-deep in the water, with drooping head and half-shut eyes, drowsed a red-coated, many-antlered buck.

On one side, beginning at the very lip of the pool, was a tiny meadow, a cool, resilient surface of green that extended to the base of the frowning wall. Beyond the pool a gentle slope of earth ran up and up to meet the opposing wall. Fine grass covered the slope—grass that was spangled with flowers, with here and there patches of color, orange and purple and golden. Below, the canyon was shut in. There was no view. The walls leaned together abruptly and the canyon ended in a chaos of rocks, moss-covered and hidden by a green screen of vines and creepers and boughs of trees. Up the canyon rose far hills and peaks, the big foothills, pine-covered and remote. And far beyond, like clouds upon the border of the sky, towered minarets of white, where the Sierra's eternal snows flashed austerely the blazes of the sun.

There was no dust in the canyon. The leaves and flowers were clean and virginal. The grass was young velvet. Over the pool three cottonwoods sent their snowy fluffs fluttering down the quiet air. On the slope the blossoms of the wine-wooded manzanita filled the air with springtime odors, while the leaves, wise with experience, were already beginning their vertical twist against the coming aridity of summer. In the open spaces on the slope, beyond the farthest shadow-reach of the manzanita, poised the mariposa lilies, like so many flights of jewelled moths suddenly arrested and on the verge of trembling into flight again. Here and there that woods harlequin, the madrone, permitting itself to be caught in the act of changing its pea-

126

green trunk to madder-red, breathed its fragrance into the air from great clusters of waxen bells. Creamy white were these bells, shaped like lilies-of-the-valley, with the sweetness of perfume that is of the springtime.

There was not a sigh of wind. The air was drowsy with its weight of perfume. It was a sweetness that would have been cloying had the air been heavy and humid. But the air was sharp and thin. It was as starlight transmuted into atmosphere, shot through and warmed by sunshine, and flower-drenched with sweetness.

An occasional butterfly drifted in and out through the patches of light and shade. And from all about rose the low and sleepy hum of mountain bees—feasting Sybarites that jostled one another good-naturedly at the board, nor found time for rough discourtesy. So quietly did the little stream drip and ripple its way through the canyon that it spoke only in faint and occasional gurgles. The voice of the stream was as a drowsy whisper, ever interrupted by dozings and silences, ever lifted again in the awakenings.

The motion of all things was a drifting in the heart of the canyon. Sunshine and butterflies drifted in and out among the trees. The hum of the bees and the whisper of the stream were a drifting of sound. And the drifting sound and drifting color seemed to weave together in the making of a delicate and intangible fabric which was the spirit of the place. It was a spirit of peace that was not of death, but of smooth-pulsing life, of quietude that was not silence, of movement that was not action, of repose that was quick with existence without being violent with struggle and travail. The spirit of the place was the spirit of the peace of the living, somnolent with the easement and content of prosperity, and undisturbed by rumors of far wars.

The red-coated, many-antlered buck acknowledged the lordship of the spirit of the place and dozed knee-deep in the cool, shaded pool. There seemed no flies to vex him and he was languid with rest. Sometimes his ears moved when the stream awoke and whispered; but they moved lazily, with foreknowledge that it was merely the stream grown garrulous at discovery that it had slept.

But there came a time when the buck's ears lifted and tensed with swift eagerness for sound. His head was turned down the canyon. His sensitive, quivering nostrils scented the air. His eyes could not pierce the green screen through which the stream rippled away, but to his ears came the voice of a man. It was a steady, monotonous, singsong voice. Once the buck heard the harsh clash of metal upon rock. At the sound he snorted with a sudden start that jerked him through the air from water to meadow, and his feet sank into the young velvet, while he pricked his ears and again scented the air. Then he stole across the tiny meadow, pausing once and again to listen, and faded away out of the canyon like a wraith, soft-footed and without sound.

The clash of steel-shod soles against the rocks began to be heard, and the man's voice grew louder. It was raised in a sort of chant and became distinct with nearness, so that the words could be heard:

"Tu'n around an' tu'n yo' face
Untoe them sweet hills of grace
  (D' pow'rs of sin yo' am scornin'!).
Look about an' look aroun'
Fling yo' sin-pack on d' groun'
  (Yo' will meet wid d' Lord in d' mornin'!)."

A sound of scrambling accompanied the song, and the spirit of the place fled away on the heels of the red-coated buck. The green screen was burst asunder, and a man peered out at the meadow and the pool and the sloping side-hill. He was a deliberate sort of man. He took in the scene with one embracing glance, then ran his eyes over the details to verify the general impression. Then, and not until then, did he open his mouth in vivid and solemn approval.

"Smoke of life an' snakes of purgatory! Will you just look at that! Wood an' water an' grass an' a side-hill! A pocket-hunter's delight an' a cayuse's paradise! Cool green for tired eyes! Pink pills for pale people ain't in it. A secret pasture for prospectors and a resting-place for tired burros. It's just booful!"

He was a sandy-complexioned man in whose face geniality and humor seemed the salient characteristics. It was a mobile face, quick-changing to inward mood and thought. Thinking was in him a visible process. Ideas chased across his face like wind-flaws across the surface of a lake. His hair, sparse and unkempt of growth, was as indeterminate and colorless as his complexion. It would seem that all the color of his frame had gone into his eyes, for they were startlingly blue. Also, they were laughing and merry eyes, within them much of the naiveté and wonder of the child; and yet, in

128

an unassertive way, they contained much of calm self-reliance and strength of purpose founded upon self-experience and experience of the world.

From out the screen of vines and creepers he flung ahead of him a miner's pick and shovel and gold-pan. Then he crawled out himself into the open. He was clad in faded overalls and black cotton shirt, with hobnailed brogans on his feet, and on his head a hat whose shapelessness and stains advertised the rough usage of wind and rain and sun and camp-smoke. He stood erect, seeing wide-eyed the secrecy of the scene and sensuously inhaling the warm, sweet breath of the canyon-garden through nostrils that dilated and quivered with delight. His eyes narrowed to laughing slits of blue, his face wreathed itself in joy, and his mouth curled in a smile as he cried aloud:

"Jumping dandelions and happy hollyhocks, but that smells good to me! Talk about your attar o' roses an' cologne factories! They ain't in it!"

He had the habit of soliloquy. His quick-changing facial expressions might tell every thought and mood, but the tongue, perforce, ran hard after, repeating, like a second Boswell.

The man lay down on the lip of the pool and drank long and deep of its water. "Tastes good to me," he murmured, lifting his head and gazing across the pool at the side-hill, while we wiped his mouth with the back of his hand. The side-hill attracted his attention. Still lying on his stomach, he studied the hill formation long and carefully. It was a practised eye that traveled up the slope to the crumbling canyon-wall and back and down again to the edge of the pool. He scrambled to his feet and favored the side-hill with a second survey.

"Looks good to me," he concluded, picking up his pick and shovel and gold-pan.

He crossed the stream below the pool, stepping agilely from stone to stone. Where the side-hill touched the water he dug up a shovelful of dirt and put it into the gold-pan. He squatted down, holding the pan in his two hands, and partly immersing it in the stream. Then he imparted to the pan a deft circular motion that sent the water sluicing in and out through the dirt and gravel. The larger and the lighter particles worked to the surface, and these, by a skilful dipping movement of the pan, he spilled out and over the edge. Occasionally, to expedite matters, he rested the pan and with his fingers raked out the large pebbles and pieces of rock.

The contents of the pan diminished rapidly until only fine dirt and the smallest bits of gravel remained. At this stage he began to work very deliberately and carefully. It was fine washing, and he washed fine and finer, with a keen scrutiny and delicate and fastidious touch. At last the pan seemed empty of everything but water; but with a quick semi-circular flirt that sent the water flying over the shallow rim into the stream, he disclosed a layer of black sand on the bottom of the pan. So thin was this layer that it was like a streak of paint. He examined it closely. In the midst of it was a tiny golden speck. He dribbled a little water in over the depressed edge of the pan. With a quick flirt he sent the water sluicing across the bottom, turning the grains of black sand over and over. A second tiny golden speck rewarded his effort.

The washing had now become very fine—fine beyond all need of ordinary placer mining. He worked the black sand, a small portion at a time, up the shallow rim of the pan. Each small portion he examined sharply, so that his eyes saw every grain of it before he allowed it to slide over the edge and away. Jealously, bit by bit, he let the black sand slip away. A golden speck, no larger than a pin-point, appeared on the rim, and by his manipulation of the water it returned to the bottom of the pan. And in such fashion another speck was disclosed, and another. Great was his care of them. Like a shepherd he herded his flock of golden specks so that not one should be lost. At last, of the pan of dirt nothing remained but his golden herd. He counted it, and then, after all his labor, sent it flying out of the pan with one final swirl of water.

But his blue eyes were shining with desire as he rose to his feet. "Seven," he muttered aloud, asserting the sum of the specks for which he had toiled so hard and which he had so wantonly thrown away. "Seven," he repeated, with the emphasis of one trying to impress a number on his memory.

He stood still a long while, surveying the hillside. In his eyes was a curiosity, new-aroused and burning. There was an exultance about his bearing and a keenness like that of a hunting animal catching the fresh scent of game.

He moved down the stream a few steps and took a second panful of dirt.

Again came the careful washing, the jealous herding of the golden specks, and the wantonness with which he sent them flying into the stream.

His golden herd diminished. "Four, five," he muttered, and repeated, "five."

He could not forbear another survey of the hill before filling the pan farther down the stream. His golden herds diminished. "Four, three, two, two, one," were his memory tabulations as he moved down the stream. When but one speck of gold rewarded his washing, he stopped and built a fire of dry twigs. Into this he thrust the gold-pan and burned it till it was blue-black. He held up the pan and examined it critically. Then he nodded approbation. Against such a color-background he could defy the tiniest yellow speck to elude him.

Still moving down the stream, he panned again. A single speck was his reward. A third pan contained no gold at all. Not satisfied with this, he panned three times again, taking his shovels of dirt within a foot of one another. Each pan proved empty of gold, and the fact, instead of discouraging him, seemed to give him satisfaction. His elation increased with each barren washing, until he arose, exclaiming jubilantly:

"If it ain't the real thing, may God knock off my head with sour apples!"

Returning to where he had started operations, he began to pan up the stream. At first his golden herds increased—increased prodigiously. "Fourteen, eighteen, twenty-one, twenty-six," ran his memory tabulations. Just above the pool he struck his richest pan—thirty-five colors.

"Almost enough to save," he remarked regretfully as he allowed the water to sweep them away.

The sun climbed to the top of the sky. The man worked on. Pan by pan, he went up the stream, the tally of results steadily decreasing.

"It's just booful, the way it peters out," he exulted when a shovelful of dirt contained no more than a single speck of gold.

And when no specks at all were found in several pans, he straightened up and favored the hillside with a confident glance.

"Ah, ha! Mr. Pocket!" he cried out, as though to an auditor hidden somewhere above him beneath the surface of the slope. "Ah, ha! Mr. Pocket! I'm a-comin', I'm a-comin', an' I'm shorely gwine to get yer! You heah me, Mr. Pocket? I'm gwine to get yer as shore as punkins ain't cauliflowers!"

He turned and flung a measuring glance at the sun poised above him in the azure of the cloudless sky. Then he went down the canyon, following the line of shovel-holes he had made in filling the pans. He crossed the stream below the pool and disappeared through the green screen. There was little opportunity for the spirit of the place to return with its quietude and repose, for the man's voice, raised in ragtime song, still dominated the canyon with possession.

After a time, with a greater clashing of steel-shod feet on rock, he returned. The green screen was tremendously agitated. It surged back and forth in the throes of a struggle. There was a loud grating and clanging of metal. The man's voice leaped to a higher pitch and was sharp with imperativeness. A large body plunged and panted. There was a snapping and ripping and rending, and amid a shower of falling leaves a horse burst through the screen. On its back was a pack, and from this trailed broken vines and torn creepers. The animal gazed with astonished eyes at the scene into which it had been precipitated, then dropped its head to the grass and began contentedly to graze. A second horse scrambled into view, slipping once on the mossy rocks and regaining equilibrium when its hoofs sank into the yielding surface of the meadow. It was riderless, though on its back was a high-horned Mexican saddle, scarred and discolored by long usage.

The man brought up the rear. He threw off pack and saddle, with an eye to camp location, and gave the animals their freedom to graze. He unpacked his food and got out frying-pan and coffeepot. He gathered an armful of dry wood, and with a few stones made a place for his fire.

"My!" he said, "but I've got an appetite. I could scoff iron-filings an' horseshoe nails an' thank you kindly, ma'am, for a second helpin'."

He straightened up, and, while he reached for matches in the pocket of his overalls, his eyes traveled across the pool to the side-hill. His fingers had clutched the match-box, but they relaxed their hold and the hand came out empty. The man wavered perceptibly. He looked at his preparations for cooking and he looked at the hill.

"Guess I'll take another whack at her," he concluded, starting to cross the stream.

"They ain't no sense in it, I know," he mumbled apologetically. "But keepin' grub back an hour ain't goin' to hurt none, I reckon."

A few feet back from his first of test-pans he started a second line. The sun dropped down the western sky, the shadows lengthened, but the man worked on. He began a third line of test-pans. He was cross-cutting the hillside, line by line, as he ascended. The center of each line produced the richest pans, while the ends came where no colors showed in the pan. And as he ascended the hillside the lines grew perceptibly shorter. The regularity with which their length diminished served to indicate that somewhere up the slope the last line would be so short as to have scarcely length at all, and that beyond could come only a point. The design was growing into an inverted "V." The converging sides of this "V" marked the boundaries of the gold-bearing dirt.

The apex of the "V" was evidently the man's goal. Often he ran his eye along the converging sides and on up the hill, trying to divine the apex, the point where the gold-bearing dirt must cease. Here resided "Mr. Pocket"— for so the man familiarly addressed the imaginary point above him on the slope, crying out:

"Come down out o' that, Mr. Pocket! Be right smart an' agreeable, an' come down!"

"All right," he would add later, in a voice resigned to determination. "All right, Mr. Pocket. It's plain to me I got to come right up an' snatch you out bald-headed. An' I'll do it! I'll do it!" he would threaten still later.

Each pan he carried down to the water to wash, and as he went higher up the hill the pans grew richer, until he began to save the gold in an empty baking powder can which he carried carelessly in his hip pocket. So engrossed was he in his toil that he did not notice the long twilight of oncoming night. It was not until he tried vainly to see the gold colors in the bottom of the pan that he realized the passage of time. He straightened up abruptly. An expression of whimsical wonderment and awe overspread his face as he drawled:

"Gosh darm my buttons! if I didn't plumb forget dinner!"

He stumbled across the stream in the darkness and lighted his long-delayed fire. Flapjacks and bacon and warmed-over beans constituted his supper. Then he smoked a pipe by the smouldering coals, listening to the night noises and watching the moonlight stream through the canyon. After that he unrolled his bed, took off his heavy shoes, and pulled the blankets up to his chin. His face showed white in the moonlight, like the face of a corpse. But it was a corpse that knew its resurrection, for the man rose suddenly on one elbow and gazed across at his hillside.

"Good night, Mr. Pocket," he called sleepily. "Good night."

He slept through the early gray of morning until the direct rays of the sun smote his closed eyelids, when he awoke with a start and looked about him until he had established the continuity of his existence and identified his present self with the days previously lived.

To dress, he had merely to buckle on his shoes. He glanced at his fireplace and at his hillside, wavered, but fought down the temptation and started the fire.

"Keep yer shirt on, Bill; keep yer shirt on," he admonished himself. "What's the good of rushin'? No use in gettin' all het up an' sweaty. Mr. Pocket 'll wait for you. He ain't a-runnin' away before you can get your breakfast. Now, what you want, Bill, is something fresh in yer bill o' fare. So it's up to you to go an' get it."

He cut a short pole at the water's edge and drew from one of his pockets a bit of line and a draggled fly that had once been a royal coachman.

"Mebbe they'll bite in the early morning," he muttered, as he made his first cast into the pool. And a moment later he was gleefully crying: "What 'd I tell you, eh? What 'd I tell you?"

He had no reel, nor any inclination to waste time, and by main strength, and swiftly, he drew out of the water a flashing ten-inch trout. Three more, caught in rapid succession, furnished his breakfast. When he came to the stepping-stones on his way to his hillside, he was struck by a sudden thought, and paused.

"I'd just better take a hike down-stream a ways," he said. "There's no tellin' who may be snoopin' around."

But he crossed over on the stones, and with a "I really oughter take that hike," the need of the precaution passed out of his mind and he fell to work.

At nightfall he straightened up. The small of his back was stiff from stooping toil, and as he put his hand behind him to soothe the protesting muscles, he said:

"Now what d'ye think of that? I clean forgot my dinner again! If I don't watch out, I'll sure be degeneratin' into a two-meal-a-day crank."

"Pockets is the hangedest things I ever see for makin' a man absent-minded," he communed that night, as he crawled into his blankets. Nor did he forget to call up the hillside, "Good night, Mr. Pocket! Good night!"

Rising with the sun, and snatching a hasty breakfast, he was early at work. A fever seemed to be growing in him, nor did the increasing richness of the test-pans allay this fever. There was a flush in his cheek other than that made by the heat of the sun, and he was oblivious to fatigue and the

134

passage of time. When he filled a pan with dirt, he ran down the hill to wash it; nor could he forbear running up the hill again, panting and stumbling profanely, to refill the pan.

He was now a hundred yards from the water, and the inverted "V" was assuming definite proportions. The width of the paydirt steadily decreased, and the man extended in his mind's eye the sides of the "V" to their meeting place far up the hill. This was his goal, the apex of the "V," and he panned many times to locate it.

"Just about two yards above that manzanita bush an' a yard to the right," he finally concluded.

Then the temptation seized him. "As plain as the nose on your face," he said, as he abandoned his laborious cross-cutting and climbed to the indicated apex. He filled a pan and carried it down the hill to wash. It contained no trace of gold. He dug deep, and he dug shallow, filling and washing a dozen pans, and was unrewarded even by the tiniest golden speck. He was enraged at having yielded to the temptation, and berated himself blasphemously and pridelessly. Then he went down the hill and took up the cross-cutting.

"Slow an' certain, Bill; slow an' certain," he crooned. "Shortcuts to fortune ain't in your line, an' it's about time you know it. Get wise, Bill; get wise. Slow an' certain's the only hand you can play; so get to it, an' keep to it, too."

As the cross-cuts decreased, showing that the sides of the "V" were converging, the depth of the "V" increased. The gold-trace was dipping into the hill. It was only at thirty inches beneath the surface that he could get colors in his pan. The dirt he found at twenty-five inches from the surface, and at thirty-five inches yielded barren pans. At the base of the "V," by the water's edge, he had found the gold colors at the grass roots. The higher he went up the hill, the deeper the gold dipped. To dig a hole three feet deep in order to get one test-pan was a task of no mean magnitude; while between the man and the apex intervened an untold number of such holes to be dug. "An' there's no tellin' how much deeper it'll pitch," he sighed, in a moment's pause, while his fingers soothed his aching back.

Feverish with desire, with aching back and stiffening muscles, with pick and shovel gouging and mauling the soft brown earth, the man toiled up the hill. Before him was the smooth slope, spangled with flowers and made sweet with their breath. Behind him was devastation. It looked like some terrible eruption breaking out on the smooth skin of the hill. His slow progress was like that of a slug, befouling beauty with a monstrous trail.

Though the dipping gold-trace increased the man's work, he found consolation in the increasing richness of the pans. Twenty cents, thirty cents, fifty cents, sixty cents, were the values of the gold found in the pans, and at nightfall he washed his banner pan, which gave him a dollar's worth of gold-dust from a shovelful of dirt.

"I'll just bet it's my luck to have some inquisitive one come buttin' in here on my pasture," he mumbled sleepily that night as he pulled the blankets up to his chin.

Suddenly he sat upright. "Bill!" he called sharply. "Now, listen to me, Bill; d'ye hear! It's up to you, to-morrow mornin', to mosey round an' see what you can see. Understand? To-morrow morning, an' don't you forget it!"

He yawned and glanced across at his side-hill. "Good night, Mr. Pocket," he called.

In the morning he stole a march on the sun, for he had finished breakfast when its first rays caught him, and he was climbing the wall of the canyon where it crumbled away and gave footing. From the outlook at the top he found himself in the midst of loneliness. As far as he could see, chain after chain of mountains heaved themselves into his vision. To the east his eyes, leaping the miles between range and range and between many ranges, brought up at last against the white-peaked Sierras—the main crest, where the backbone of the Western world reared itself against the sky. To the north and south he could see more distinctly the cross-systems that broke through the main trend of the sea of mountains. To the west the ranges fell away, one behind the other, diminishing and fading into the gentle foothills that, in turn, descended into the great valley which he could not see.

And in all that mighty sweep of earth he saw no sign of man nor of the handiwork of man—save only the torn bosom of the hillside at his feet. The man looked long and carefully. Once, far down his own canyon, he thought he saw in the air a faint hint of smoke. He looked again and decided that it was the purple haze of the hills made dark by a convolution of the canyon wall at its back.

"Hey, you, Mr. Pocket!" he called down into the canyon. "Stand out from under! I'm a-comin', Mr. Pocket! I'm a-comin'!"

The heavy brogans on the man's feet made him appear clumsy-footed, but he swung down from the giddy height as lightly and airily as a mountain goat. A rock, turning under his foot on the edge of the precipice, did not disconcert him. He seemed to know the precise time required for the turn to culminate in disaster, and in the meantime he utilized the false footing itself for the momentary earth-contact necessary to carry him on into safety. Where the earth sloped so steeply that it was impossible to stand for a second upright, the man did not hesitate. His foot pressed the impossible surface for but a fraction of the fatal second and gave him the bound that carried him onward. Again, where even the fraction of a second's footing was out of the question, he would swing his body past by a moment's hand-grip on a jutting knob of rock, a crevice, or a precariously rooted shrub. At last, with a wild leap and yell, he exchanged the face of the wall for an earthslide and finished the descent in the midst of several tons of sliding earth and gravel.

His first pan of the morning washed out over two dollars in coarse gold. It was from the centre of the "V." To either side the diminution in the values of the pans was swift. His lines of cross-cutting holes were growing very short. The converging sides of the inverted "V" were only a few yards apart. Their meeting-point was only a few yards above him. But the pay-streak was dipping deeper and deeper into the earth. By early afternoon he was sinking the test-holes five feet before the pans could show the gold-trace.

For that matter, the gold-trace had become something more than a trace; it was a placer mine in itself, and the man resolved to come back after he had found the pocket and work over the ground. But the increasing richness of the pans began to worry him. By late afternoon the worth of the pans had grown to three and four dollars. The man scratched his head perplexedly and looked a few feet up the hill at the manzanita bush that marked approximately the apex of the "V." He nodded his head and said oracularly:

"It's one o' two things, Bill: one o' two things. Either Mr. Pocket's spilled himself all out an' down the hill, or else Mr. Pocket's so rich you maybe won't be able to carry him all away with you. And that'd be an awful shame, wouldn't it, now?" He chuckled at contemplation of so pleasant a dilemma.

Nightfall found him by the edge of the stream, his eyes wrestling with the gathering darkness over the washing of a five-dollar pan.

"Wisht I had an electric light to go on working," he said.

He found sleep difficult that night. Many times he composed himself and closed his eyes for slumber to overtake him; but his blood pounded with too strong desire, and as many times his eyes opened and he murmured wearily, "Wisht it was sun-up."

Sleep came to him in the end, but his eyes were open with the first paling of the stars, and the gray of dawn caught him with breakfast finished and climbing the hillside in the direction of the secret abiding-place of Mr. Pocket.

The first cross-cut the man made, there was space for only three holes, so narrow had become the pay-streak and so close was he to the fountainhead of the golden stream he had been following for four days.

"Be ca'm, Bill; be ca'm," he admonished himself, as he broke ground for the final hole where the sides of the "V" had at last come together in a point.

"I've got the almighty cinch on you, Mr. Pocket, an' you can't lose me," he said many times as he sank the hole deeper and deeper.

Four feet, five feet, six feet, he dug his way down into the earth. The digging grew harder. His pick grated on broken rock. He examined the rock. "Rotten quartz," was his conclusion as, with the shovel, he cleared the bottom of the hole of loose dirt. He attacked the crumbling quartz with the pick, bursting the disintegrating rock asunder with every stroke.

He thrust his shovel into the loose mass. His eye caught a gleam of yellow. He dropped the shovel and squatted suddenly on his heels. As a farmer rubs the clinging earth from fresh-dug potatoes, so the man, a piece of rotten quartz held in both hands, rubbed the dirt away.

"Sufferin' Sardanopolis!" he cried. "Lumps an' chunks of it! Lumps an' chunks of it!"

It was only half rock he held in his hand. The other half was virgin gold. He dropped it into his pan and examined another piece. Little yellow was to be seen, but with his strong fingers he crumbled the rotten quartz away till both hands were filled with glowing yellow. He rubbed the dirt away from fragment after fragment, tossing them into the gold-pan. It was a treasure-hole. So much had the quartz rotted away that there was less of it than there was of gold. Now and again he found a piece to which no rock clung— a piece that was all gold. A chunk, where the pick had laid open the heart of the gold, glittered like a handful of yellow jewels, and he cocked his head at

138

it and slowly turned it around and over to observe the rich play of the light upon it.

"Talk about yer Too Much Gold diggin's!" the man snorted contemptuously. "Why, this diggin' 'd make it look like thirty cents. This diggin' is All Gold. An' right here an' now I name this yere canyon 'All Gold Canyon,' b' gosh!"

Still squatting on his heels, he continued examining the fragments and tossing them into the pan. Suddenly there came to him a premonition of danger. It seemed a shadow had fallen upon him. But there was no shadow. His heart had given a great jump up into his throat and was choking him. Then his blood slowly chilled and he felt the sweat of his shirt cold against his flesh.

He did not spring up nor look around. He did not move. He was considering the nature of the premonition he had received, trying to locate the source of the mysterious force that had warned him, striving to sense the imperative presence of the unseen thing that threatened him. There is an aura of things hostile, made manifest by messengers too refined for the senses to know; and this aura he felt, but knew not how he felt it. His was the feeling as when a cloud passes over the sun. It seemed that between him and life had passed something dark and smothering and menacing; a gloom, as it were, that swallowed up life and made for death—his death.

Every force of his being impelled him to spring up and confront the unseen danger, but his soul dominated the panic, and he remained squatting on his heels, in his hands a chunk of gold. He did not dare to look around, but he knew by now that there was something behind him and above him. He made believe to be interested in the gold in his hand. He examined it critically, turned it over and over, and rubbed the dirt from it. And all the time he knew that something behind him was looking at the gold over his shoulder.

Still feigning interest in the chunk of gold in his hand, he listened intently and he heard the breathing of the thing behind him. His eyes searched the ground in front of him for a weapon, but they saw only the uprooted gold, worthless to him now in his extremity. There was his pick, a handy weapon on occasion; but this was not such an occasion. The man realized his predicament. He was in a narrow hole that was seven feet deep. His head did not come to the surface of the ground. He was in a trap.

He remained squatting on his heels. He was quite cool and collected;

but his mind, considering every factor, showed him only his helplessness. He continued rubbing the dirt from the quartz fragments and throwing the gold into the pan. There was nothing else for him to do. Yet he knew that he would have to rise up, sooner or later, and face the danger that breathed at his back. The minutes passed, and with the passage of each minute he knew that by so much he was nearer the time when he must stand up, or else—and his wet shirt went cold against his flesh again at the thought—or else he might receive death as he stooped there over his treasure.

Still he squatted on his heels, rubbing dirt from gold and debating in just what manner he should rise up. He might rise up with a rush and claw his way out of the hole to meet whatever threatened on the even footing above ground. Or he might rise up slowly and carelessly, and feign casually to discover the thing that breathed at his back. His instinct and every fighting fibre of his body favored the mad, clawing rush to the surface. His intellect, and the craft thereof, favored the slow and cautious meeting with the thing that menaced and which he could not see. And while he debated, a loud, crashing noise burst on his ear. At the same instant he received a stunning blow on the left side of his back, and from the point of impact felt a rush of flame through his flesh. He sprang up in the air, but halfway to his feet collapsed. His body crumpled in like a leaf withered in sudden heat, and he came down, his chest across his pan of gold, his face in the dirt and rock, his legs tangled and twisted because of the restricted space at the bottom of the hole. His legs twitched convulsively several times. His body was shaken with a mighty ague. There was a slow expansion of the lungs, accompanied by a deep sigh. Then the air was slowly, very slowly, exhaled, and his body as slowly flattened itself down into inertness.

Above, revolver in hand, a man was peering down over the edge of the hole. He peered for a long time at the prone and motionless body beneath him. After a while the stranger sat down on the edge of the hole so that he could see into it, and rested the revolver on his knee. Reaching his hand into a pocket, he drew out a wisp of brown paper. Into this he dropped a few crumbs of tobacco. The combination became a cigarette, brown and squat, with the ends turned in. Not once did he take his eyes from the body at the bottom of the hole. He lighted the cigarette and drew its smoke into his lungs with a caressing intake of the breath. He smoked slowly. Once the cigarette went out and he relighted it. And all the while he studied the body beneath him.

In the end he tossed the cigarette stub away and rose to his feet. He moved to the edge of the hole. Spanning it, a hand resting on each edge, and with the revolver still in the right hand, he muscled his body down into the hole. While his feet were yet a yard from the bottom he released his hands and dropped down.

At the instant his feet struck bottom he saw the pocket-miner's arm leap out, and his own legs knew a swift, jerking grip that overthrew him. In the nature of the jump his revolver-hand was above his head. Swiftly as the grip had flashed about his legs, just as swiftly he brought the revolver down. He was still in the air, his fall in process of completion, when he pulled the trigger. The explosion was deafening in the confined space. The smoke filled the hole so that he could see nothing. He struck the bottom on his back, and like a cat's the pocket-miner's body was on top of him. Even as the miner's body passed on top, the stranger crooked in his right arm to fire; and even in that instant the miner, with a quick thrust of elbow, struck his wrist. The muzzle was thrown up and the bullet thudded into the dirt of the side of the hole.

The next instant the stranger felt the miner's hand grip his wrist. The struggle was now for the revolver. Each man strove to turn it against the other's body. The smoke in the hole was clearing. The stranger, lying on his back, was beginning to see dimly. But suddenly he was blinded by a handful of dirt deliberately flung into his eyes by his antagonist. In that moment of shock his grip on the revolver was broken. In the next moment he felt a smashing darkness descend upon his brain, and in the midst of the darkness even the darkness ceased.

But the pocket-miner fired again and again, until the revolver was empty. Then he tossed it from him and, breathing heavily, sat down on the dead man's legs.

The miner was sobbing and struggling for breath. "Measly skunk!" he panted; "a-campin' on my trail an' lettin' me do the work, an' then shootin' me in the back!"

He was half crying from anger and exhaustion. He peered at the face of the dead man. It was sprinkled with loose dirt and gravel, and it was difficult to distinguish the features.

"Never laid eyes on him before," the miner concluded his scrutiny. "Just a common an' ordinary thief, hang him! An' he shot me in the back! He shot me in the back!"

He opened his shirt and felt himself, front and back, on his left side.

"Went clean through, and no harm done!" he cried jubilantly. "I'll bet he aimed all right all right; but he drew the gun over when he pulled the trigger—the cur! But I fixed 'm! Oh, I fixed 'm!"

His fingers were investigating the bullet-hole in his side, and a shade of regret passed over his face. "It's goin' to be stiffer'n hell," he said. "An' it's up to me to get mended an' get out o' here."

He crawled out of the hole and went down the hill to his camp. Half an hour later he returned, leading his pack-horse. His open shirt disclosed the rude bandages with which he had dressed his wound. He was slow and awkward with his left-hand movements, but that did not prevent his using the arm.

The bight of the pack-rope under the dead man's shoulders enabled him to heave the body out of the hole. Then he set to work gathering up his gold. He worked steadily for several hours, pausing often to rest his stiffening shoulder and to exclaim:

"He shot me in the back, the measly skunk! He shot me in the back!"

When his treasure was quite cleaned up and wrapped securely into a number of blanket-covered parcels, he made an estimate of its value.

"Four hundred pounds, or I'm a Hottentot," he concluded. "Say two hundred in quartz an' dirt—that leaves two hundred pounds of gold. Bill! Wake up! Two hundred pounds of gold! Forty thousand dollars! An' it's yourn—all yourn!"

He scratched his head delightedly and his fingers blundered into an unfamiliar groove. They quested along it for several inches. It was a cease through his scalp where the second bullet had ploughed.

He walked angrily over to the dead man.

"You would, would you?" he bullied. "You would, eh? Well, I fixed you good an' plenty, an' I'll give you a decent burial, too. That's more'n you'd have done for me."

He dragged the body to the edge of the hole and toppled it in. It struck the bottom with a dull crash, on its side, the face twisted up to the light. The miner peered down at it.

"An' you shot me in the back!" he said accusingly.

With pick and shovel he filled the hole. Then he loaded the gold on his horse. It was too great a load for the animal, and when he had gained his camp he transferred part of it to his saddle-horse. Even so, he was compelled to abandon a portion of his outfit—pick and shovel and gold-pan, extra food and cooking utensils, and divers odds and ends.

The sun was at the zenith when the man forced the horses at the screen of vines and creepers. To climb the huge boulders the animals were compelled to uprear and struggle blindly through the tangled mass of vegetation. Once the saddle-horse fell heavily and the man removed the pack to get the animal on its feet. After it started on its way again the man thrust his head out from among the leaves and peered up at the hillside.

"The measly skunk!" he said, and disappeared.

There was a ripping and tearing of vines and boughs. The trees surged back and forth, marking the passage of the animals through the midst of them. There was a clashing of steel-shod hoofs on stone, and now and again a sharp cry of command. Then the voice of the man was raised in song:—

"Tu'n around an' tu'n yo' face
Untoe them sweet hills of grace
    (D' pow'rs of sin yo' am scornin'!).
Look about an' look aroun'
Fling yo' sin-pack on d' groun'
    (Yo' will meet wid d' Lord in d' mornin'!)."

The song grew faint and fainter, and through the silence crept back the spirit of the place. The stream once more drowsed and whispered; the hum of the mountain bees rose sleepily. Down through the perfume-weighted air fluttered the snowy fluffs of the cottonwoods. The butterflies drifted in and out among the trees, and over all blazed the quiet sunshine. Only remained the hoof-marks in the meadow and the torn hillside to mark the boisterous trail of the life that had broken the peace of the place and passed on.

Buck Fanshaw's Funeral

MARK TWAIN

Somebody has said that in order to know a community, one must observe the style of its funerals and know what manner of men they bury with most ceremony. I cannot say which class we buried with most éclat in our "flush times," the distinguished public benefactor or the distinguished rough—possibly the two chief grades or grand divisions of society honored their illustrious dead about equally; and hence, no doubt, the philosopher I have quoted from would have needed to see two representative funerals in Virginia before forming his estimate of the people.

There was a grand time over Buck Fanshaw when he died. He was a representative citizen. He had "killed his man"—not in his own quarrel, it is true, but in defense of a stranger unfairly beset by numbers. He had kept a sumptuous saloon. He had been the proprietor of a dashing helpmeet whom he could have discarded without the formality of a divorce. He had held a high position in the fire department and been a very Warwick in politics. When he died there was great lamentation throughout the town, but especially in the vast bottom-stratum of society.

On the inquest it was shown that Buck Fanshaw, in the delirium of a wasting typhoid fever, had taken arsenic, shot himself through the body, cut his throat, and jumped out of a four-story window and broken his neck—and after due deliberation, the jury, sad and tearful, but with intelligence unblinded by its sorrow, brought in a verdict of death "by the visitation of God." What could the world do without juries?

Prodigious preparations were made for the funeral. All the vehicles in town were hired, all the saloons put in mourning, all the municipal and fire-company flags hung at half-mast, and all the firemen ordered to muster in uniform and bring their machines duly draped in black. Now—let us remark in parenthesis—as all the peoples of the earth had representative adventurers in the Silverland, and as each adventurer had brought the slang of his nation or his locality with him, the combination made the slang of Nevada the richest and the most infinitely varied and copious that had ever existed anywhere in the world, perhaps, except in the mines of California in the "early days." Slang was the language of Nevada. It was hard to preach a sermon without it, and be understood. Such phrases as "You bet!" "Oh, no, I reckon not!" "No Irish need apply," and a hundred others, became so common as to fall from the lips of a speaker unconsciously—and very often when they did not touch the subject under discussion and consequently failed to mean anything.

After Buck Fanshaw's inquest, a meeting of the short-haired brotherhood was held, for nothing can be done on the Pacific coast without a public meeting and an expression of sentiment. Regretful resolutions were passed and various committees appointed; among others, a committee of one was deputed to call on the minister, a fragile, gentle, spiritual new fledgling from an Eastern theological seminary, and as yet unacquainted with the ways of the mines. The committeeman, "Scotty" Briggs, made his visit; and in after days it was worth something to hear the minister tell about it. Scotty was a stalwart rough, whose customary suit, when on weighty official business, like committee work, was a fire helmet, flaming red flannel shirt, patent leather belt with spanner and revolver attached, coat hung over arm, and pants stuffed into boot tops. He formed something of a contrast to the pale theological student. It is fair to say of Scotty, however, in passing, that he had a warm heart, and a strong love for his friends, and never entered into a quarrel when he could reasonably keep out of it. Indeed, it was commonly said that whenever one of Scotty's fights was investigated, it always turned out that it had originally been no affair of his, but that out of native goodheartedness he had dropped in of his own accord to help the man who was getting the worst of it. He and Buck Fanshaw were bosom friends, for years, and had often taken adventurous "potluck" together. On one occasion, they had thrown off their coats and taken the weaker side in a fight among strangers, and after gaining a hard-earned victory, turned and found that the men they were helping had deserted early, and not only that, but had stolen their coats and made off with them! But to return to Scotty's visit to the minister. He was on a sorrowful mission, now, and his face was the picture of woe. Being admitted to the presence he sat down before the clergyman, placed his fire-hat on an unfinished manuscript sermon under the minister's nose, took from it a red silk handkerchief, wiped his brow and heaved a sigh of dismal impressiveness, explanatory of his business. He choked, and even shed tears; but with an effort he mastered his voice and said in lugubrious tones:

"Are you the duck that runs the gospel-mill next door?"

"Am I the—pardon me, I believe I do not understand?"

With another sigh and a half-sob, Scotty rejoined:

"Why you see we are in a bit of trouble, and the boys thought maybe you would give us a lift, if we'd tackle you—that is, if I've got the rights of it and you are the head clerk of the doxology-works next door."

"I am the shepherd in charge of the flock whose fold is next door."

"The which?"

"The spiritual adviser of the little company of believers whose sanctuary adjoins these premises."

Scotty scratched his head, reflected a moment, and then said:

"You ruther hold over me, pard. I reckon I can't call that hand. Ante and pass the buck."

"How? I beg pardon. What did I understand you to say?"

"Well, you've ruther got the bulge on me. Or maybe we've both got the bulge, somehow. You don't smoke me and I don't smoke you. You see, one of the boys has passed in his checks, and we want to give him a good send-off, and so the thing I'm on now is to roust out somebody to jerk a little chin-music for us and waltz him through handsome."

"My friend, I seem to grow more and more bewildered. Your observations are wholly incomprehensible to me. Cannot you simplify them in some way? At first I thought perhaps I understood you, but I grope now. Would it not expedite matters if you restricted yourself to categorical statements of fact unencumbered with obstructing accumulations of metaphor and allegory?"

Another pause, and more reflection. Then, said Scotty:

"I'll have to pass, I judge."

"How?"

"You've raised me out, pard."

"I still fail to catch your meaning."

"Why, that last lead of yourn is too many for me—that's the idea. I can't neither trump nor follow suit."

The clergyman sank back in his chair perplexed. Scotty leaned his head on his hand and gave himself up to thought. Presently his face came up, sorrowful but confident.

"I've got it now, so's you can savvy," he said. "What we want is a gospel-sharp. See?"

"A what?"

"Gospel-sharp, Parson."

"Oh! Why did you not say so before? I am a clergyman—a parson."

"Now you talk! You see my blind and straddle it like a man. Put it there!"—extending a brawny paw, which closed over the minister's small hand and gave it a shake indicative of fraternal sympathy and fervent gratification.

"Now we're all right, pard. Let's start fresh. Don't you mind my snuffing a little—becuz we're in a power of trouble. You see, one of the boys has gone up the flume—"

"Gone where?"

"Up the flume—throwed up the sponge, you understand."

"Thrown up the sponge?"

"Yes—kicked the bucket—"

"Ah—has departed to that mysterious country from whose bourne no traveler returns."

"Return! I reckon not. Why, pard, he's *dead!*"

"Yes, I understand."

"Oh, you do? Well I though maybe you might be getting tangled some more. Yes, you see he's dead again—"

"*Again!* Why, has he ever been dead before?"

"Dead before? No! Do you reckon a man has got as many lives as a cat? But you bet you he's awful dead now, poor old boy, and I wish I'd never seen this day. I don't want no better friend than Buck Fanshaw. I knowed him by the back; and when I know a man and like him, I freeze to him— you hear *me.* Take him all round, pard, there never was a bullier man in the mines. No man ever knowed Buck Fanshaw to go back on a friend. But it's all up, you know, it's all up. It ain't no use. They've scooped him."

"Scooped him?"

"Yes—death has. Well, well, well, we've got to give him up. Yes, indeed. It's a kind of a hard world, after all, *ain't* it? But pard, he was a rustler! You ought to seen him get started once. He was a bully boy with a

147

glass eye! Just spit in his face and give him room according to his strength, and it was just beautiful to see him peel and go in. He was the worst son of a thief that ever drawed breath. Pard, he was *on* it! He was on it bigger than an Injun!"

"On it? On what?"

"On the shoot. On the shoulder. On the fight, you understand. *He* didn't give a continental for *any*body. *Beg* your pardon, friend, for coming so near saying a cuss-word—but you see I'm on an awful strain, in this palaver, on account of having to cramp down and draw everything so mild. But we've got to give him up. There ain't any getting around that, I don't reckon. Now if we can get you to help plant him—"

"Preach the funeral discourse? Assist at the obsequies?"

"Obs'quies is good. Yes. That's it—that's our little game. We are going to get the thing up regardless, you know. He was always nifty himself, and so you bet you his funeral ain't going to be no slouch—solid silver door-plate on his coffin, six plumes on the hearse, and a nigger on the box in a biled shirt and a plug hat—how's that for high? And we'll take care of *you*, pard. We'll fix you all right. There'll be a kerridge for you; and whatever you want, you just 'scape out and we'll 'tend to it. We've got a shebang fixed up for you to stand behind, in No. 1's house, and don't you be afraid. Just go in and toot your horn, if you don't sell a clam. Put Buck through as bully as you can, pard, for anybody that knowed him will tell you that he was one of the whitest men that was ever in the mines. You can't draw it too strong. He never could stand it to see things going wrong. He's done more to make this town quiet and peaceable than any man in it. I've seen him lick four Greasers in eleven minutes, myself. If a thing wanted regulating, *he* warn't a man to go browsing around after somebody to do it, but he would prance in and regulate it himself. He warn't a Catholic. Scasely. He was down on 'em. His word was, 'No Irish need apply!' But it didn't make no difference about that when it came down to what a man's rights was—and so, when some roughs jumped the Catholic boneyard and started in to stake out town-lots in it he *went* for 'em! And he *cleaned* 'em, too! I was there, pard, and I seen it myself."

"That was very well indeed—at least the impulse was—whether the act was strictly defensible or not. Had deceased any religious convictions? That is to say, did he feel a dependence upon, or acknowledge allegiance to a higher power?"

More reflection.

"I reckon you've stumped me again, pard. Could you say it over once more, and say it slow?"

"Well, to simplify it somewhat, was he, or rather had he ever been connected with any organization sequestered from secular concerns and devoted to self-sacrifice in the interests of morality?"

"All down but nine—set 'em up on the other alley, pard."

"What did I understand you to say?"

"Why, you're most too many for me, you know. When you get in with your left I hunt grass every time. Every time you draw, you fill; but I don't seem to have any luck. Let's have a new deal."

"How? Begin again?"

"That's it."

"Very well. Was he a good man, and—"

"There— I see that; don't put up another chip till I look at my hand. A good man, says you? Pard, it ain't no name for it. He was the best man that ever—pard, you would have doted on that man. He could lam any galoot of his inches in America. It was him that put down the riot last election before it got a start; and everybody said he was the only man that could have done it. He waltzed in with a spanner in one hand and a trumpet in the other, and sent fourteen men home on a shutter in less than three minutes. He had that riot all broke up and prevented nice before anybody ever got a chance to strike a blow. He was always for peace, and he would *have* peace—he could not stand disturbances. Pard, he was a great loss to this town. It would please the boys if you could chip in something like that and do him justice. Here once when the Micks got to throwing stones through the Methodis' Sunday-school windows, Buck Fanshaw, all of his own notion, shut up his saloon and took a couple of six-shooters and mounted guard over the Sunday-school. Says he, 'No Irish need apply!' And they didn't. He was the bulliest man in the mountains, pard! He could run faster, jump higher, hit harder, and hold more tanglefoot whisky without spilling it than any man in seventeen counties. Put that in, pard—it'll please the boys more than anything you could say. And you can say, pard, that he never shook his mother."

"Never shook his mother?"

"That's it—any of the boys will tell you so."

"Well, but why *should* he shake her?"

"That's what *I* say—but some people does."

"Not people of any repute?"

"Well, some that averages pretty so-so."

"In my opinion the man that would offer personal violence to his own mother, ought to—"

"Cheese it, pard; you've banked your ball clean outside the string. What I was a drivin' at, was, that he never *throwed off* on his mother—don't you see? No indeedy. He give her a house to live in, and town lots, and plenty of money; and he looked after her and took care of her all the time; and when she was down with the smallpox I'm d——d if he didn't set up nights and nuss her himself! *Beg* your pardon for saying it, but it hopped out too quick for yours truly. You've treated me like a gentleman, pard, and I ain't the man to hurt your feelings intentional. I think you're white. I think you're a square man, pard. I like you, and I'll lick any man that don't. I'll lick him till he can't tell himself from a last year's corpse! Put it *there!*" [Another fraternal hand-shake—and exit.]

The obsequies were all that "the boys" could desire. Such a marvel of funeral pomp had never been seen in Virginia. The plumed hearse, the dirge-breathing brass bands, the closed marts of business, the flags drooping at half-mast, the long, plodding procession of uniformed secret societies, military battalions and fire companies, draped engines, carriages of officials, and citizens in vehicles and on foot, attracted multitudes of spectators to the sidewalks, roofs, and windows; and for years afterward, the degree of grandeur attained by any civic display in Virginia was determined by comparison with Buck Fanshaw's funeral.

Scotty Briggs, as a pall-bearer and a mourner, occupied a prominent place at the funeral, and when the sermon was finished and the last sentence of the prayer for the dead man's soul ascended, he responded, in a low voice, but with feeling:

"Amen. No Irish need apply."

As the bulk of the response was without apparent relevancy, it was probably nothing more than a humble tribute to the memory of the friend that was gone; for, as Scotty had once said, it was "his word."

Scotty Briggs, in after days, achieved the distinction of becoming the only convert to religion that was ever gathered from the Virginia roughs; and it transpired that the man who had it in him to espouse the quarrel of the weak out of inborn nobility of spirit was no mean timber whereof to construct a Christian. The making him one did not warp his generosity or diminish his courage; on the contrary it gave intelligent direction to the one and a broader field to the other. If his Sunday-school class progressed faster than the other classes, was it matter for wonder? I think not. He talked to his pioneer small-fry in a language they understood! It was my large privilege, a month before he died, to hear him tell the beautiful story of Joseph and his brethren to his class "without looking at the book." I leave it to the reader to fancy what it was like, as it fell, riddled with slang, from the lips of that grave, earnest teacher, and was listened to by his little learners with a consuming interest that showed that they were as unconscious as he was that any violence was being done to the sacred proprieties!

Not A Chinaman's Chance

W. EUGENE HOLLON

Throughout the West, wherever the Chinese went, prejudice and violence followed. Among the common charges against them were that they lived in filth and squalor, defied the laws of the land, kept up the manners and customs of China, were addicted to opium, and could never become citizens or Christians. Some of these points obviously were true: the Chinese rarely drank alcohol, but they did enjoy smoking opium, and most of their women in the early days were harlots. But authorities generally agree that the Chinese were able to exercise better control over opium than most white miners could over whiskey, and that they seemed no better or worse for the habit.

There were prostitutes of every nationality in California in the early days, but the Chinese professionals experienced no shortage of white customers. And, as for living in filth and squalor, some unbiased observers maintained that the Chinese generally were more careful about personal cleanliness than the Anglos were. Furthermore, nearly all agreed that, whatever faults the Orientals might have had, they were steady and dependable workers. "A disorderly Chinaman is rare and a lazy one does not exist," Mark Twain wrote in *Roughing It*.

The Chinese had no opportunity to become Americanized until the twentieth century, for whenever they reached sizable numbers in any Western community they became the victims of flagrant discrimination. In 1879, Robert Louis Stevenson crossed the American continent on the Union Pacific's third-class immigrant cars. He was appalled at the attitude of the Americans toward the Chinese passengers, who were segregated in a separate car. "Of all the stupid ill-feeling, the sentiment of fellow Caucasians toward our companions in the Chinese car was the most stupid and the worst. They seemed never to have looked at them, listened to them or thought of them, but hated them *a priori*." Little wonder the Chinese found it difficult, if not impossible, to assimilate the Anglos' ideas of citizenship or religion.

152

Armies of Protestant missionaries failed miserably in their efforts to Christianize the "heathens," for the Chinese maintained their own temples and shrines wherever they settled. "They were unable to distinguish between our mobs and our Christian workers and could not be expected to favor or tolerate our religion," one missionary complained. "They had no way of knowing that Christianity was a religion of love, not one of bowie knife, insult, and the worst oppression the world has yet seen." Henry Ward Beecher put it more sarcastically: "We have clubbed them, stoned them, burned their houses and murdered some of them; yet they refuse to be converted. I do not know any way, except to blow them up with nitroglycerin, if we are ever to get them to Heaven."

More basic to the development of anti-Chinese feeling which contributed to several senseless massacres was "the cruel and treacherous battlefield of money," as Robert Louis Stevenson put it. An official spokesman for the city of San Francisco summed it all up before a Special Committee of Congress in 1876:

> The burden of our accusation against them is that they come in conflict with our labor interest; that they can never assimilate with us; that they were a perpetual, unchanging, and unchangeable alien element . . . a degraded labor class, without desire for citizenship, without education, and without interest in the country it inhabits, is an element both demoralizing and dangerous to the community within which it exists.

The Chinese sometimes were charged with robbing the sluice boxes of the other miners, who administered twenty-five to fifty lashes upon the accused and sometimes cut off their queues, or pigtails. The latter was a supreme punishment, for the average Oriental treasured his pigtail and groomed it with considerable care. So many observers have testified to his patient and law-abiding qualities that many of the charges of theft and other crimes levied against him are highly suspect. In the letters and diaries of the forty-niners one reads over and over of Chinese workers being robbed, beaten, and even killed by whites, and of the sheriff and other elected officials taking little or no trouble to ascertain the particulars of such cases.

"Not having a Chinaman's chance" quickly took on a grim, literal meaning, and derogatory jokes about "chinks" became part of the folklore of the West. Even J. Frank Dobie, a humanist and fighter for civil rights in Texas during a generation when it took real courage to be one, regularly told the

153

story, to his classes in Southwestern literature, about a Texan who shot and killed a Chinese worker on the Southern Pacific Railroad in 1883 near Langtry, Texas, and who was brought to trial before Judge Roy Bean, the self-appointed "Law West of the Pecos." Judge Bean looked through two or three dilapidated law books before remarking that he'd be damned if he could find any law against killing a Chinaman. He then discharged the prisoner on condition that he pay for the "Chink's" burial—and that he buy drinks for the house.

If Chinese workers were allowed to remain in an area dominated by whites, they could expect to be the butt of frequent practical jokes. Sometimes the jokes were sadistic, like one at a mining camp near present Butte, Montana, in 1868, when the miners got drunk and celebrated the occasion by hanging one of the Chinese workers. "It was not a judicial execution," the *Anaconda Standard* explained many years later. "It was simply the cool, premeditated act of disheartened, yet patriotic and Fourth of July conscious miners who hanged the Chinaman to a cottonwood tree just for the devilment and in hopes that it might bring luck." Obviously, the victim did not appreciate either the humor or the patriotic fervor of the occasion.

How many innocent Chinese were strung up by exuberant mobs throughout the mining frontier is impossible to determine at this date. In the cemetery at Florence, Idaho, these words appear on the gravestone of a former Chinese resident: "Hung by mistake." The victim may or may not have been the inspiration for a popular ballad written sometime before 1900 and still sung by folksingers through the Northwest:

> Old John Martin Duffy was judge of the court
> In a small mining town in the West;
> Although the knew nothing about rules of the law,
> At judging he was one of the best.
>
> One night in the winter a murder occurred,
> And the blacksmith was accused of the crime;
> We caught him red-handed and give him three trials,
> But the verdict was "guilty" each time.
>
> Now he was the only good blacksmith we had
> And we wanted to spare him his life,

So Duffy stood up in the court like a lord
And with these words he settled the strife:

"I move we dismiss him, he's needed in town";
Then he spoke out these words which have gained him renown:
"We've got two Chinese laundrymen, everyone knows;
Why not save the poor blacksmith and hang one of those?"

Bob Rumsey's Place, James Bama

The Homesteader's Marriage and a Little Funeral

ELINORE PRUITT STEWART

December 2, 1912.

Dear Mrs. Coney,—

Every time I get a new letter from you I get a new inspiration, and I am always glad to hear from you.

I have often wished I might tell you all about my Clyde, but have not because of two things. One is I could not even begin without telling you what a good man he is, and I didn't want you to think I could do nothing but brag. The other reason is the haste I married in. I am ashamed of that. I am afraid you will think me a Becky Sharp of a person. But although I married in haste, I have no cause to repent. That is very fortunate because I have never had one bit of leisure to repent in. So I am lucky all around. The engagement was powerfully short because both agreed that the trend of events and ranch work seemed to require that we be married first and do our "sparking" afterward. You see, we had to chink in the wedding between times, that is, between planting the oats and other work that must be done early or not at all. In Wyoming ranchers can scarcely take time even to be married in the springtime. That having been settled, the license was sent for by mail, and as soon as it came Mr. Stewart saddled Chub and went down to the house of Mr. Pearson, the justice of the peace and a friend of long standing. I had never met any of the family and naturally rather dreaded to have them come, but Mr. Stewart was firm in wanting to be married at home, so he told Mr. Pearson he wanted him and his family to come up the following Wednesday and serve papers on the "wooman i' the hoose." They were astonished, of course, but being such good friends they promised him all the assistance they could render. They are quite the dearest, most interesting family! I have since learned to love them as my own.

Well, there was no time to make wedding clothes, so I had to "do up" what I did have. Is n't it queer how sometimes, do what you can, work will keep getting in the way until you can't get anything done? That is how it was with me those few days before the wedding; so much so that when Wednesday dawned everything was topsy-turvy and I had a very strong desire to run away. But I always did hate a "piker," so I stood pat. Well, I had most of the dinner cooked, but it kept me hustling to get the house into anything like decent order before the old dog barked, and I knew my moments of liberty were limited. It was blowing a perfect hurricane and snowing like midwinter. I had bought a beautiful pair of shoes to wear on that day, but my vanity had squeezed my feet a little, so while I was so busy at work I had kept on a worn old pair, intending to put on the new ones later; but when the Pearsons drove up all I thought about was getting them into the house where there was fire, so I forgot all about the old shoes and the apron I wore.

I had only been here six weeks then, and was a stranger. That is why I had no one to help me and was so confused and hurried. As soon as the newcomers were warm, Mr. Stewart told me I had better come over by him and stand up. It was a large room I had to cross, and how I did it before all those strange eyes I never knew. All I can remember very distinctly is hearing Mr. Stewart saying, "I will," and myself chiming in that I would, too. Happening to glance down, I saw that I had forgotten to take off my apron or my old shoes, but just then Mr. Pearson pronounced us man and wife, and as I had dinner to serve right away I had no time to worry over my odd toilet. Anyway the shoes were comfortable and the apron white, so I suppose it could have been worse; and I don't think it has ever made any difference with the Pearsons, for I number them all among my most esteemed friends.

It is customary here for newlyweds to give a dance and supper at the hall, but as I was a stranger I preferred not to, and so it was a long time before I became acquainted with all my neighbors. I had not thought I should ever marry again. Jerrine was always such a dear little pal, and I wanted to just knock about foot-loose and free to see life as a gypsy sees it. I had planned to see the Cliff-Dwellers' home; to live right there until I caught the spirit of the surroundings enough to live over their lives in imagination anyway. I had planned to see the old missions and to go to Alaska; to hunt in Canada. I even dreamed of Honolulu. Life stretched out before me one long, happy jaunt. I aimed to see all the world I could, but to travel unknown bypaths to do it. But first I wanted to try homesteading.

158

But for my having the grippe, I should never have come to Wyoming. Mrs. Seroise, who was a nurse at the institution for nurses in Denver while I was housekeeper there, had worked one summer at Saratoga, Wyoming. It was she who told me of the pine forests. I had never seen a pine until I came to Colorado; so the idea of a home among the pines fascinated me. At that time I was hoping to pass the Civil-Service examination, with no very definite idea as to what I would do, but just to be improving my time and opportunity. I never went to a public school a day in my life. In my childhood days there was no such thing in the Indian Territory part of Oklahoma where we lived, so I have had to try hard to keep learning. Before the time came for the examination I was so discouraged because of the grippe that nothing but the mountains, the pines, and the clean, fresh air seemed worth while; so it all came about just as I have written you.

So you see I was very deceitful. Do you remember, I wrote you of a little baby boy dying? That was my own little Jamie, our first little son. For a long time my heart was crushed. He was such a sweet, beautiful boy. I wanted him so much. He died of erysipelas. I held him in my arms till the last agony was over. Then I dressed the beautiful little body for the grave. Clyde is a carpenter; so I wanted him to make the little coffin. He did it every bit, and I lined and padded it, trimmed and covered it. Not that we couldn't afford to buy one or that our neighbors were not all that was kind and willing; but because it was a sad pleasure to do everything for our little first-born ourselves.

As there had been no physician to help, so there was no minister to comfort, and I could not bear to let our baby leave the world without leaving any message to a community that sadly needed it. His little message to us had been love, so I selected a chapter from John and we had a funeral service, at which all our neighbors for thirty miles around were present. So you see, our union is sealed by love and welded by a great sorrow.

Little Jamie was the first little Stewart. God has given me two more precious little sons. The old sorrow is not so keen now. I can bear to tell you about it, but I never could before. When you think of me, you must think of me as one who is truly happy. It is true, I want a great many things I haven't got, but I don't want them enough to be discontented and not enjoy the many blessings that are mine. I have my home among the blue mountains, my healthy, well-formed children, my clean, honest husband, my kind, gentle milk cows, my garden which I make myself. I have loads and loads of flowers which I tend myself. There are lots of chickens, turkeys, and pigs which are my own special care. I have some slow old gentle horses and an old wagon. I can load up the kiddies and go where I please any time. I have the best, kindest neighbors and I have my dear absent friends. Do you wonder I am so happy? When I think of it all, I wonder how I can crowd all my joy into one short life. I don't want you to think for one moment that you are bothering me when I write you. It is a real pleasure to do so. You're always so good to let me tell you everything. I am only afraid of trying your patience too far. Even in this long letter I can't tell you all I want to; so I shall write you again soon. Jerrine will write too. Just now she has very sore fingers. She has been picking gooseberries, and they have been pretty severe on her brown little paws.

With much love to you, I am
"Honest and truly" yours,
Elinore Rupert Stewart.

Oregon Trail

LOREN EISELEY

It is spring somewhere beyond
                    Chimney Rock
                    on the old
                    Oregon trail now.
I remember the time
                    when the ruts of the wagons
                          could still be seen across
                                    a half mile
                  of unbroken short-grass prairie
as though
              in that high air
              they had just passed,
the rolling Conestoga wagons
                  heavy-freighted
                    for the Sierras,
                    as though time was
only yesterday,
                as though, if one hurried,
a fast horse
              with good wind
              would bring you
                  to the buckskinned outriders
                  and the lined brown women
                  with sunbonnets,

Pioneers and Settlers

the grandmothers,
                    the fathers,
                    children who became
                    the forest cutters,
                    wheat raisers,
                                gold seekers,
                                sharpshooters,
                    range killers,
                      users of
                      the first Colts in
                      the cattle wars
                      or at the gamblers' tables—
a time a fast horse
            might still catch up with
almost anything.

I whirl my animal
three times about
and bend over the tracks
trampling uncertainly.
            It is time to go home.
But the other time is there
                    tempting
            just beyond the horizon.
I back off reluctantly
                    and out of some shamed courtesy
                    slip my spectacles
                    into my pocket
                      and raise my hand
                      saying a wordless
                                goodbye.

Cowpokes and Gunfighters

They went thattaway—GABBY HAYES

The mythic figure of the West, celebrated in pulp fiction and glamorized by countless Hollywood movies, actually accounted for a small percentage of the frontier population. These men on horseback, equipped with Samuel Colt's .44 calibre appliance which was claimed to make all men equal, generated legends so potent that every child in America grows up in their shadow.

After the extermination of the buffalo, the end of the Civil War, and removal of the Indian, western plains opened up and the cattle industry boomed. Herds moved from Texas up the Chisholm Trail to Kansas railheads and on to the new ranges of Wyoming and Montana. The historical cowboy was a hired hand on horseback who worked in the saddle, slept on the ground, and ate plentifully of dust and beans. The mythic cowboy, riding limitless plains with solemn, virtuous, masculine authority, moved into our permanent imagination in the 1880s, following Buffalo Bill's Wild West Show, embodying the universal impulse to get clear of the restraints of civilization. With horse and gun and the society of cattle, he came to represent a code of such powerful simplicity and wide appeal that John Wayne, Gary Cooper, and Clint Eastwood have ridden down his trail to fortunes unimaginable to nineteenth-century cowhands. So compelling is his romantic image that westerners who have been no closer to beef than their dinner plates pay him the homage of imitation.

Today, with brokers and computers managing the range, the real cowboy has become another displaced person in his own homeland,

163

reduced to the annual rodeo and the commercial image of Marlboro Man. Tall in the saddle and ready for trouble, he rests on his mount, chiseled, grizzled, squinting into the hard, clear light, wondering where in tarnation the West went.

The gunfighter stands out as pure melodrama in the legendary landscape. Unsettled conditions on the frontier, particularly the rowdyism of the Kansas cow towns, provided fertile ground for violence, and shootists soon began to make local headlines and obituary notices. Parties on both sides of the law subscribed to that article in the Code of the West which held, "A man's gotta do what a man's gotta do," even when it included ventilating his neighbor. If one is to half believe the pulps, life in a frontier town was one sustained hold-up, walk-down, shoot-out, relieved at intervals by campfire ballads, saloon brawls, romantic interludes with the schoolmarm, and meetings of the local vigilance committee and uplift society. Yet Tombstone, the O.K. Corral, and Boot Hill were lurid exceptions. Against the dusty handful of robbers, bushwhackers, and low-down, sidewinding varmints whose notoriety was translated into enduring fame, most westerners maintained a decent respect for the law. Despite the great folklore factory's insistence in transforming every other scoundrel into a sagebrush Robin Hood and every tenth homicidal psychopath into a misunderstood rebel, the whole tribe from the James Boys to Billy the Kid (some boys and kids) properly deserves oblivion. Even the lawmen were not always respectable characters. Wild Bill Hickock and Wyatt Earp owe more to the dime novels for their six-shooter fame than to the towns they protected. Yet the fable cast them in roles of lonely, embattled outsiders, who lived in continual danger, and ended up dying or moving on. Ironically, the order that the gun imposed left no room for the gunman; the law bloodily upheld, the lawman headed out for the next (unpacified) town where disputes could be settled by gunfire.

Without stretching the point too far, this set of attitudes in the Old West made women a distinct minority. Initially scarce in the raw frontier settlements and boom towns, women folk were prized creatures. Still the role assigned to them, whether in a saloon or on a homestead, was paradoxical. They represented civilization, comfort, and morality and at the same time stood for softness, weakness, and the loss of select masculine freedoms. As long as women kept home, the culture was preserved and men could go off "with the boys" to defy it. When women finally established their presence, towns tended to settle down, wildness and lawlessness declined, and family life replaced the wooly romance of cow culture. The West, if not completely domesticated, was tamed somewhat.

Nonetheless, out of all this sentimental haze ride the fictional knights on horseback, from Owen Wister's Virginian to Jack Schaefer's Shane, dutifully to enact ritual horse opera.

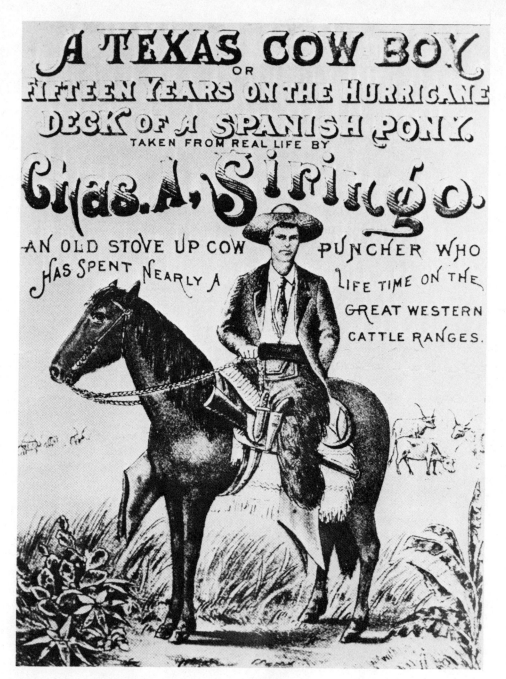

Charles Siringo's *A Texas Cow Boy* (Book cover)

Up The Trail

BAYLIS JOHN FLETCHER

On the morning of April 11,* a supreme moment for us, we started up the trail to Cheyenne, Wyoming. To gather the cattle in the pasture into one great herd took up the forenoon. In the afternoon we made only about five miles, bedding our cattle that night just south of Victoria, near the Guadalupe River. On the following morning we forded the river, which was low.

When we were passing through the streets of Victoria, a lady, fearful that the cattle would break down her fence and ruin her roses, ran out to the pickets and, waving her bonnet frantically at the cattle, stampeded those in front. With a dull roar, they charged back upon the rear of the herd, and but for the discreet management of boss Arnett, heavy damage to city property would have resulted.

"Give way at all street crossings and let the cattle have room," he shouted as he galloped about, giving orders to save the City of Roses from a disaster.

We complied quickly and soon had half a dozen residence blocks surrounded by excited and infuriated cattle. Soon they became so confused that the stampede was ended. We gave their fears time to subside, then drove them quietly out of the city without doing any serious damage.

On the second night, when we were camped near the source of Spring Creek, a real midnight stampede occurred. All hands were called to the saddle, and it was near dawn before we could return to our pallets for rest. We proceeded to the north and, in a few days, reached the mouth of Peach Creek, north of Cuero, where we paid for the privilege of watering in the big Kokernot pasture.

Here water was procured in the Guadalupe River, and we stopped on its banks to rest our cattle and eat dinner. While grazing the cattle along the

---

*The year was 1879.

bank of the river, we discovered a big alligator idly floating on the water's surface. All hands were attracted by the strange sight and began shouting at the big saurian, who protected himself by sinking out of sight in the turbid waters.

After dinner Joe Felder took off his boots and washed his feet in the river. Then he sat on the root of a big tree facing the stream and fell asleep. Manuel García, our cook, with that levity characteristic of the Mexican, conceived a practical joke. Throwing a log so that it fell into the river just in front of the sleeping Joe, he shouted, "Alligator!" In a quick effort to rise, Joe slipped into the river, going entirely under and rising by the side of the floating log, which he mistook for the alligator. He screamed for help, and stake ropes were thrown him, which he seized frantically, to be drawn out, as he thought, from the jaws of death. His disgust was profound when he discovered that he was escaping only from a rotten log.

On the following night we bedded our cattle in a short, wide lane between high rail fences a few miles east of Gonzales. This was a thickly settled region, timbered with a variety of oaks, and the surface was covered with gravel. My shift at guard duty was the last in the night, and at about two A.M., Sam Allen, Carteman García, and I were called to go on herd. Allen and I were stationed at the east end of the lane, while the Mexican guarded the other end. The night was frosty, and as the cattle seemed to be sleeping soundly, Sam and I dismounted and built a fire of dry branches by which to warm. At first we would warm by turns and ride time about. But everything was so still that we became careless and both dismounted at the fire, where we began to spin yarns. As the bright fire lit up the scene, it was beautiful to behold. Two thousand cattle rested quietly, lying down and chewing their cuds.

Suddenly there was a loud and ominous roar, while a cloud of dust obscured our vision.

"Stampede!" shouted Sam as he let loose his bridle reins and sprang behind an oak, which he hugged with both hands. I did not have time to turn Happy Jack loose but threw my arms around Allen on the side of the tree opposite the herd. We were none too quick, for now the horns of the stampeding bovines were raking the bark from the opposite side of the oak as they rushed madly past us. It was a moment of supreme terror, but only a moment. In less time than it takes to relate it, the cattle had passed us and, mounting Happy Jack, I was in full pursuit.

I soon overtook the cattle, pressed on past them, and turned their leaders back. They now formed a circle, where they milled in one great wheel, revolving with almost lightning velocity. By holding them in this mill, I soon had them confused, and they began to bellow to one another. I had learned that these were welcome sounds in a stampede. As soon as the bellowing becomes general, the run begins to subside. Of course, such a revolving wheel cannot be stopped suddenly. The momentum they have acquired makes it necessary to slow down the cattle gradually, or else the ones that stopped first would be trampled to death.

I now heard a voice shouting, "Stay with them, Fletcher." In a moment I was joined by Mr. Snyder, riding one of the wagon horses bareback and with a blind bridle. "Where is Sam?" he asked. But I did not know.

We soon had the cattle quiet, and as it now was about dawn, we drove them back to the bed ground. I learned from Mr. Snyder that something had frightened the cattle in about the middle of the lane where we had bedded them and that I was holding only a part of the herd, the remainder having run out of the other end of the lane past García. Thinking that the whole herd had gone that way, the cowboys had all gone to the aid of García, but when Allen and I were missed, Mr. Snyder had gone in search of us. When Allen's horse was found loose with the saddle on, it was supposed that the horse had fallen with him as he rode out ahead of the cattle and that he had narrowly escaped being trampled to death.

We did not confess until long afterward that we had been caught off our horses by the stampede and that Allen had let his horse go. Such admissions were not expected on the trail. After getting the fragments of our herd together, we strung them out in a thin line, and as they passed a certain point, the cattle were counted. It was found that we were about one hundred head short. That many evidently had escaped in the stampede.

While we were discussing the feasibility of recovering the lost cattle, four hard-looking citizens rode up and said, "Had a stampede last night, did you?" We answered in the affirmative. Then the strangers offered their services to help put the cattle back in the herd. Their offer was to bring in all they could for one dollar per head. Mr. Snyder then offered them fifty cents per head, to which they readily agreed. It seemed plain to us that these accommodating gentry had stampeded our herd for this revenue.

They were joined by recruits, and during the day they delivered sixty cattle bearing our road brand. We still were forty short, but time was

169

precious. Mr. Snyder said that the missing ones would go back to the range near Victoria and be gathered there for his account and that we must proceed. Later our own scouts brought in about twenty additional renegades, so that we were only about twenty short when we started forward on the following day.

Moving a large herd through a timbered country was attended with many difficulties. Sometimes a stubborn brute would take to a thicket and fight with wild fury any puncher who tried to dislodge him. In a rocky thicket near Plum Creek one old cow took refuge, and when Poinsett Barton entered on foot to drive her out, she made a desperate lunge to gore him. Barton hurled a stone, striking her in the forehead. Her skull was crushed, and she fell dead. Barton was brought before the boss for killing a cow, but he pleaded self-defense and was acquitted, with a warning not to place himself again in such a position as to make the death of a cow necessary to protect his life.

Suitable bed grounds were difficult to find on this part of the trail. We made use of a line of picket corrals which enterprising residents had erected, and regular herders were stationed around the big pen to watch that the cattle did not escape. For awhile all was quiet, but late in the night the herd stampeded and broke down the fence, giving us another night in the saddle for all hands.

In this stampede, which was on a Saturday night, I lost my hat. On the following morning we came to a country store just south of Lockhart. I called at the home of the merchant and asked him if he kept hats. He said he did. Then I told him of my predicament and asked him to sell me one. He replied that he was sorry for me but that under no circumstances would he sell a hat on the Sabbath. I implored him, speaking of "the ox in the ditch," but he was inexorable in his determination. So I had to ride all day bareheaded. On the next day we arrived at Lockhart, where I rode into town and bought a hat.

The weather in the spring of 1879 was extremely dry. The supply of water along the trail was so scant that often we had to fill our barrel for drinking water from tanks, as the dirty ponds made by the damming of ravines were called. Since this water was contaminated, we were attacked by sickness in the camp. I had fever several days but kept it secret from fear of being sent home.

Anderson Pickett, a Negro Mr. Snyder took along as his servant, came

170

to me one night while I was on herd and said, "Look heah, boy, I know youse sick, ain't yer?"

"Yes," I said. "I'm sick tonight."

"Den you des' let me herd in yo' place. You des' lay down here under dis here mesquite tree, an' I wake you up 'fo' day." I was too sick to refuse the proffered aid. Dismounting, I gave the reins of old Happy Jack to Anderson, who faithfully did my guard duty until dawn, waking me as promised in time to prevent detection. This relief was of great benefit to me.

We forded the Colorado River at old Webberville, a few miles below Austin. As we drove our cattle across the river, we heard the booming of a cannon in the direction of the capital city. It was April 21, and the people were celebrating the anniversary of the battle of San Jacinto, which had changed the course of Texas history just forty-three years earlier.

We camped near Manor, where I went to a physician and had a prescription filled. My fever, however, continued to rise every day, and my legs were so swollen that I had to split the uppers of my boots to get them on. My condition was such that I could no longer conceal it. And now it began to rain. All night long the rain poured in torrents. We had reached Brushy Creek north of Manor and near Hutto Station. The pain from inflammatory rheumatism in my ankles was excruciating. We forded Brushy at Rice's Crossing, and Mr. Snyder, learning of my condition, told the faithful Anderson to take me to some farmhouse where I could be cared for and kept dry.

The Negro did his best to comply, but every application for shelter was refused, until we became discouraged. I thought I should have to give up and die of exposure in the cold, blinding April rain. But Anderson persevered. "Yonder is a little rent house," said he. "Mebbe-so we kin git you in dar." Sure enough, the poor renter had not the heart to drive me away. My host and hostess, who had recently married, received me kindly.

Anderson explained that I was one of Tom Snyder's cowboys and that I was sick. The big young fellow said, "Bring him in. We have only one room and are not fixed to entertain, but I have been on the trail myself, and I can't turn off a sick puncher in this rain." I was helped into the cabin as Anderson led my horse away.

Seeing how I was suffering, the tender-hearted young woman burst into tears. "Take our bed, and we will sit up for you," she said.

171

"No," said I, "just spread my blanket and slicker on the floor. That's all the bed I need."

That night, when all was still and I was supposed to be asleep, I overheard my case discussed by my hosts. "Oh, goodness, John! The boy can't live. Oh, it's awful to be sick on the trail. We could not turn him off to die in this rain. Do you think he will live?"

"You can't tell anything about it, Lucy," came the deep drawl of the husband. "I have been mighty sick on the trail, but I never died. We must do our duty and take care of him until he dies or gets better. That's all we can do."

The cabin had a fireplace, and my host kept a fire all night near my feet. The next morning I felt much improved, but my feet were so swollen that I could not put on my boots. A hot foot bath reduced the swelling, and in the afternoon I was able to sit up. Reaction was now so favorable that on the second morning, at my request, my host carried me on one of his horses to our camp. He refused to accept any pay for my entertainment.

The rainstorm had passed away, and the sun was shining when I rejoined our outfit. Mr. Snyder said I must go home on a sick discharge, as I would not be able to endure the hardships of the trail. I begged him not to dismiss me. He finally agreed to try me awhile longer but told Mr. Arnett to discharge me when we reached Fort Worth if I were not well. My health, however, gave me no more trouble.

Sam Allen, Andy Marcus, and John Ledbetter quit the outfit at Hutto, where new men were hired to take their places. Mr. Snyder also went back to his home at Liberty Hill, turning over the entire responsibility of the trip to our foreman, George Arnett. His faithful Negro, Anderson Pickett, also left us, finding work with a drove of saddle horses bound for Wyoming.

We forded the San Gabriel River near Jonah, a few miles east of Georgetown. Crossing Possum Creek, we followed the Belton road to a bridge on the Lampasas River. Fearing to risk the bridge, we made a detour of several miles and crossed the stream at Saul's Mill. Just as the leaders of our herd came opposite the mill, they took fright at the noise of the machinery and rushed back on the rear cattle. For half an hour the whole herd milled on the bank before we could force them to cross the stream.

Our next camp was on Salado Creek near the village of Salado. There, on the night of May 4, we were caught in a hailstorm that made our cattle drift badly. The severe hail lasted only a few moments, but our heads and shoulders were bruised by the falling ice, and it was many hours before we could quiet the excited cattle. We found the next day that a few miles north of us the hail was so severe that birds, rabbits, and domestic fowls were beaten to death and many crops destroyed. During the hail our saddle horses had stampeded, and we found on taking stock the next morning that two horses were missing. I was detailed to hunt for them and to follow the herd, which crossed the Leon River at Belton. I found only one of the runaways, and by hard riding I overtook the herd that night.

We now entered a more broken country among the hills of McLennan County. We passed to the west of Waco, entering Bosque County at Valley Mills. While camped on Steele's Creek in Bosque County, we had one of the biggest stampedes of the entire trip. That night a coyote was seen to enter the bed ground of the herd, frightening the cattle and causing them to run. The country was open, and the only loss we suffered was that of a much-needed night's rest. We halted here a day or two to look for a saddle horse that had escaped from Poinsett Barton with a long stake rope attached to it. It was the best horse allotted to him and never was recovered. Perhaps it became entangled by the stake rope in the thickets which covered the hills in that section and perished from starvation.

We were now having a great deal of trouble finding pasturage for our cattle. As long as we kept to the plain beaten trail, we were not molested. But the moment we turned aside to graze our cattle, the settlers came to us, claimed the land upon which our herd was grazing, and ordered us to get off the grass. Under the law, we had to comply quickly or sustain an action for damages. We often doubted the ownership claimed to the grazing lands, but as we had no time to investigate titles, the only safe thing we could do was to move on. We crossed the Brazos River at the old mountain village of Kimball and passed through Johnson County just west of Cleburne. We now had a delightful stretch of prairie, sparsely settled, until we neared Fort Worth. Grass was abundant, and we were rarely molested while seeking forage for our herd.

Fort Worth, with a population of about ten thousand, was then the terminus of the Texas and Pacific Railway and was the last trading point where we could buy supplies on the trail until we should reach Dodge City, Kansas. We were given a day of rest, and, dividing the hands into two shifts,

Mr. Arnett said he would allow each of us half a day in town. He planned to buy provisions to last two months. By the Chisholm Trail it was five hundred miles from Fort Worth to Dodge.

Solicitors from the big grocery stores of Fort Worth met us on horseback several miles from the city, bringing such gifts as bottles of whisky and boxes of fine cigars. Steve Pointer, known as Shug in our outfit, was the oldest cowpuncher we had, and looking older than Mr. Arnett, he often was mistaken for the boss. Frequently the mistake worked to Shug's advantage, though there would come a time when he regretted that he did not look more like a cowpuncher.

The drummers from Fort Worth all wanted to see the boss, who was purchasing agent for the outfit, and by previous arrangement Shug played his part well, accepting a box of fine cigars, some whisky, and other blandishments. Mr. Arnett quietly trailed the cattle while Shug stopped to talk with the drummers. After he thought Shug had accepted all that was due him, Will Bower rode swiftly to the rear and shouted to the erstwhile boss, "Shug, the boss says come on, you lazy cuss, and get to work, or he'll turn you off at Fort Worth." It then dawned upon the solicitors that they had been buncoed and that they would need a new supply of gifts to corral the real boss when he was identified. Shug became angry at Will for interrupting his game and made some uncomplimentary remarks.

Leaving Fort Worth, we followed the trail north, passing in sight of Decatur to our left and Saint Jo to our right, crossing parts of Wise, Denton, Cook, and Montague counties. Since Montague was a border county, we were told that we could wear side arms without fear of arrest, so every cowpuncher who had a six-shooter buckled it on just to enjoy the privilege of carrying a weapon.

As we passed a farmhouse near Saint Jo, a fine Shorthorn bull broke out of a pasture and joined our herd. We cut him repeatedly, but he followed on about a mile to a point where we bedded our cattle for the night. The next morning the indignant owner came to us and demanded we take his bull back to the pasture, threatening to prosecute us if we did not. We advised him to take the animal back with him, but he haughtily refused to do so and threatened to have us arrested for carrying pistols in Montague County. We promised that we would carry the animal no farther but did not agree to take him back. He rode away in a great rage, continuing his threats. After he had gone we roped the bull, threw him down, hogged his

174

feet together with strong cords, and left him lying on the ground as we moved our herd down the valley of Farmer's Creek to Spanish Fort, where we were to cross the Red River and enter the Indian Territory.

On or about the first day of June we came in sight of the Red River Valley, beyond which we could see the Indian Territory. The country ahead was then a wilderness, without a human habitation in view of the Chisholm Trail to the line of Kansas, nearly three hundred miles away by the meanderings of our route.

As we were gazing upon this distant prospect, several well-mounted horsemen rode up, and their leader informed Mr. Arnett that he was a cattle inspector, whose duty it was to inspect carefully every herd crossing the northern boundary of Texas, cutting out any estrays that might be in the herd not bearing the road brand of the outfit. We were instructed to string the cattle out in a line, so that they might be passed one or two at a time between the inspector and one of his assistants, to be examined carefully as to their ownership.

Four or five little dogies, as poor little orphan yearlings were called, had escaped our vigilance in cutting out strays, and they were taken out of the herd by the inspector and turned over to his assistants. After the inspection was over, Mr. Arnett paid the inspector his per capita fee for examining the herd, which in our case amounted to about seventy-five dollars.

Having undergone this inspection, our herd was given a clean bill of health, and we were permitted to take the cattle across the Red River, which at this point was low and easily forded. The prospect of entering an uninhabited wilderness was a source of great joy to the cowboys. Civilization and cattle trailing were not congenial, and we had been greatly annoyed in the settled districts of Texas. Depending entirely on free grass for forage for our cattle and horses, we had constantly come in collision with the farmers, who wanted the grass for their domestic animals.

We were not alone on the trail. The big drive northward was at its height, and that spring there were probably 500,000 cattle and horses moving up the one universal trail from South Texas. Often we had been driven by angry men, with ferocious dogs, from tract to tract of grazing land, but our movements were so deliberate that the cattle got enough to live upon. The Indian Territory was the cowpuncher's paradise. Now we would have no more lanes, no more obstructing fences, but one grand expanse of free grass. It was a delightful situation to contemplate.

The Johnson County War

HELENA HUNTINGTON SMITH

On a blizzardy April morning in 1892, fifty armed men surrounded a cabin on Powder River in which two accused cattle rustlers had been spending the night. The first rustler was shot as he came down the path for the morning bucket of water; he was dragged over the doorstep by his companion, to die inside. The second man held out until afternoon, when the besiegers fired the house. Driven out by the flames, he went down with twenty-eight bullets in him. He was left on the bloodstained snow with a card pinned to his shirt, reading: "Cattle thieves, beware!"

So far the affair follows the standard pattern of frontier heroics, a pattern popularized by Owen Wister and justified to some extent by the facts of history if you don't look too closely: strong men on a far frontier, in the absence of law, make their own law for the protection of society, which generally approves.

Thus runs the cliché, but in Wyoming this time it went awry. In the first place the attackers were not crude frontiersmen taking the law into their own hands. They were men of means and education, predominantly eastern, who really should have known better; civilized men, at home in drawing rooms and familiar with Paris. Two were Harvard classmates of the year '78, the one a Boston blue blood, the other a member of a Wall Street banking family. Hubert E. Teschemacher and Fred DeBillier had come west after graduation to hunt elk, as so many gilded youths from both sides of the Atlantic were doing; had fallen in love with the country; and had remained as partners in a half-million-dollar ranching enterprise.

Our fifty vigilantes were truly a strange company to ride through the land slaughtering people. The instigators dominated the cattle business and the affairs of the former territory, which had recently been elevated to statehood, and more than half of them had served in the legislature. Their leader, Major Frank Wolcott, was a fierce little pouter pigeon of a man, a Kentuckian lately of the Union Army, whose brother was United States senator from Colorado. Accompanying the party as surgeon was a socially prominent Philadelphian, Dr. Charles Bingham Penrose, who had come to Wyoming for his health. It was not improved by his experiences.

These gentlemen had no thought of the danger to themselves as they set out, without benefit of the law, to liquidate their enemies. Convinced of their own righteousness, they expected nine-tenths of the people of Wyoming to be on their side, and they even looked for a popular uprising to assist them. Instead, thirty-six hours after their sanguinary victory on Powder River, they were surrounded in their turn by an enraged horde of citizens, and just missed being lynched themselves. They were saved only by the intervention of the President of the United States, who ordered federal troops to their aid. But it wasn't quite the usual scene of the cavalry riding to the rescue at the end of the movie, for while the cattlemen were snatched from imminent death, they were also arrested for the murder of the two men and marched off in custody of the troops—the latter all making clear that personally they regretted the rescue.

So ended the Johnson County War—tragic, bizarre, unbelievable. It was a sequel to the great beef bonanza, which began around 1880. The cattle boom combined the most familiar features of the South Sea Bubble and the 1929 bull market—such as forty per cent dividends that would never cease—with some special features of its own—such as a rash of adventuring English Lords and Honorables, free grass, and the blessings of "natural increase" provided by the prolific Texas cow. A man could grow rich without his lifting a finger.

Instead of the old-style cow outfit with its headquarters in a dugout and a boss who ate beef, bacon, and beans, there were cattle companies with offices in Wall Street, London, or Edinburgh; champagne parties; thoroughbred racing on the plains; and younger sons who were shipped out west to mismanage great ranches at fancy salaries. In a raw new city sprawled along the Union Pacific tracks, the Cheyenne Club boasted the best steward of any club in the United States, and its members were drawn from a roster of aristocracy on both sides of the Atlantic. Burke's Peerage and the Social Register mingled, though not intimately, with common cowhands from Texas, but only the latter knew anything about cattle.

To be sure, some of what they knew was a trifle shady: they knew how to handle a long rope and a running iron; how to brand a maverick right out from under the noses of the lords. But the mavericks, unbranded animals of uncertain ownership, were rather casually regarded anyhow; "finders keepers" was the unwritten rule which had governed their disposition in the early days, and they had been a source of controversy and bloodshed throughout the history of the West. While they were now claimed by the big cattle companies, the Texas cowboys were not impressed.

The boom crashed into ruin in the awful winter of 1886–87. Snow fell and drifted and thawed and froze and fell again, clothing the ground with an iron sheath of white on which a stagecoach could travel and through which no bovine hoof could paw for grass; and since the plains were heavily overstocked and the previous summer had been hot and dry, there was no grass anyway. Moaning cattle wandered into the outskirts of towns, trying to eat frozen garbage and the tar paper off the eaves of the shacks; and when the hot sun of early summer uncovered the fetid carcasses piled in the creek bottoms, the bark of trees and brush was gnawed as high as a cow could reach. Herd losses averaged fifty per cent, with ninety per cent for unacclimated southern herds, and some moral revulsion set in, even the Cheyenne *Daily Sun* remarking that a man who turned animals out on a barren plain without food or shelter would suffer loss of respect of the community in which he lived.

Meanwhile there were gloomy faces at the Cheyenne Club. "Cheer up, boys," quipped the bartender across the street, setting out a row of glasses, "the books won't freeze."

In the heyday of the beef bonanza, herds had been bought and sold by "book count," based on a back-of-an-envelope calculation of "natural increase," with no pother about a tally on the range. As the day of reckoning dawned, it turned out that many big companies had fewer than half the number of cattle claimed on their books. Now the terrible winter cut this half down to small fractions: faraway directors, grown glacial as the weather, hinted that blizzards were the fault of their underlings in Cheyenne; while the few surviving cows, instead of giving birth to sextuplets as was their clear duty, produced a correspondingly diminished calf crop to fatten on the gorgeous grass that sprang up after the snows.

In their bitterness, the cattlemen believed that the damned thieves were to blame. Obsessed with this idea, they now proceeded to bring upon themselves an epidemic of stealing without parallel in the West. At least that was what they called it, though to a cool-headed observer from Nebraska it looked more like "the bitter conflict which has raged incessantly between large and small owners."

In fact it was even more. For Wyoming in the nineties shared the outlook of that decade everywhere else; a decade of economic and moral monopoly, when righteousness belonged exclusively to the upper class, along with the means of production; a decade when the best people simply could not be wrong. The best people in this case were the Wyoming Stock Growers Association and their several rich and prominent eastern friends, and the climate of opinion they breathed was startlingly revealed in the hanging of Jim Averill and Cattle Kate. When the cattlemen shed crocodile tears because thieves went unwhipped, they forgot that thieves were not the worst to go free. At least six persons were shot or hanged in the years before the final flare-up, but not one person was ever brought to trial for the crimes—not even in the case of Jim Averill and the woman whose real name was Ella, who were hanged on the Sweetwater in 1889.

Averill and Ella ran a log-cabin saloon and road ranch up a desolate little valley off the Sweetwater, and they were nuisances. The man was articulate and a Populist of sorts, and had attacked the big cattlemen in a letter to the local press; the woman was a cowboys' prostitute who took her pay in stolen cattle. From this, aristocratic Dr. Penrose could argue later that "she had to die for the good of the country."

Die she did, with her paramour, at the end of a rope thrown over a tree limb and swung out over a gulch. There were three eyewitnesses to the abduction and one to the actual hanging, and a coroner's jury named four prominent cattlemen among the perpetrators. But before the case reached the grand jury three of the witnesses had vanished and the fourth had conveniently died. Afterward two of the men whose hands were filthy from this affair continued to rub elbows with the fastidious Teschemacher on the executive committee of the Stock Growers Association, and nauseating jokes about the last moments of Kate were applauded at the Cheyenne Club. Even Owen Wister joined in the applause, noting in his diary for October 12, 1889: "Sat yesterday in smoking car with one of the gentlemen indicted [*sic*] for lynching the man and the woman. He seemed a good solid citizen and I hope he'll get off."

The association tightened its blacklist. In a cattle economy where cows were the only means of getting ahead, the cowboys had long been forbidden to own a brand or a head of stock on their own, lest they be tempted to brand a maverick. Now more and more of them were "blackballed" on suspicion from all lawful employment within the territory. Likewise the association made the rules of the range, ran the roundups to suit itself, and kept out the increasing number of people it didn't like; hence many small stockmen, suspect of misbehavior by their very smallness, were also relegated to a shady no man's land outside the law.

If you call a man a thief, and deprive him of all chance to earn a living honestly, he will soon become a thief.

By 1890 a thin colony of blackballed cowboys had settled on the rivers and creeks of Johnson County and were waging war with rope and running iron on the big outfits. Then early in 1892 a group calling themselves the Northern Wyoming Farmers' and Stockgrowers' Association announced in the press their intention of holding an independent roundup, in defiance of the state law and the Wyoming Stock Growers Association. This was provocative, insolent, outrageous if you like; it was hardly the furtive behavior of ordinary thieves.

Also announced in the press were the names of two foremen for what was now being called the "shotgun roundup." One was a Texan, known as a skilled cowhand, who was lightning with a gun. His name was Nathan D. Champion.

Meanwhile the storied walls of the Cheyenne Club beheld the amazing spectacle of nineteenth century gentlemen plotting wholesale murder. The declared object of their expedition was the "extermination"—not "arrest," but "extermination"—of various undesirable persons in the northern part of the state. The death list stood at seventy. In addition to a hard core of nineteen most-wanted rustlers, it almost certainly included a large number who were merely thought to be too close to the rustler faction, among them the sheriff of Johnson County and the three county commissioners.

This incredible project was fully known in advance to Acting Governor Amos W. Barber, to United States Senators Joseph M. Carey and Francis E. Warren, and to officials of the Union Pacific Railroad, whose consent to run a special train was obtained; and none of whom found anything questionable in the undertaking. Twenty-five hired gunfighters from Texas raised the manpower complement to fifty, since the local cowboys were thoroughly disaffected and would not have pulled a trigger for their employers. A smart Chicago newsman, Sam T. Clover, had heard about the impending necktie party and was in Cheyenne determined to get the story for the *Herald*. He and a local reporter were taken along just as though the expedition were legal; it apparently had not occurred to the planners that they were inviting witnesses to murder.

They got started the afternoon of April 5, on board a train loaded with men, arms, equipment, horses, and three supply wagons. An overnight run landed them in Casper, two hundred miles to the northwest, where they descended, saddled their horses, and were off before the townspeople were up—except for enough of the latter to start talk. Their objective was Buffalo, the county seat of Johnson County, but when they arrived at a friendly ranch on the second night, they received new intelligence which determined them to change their course: Nate Champion and possibly a good catch of other rustlers were at a cabin on the Middle Fork of Powder River, only twelve miles away. They decided to detour and finish this group off before proceeding to Buffalo.

Rumors have come down to us of the drinking and dissension that accompanied this decision: faced with the actuality of shooting trapped men in a cabin the next morning, stomachs began to turn over, and three members of the party pulled out, including the doctor and the local newsman. But that night the main body rode on to the attack, through one of the worst April blizzards in memory. They plodded along without speaking, while beards and mustaches became coated with ice, and the wind lashed knife-edged snow in their faces. Halting before daybreak to thaw out around sagebrush fires, they went on until they looked down over a low bluff at the still-sleeping KC ranch.

Two innocent visitors, trappers, had been spending the night in the cabin. As first one and then the other sauntered forth into the gray morning air, he was recognized as not among the wanted men, and as soon as a corner of the barn hid him from the house, each was made prisoner. After a long wait Champion's friend Nick Ray finally appeared and was shot down. The door opened, and Champion himself faced a storm of bullets to drag Ray inside.

The fusillade went on for hour after hour. In the log shack Nate Champion was writing, with a cramped hand in a pocket notebook, the record of his last hours.

Me and Nick was getting breakfast when the attack took place. Two men was with us—Bill Jones and another man. The old man went after water and did not come back. His friend went to see what was the matter and he did not come back. Nick started out and I told him to look out, that I thought there was someone at the stable and would not let them come back.

Nick is shot but not dead yet. He is awful sick. I must go and wait on him.

It is now about two hours since the first shot. Nick is still alive.

They are still shooting and are all around the house, Boys, there is bullets coming in here like hail.

Them fellows is in such shape I can't get at them. They are shooting from the stable and river and back of the house.

Nick is dead. He died about 9 o'clock.

Hour after hour the hills crackled with rifle fire, and such was the emptiness of the country that while the besiegers were on a main road, such as it was, connecting civilization with a little settlement at the back of beyond, they could bang away all day without fear of interruption. Or almost. As it happened there was a slight interruption in midafternoon.

Jack Flagg, a rustler intellectual of sorts, had left his ranch eighteen miles up the Red Fork of Powder River on this snowy morning of April 9, on his way to the Democratic state convention at Douglas, to which he was a delegate from Johnson County. It was one of the oddities of the situation that the thieves were all Democrats, and the murderers were all Republicans. A rancher, newspaper editor, and schoolteacher, Flagg was an accomplished demagogue who had twisted the tails of the big outfits by means fair and foul. He was very much on the wanted list.

He was riding about fifty yards or so behind a wagon driven by his seventeen-year-old stepson; and since the invaders had withdrawn into a strategy huddle and pulled in their pickets, there was no sound of firing to warn him as the wagon rattled downhill to the bridge by the KC. Flagg started over to the house to greet his friends, and was ordered to halt by someone who failed to recognize him.

"Don't shoot me, boys, I'm all right," he called gaily, taking it for a joke. Under the hail of bullets which disabused him, he fled back to the wagon and slashed the tugs holding one of the team, and he and the boy made their miraculous escape.

182

The wagon Flagg left behind was put to use by the invaders. Since hours of cannonading had failed to dislodge Champion, they loaded it with old hay and dry chips and pushed it up to the cabin, where they set it afire. Flames and smoke rolled skyward until they wondered if the man inside had cheated them by shooting himself. Champion, however, was still writing.

> I heard them splitting wood. I guess they are going to fire the house to-night.
> I think I will make a break when night comes if alive.
> It's not night yet.
> The house is all fired. Goodbye boys, if I never see you again.—Nathan D. Champion.

Finally, he broke through the roof at one end of the house and sprinted desperately for the cover of a little draw, which he never reached.

Pawing over the body, the invaders found and read the diary, after which it was presented to the Chicago newsman. Its contents survived, to become a classic of raw courage in the annals of the West.

Next day, Sunday, April 10, the invaders were approaching Buffalo when they were met by a rider on a lathered horse, who warned them that the town was in an uproar and they had better turn back if they valued their lives. They had just made a rest halt at the friendly TA ranch. Their only hope was to return there and dig in.

Sam Clover, ace reporter, was too smart for that trap. Deciding to take his chance with the aroused local population, he left the now deflated avengers and rode on into Buffalo, where he did some fast talking and finally got himself under the wing of his old friend Major Edmond G. Fechet of the 6th Cavalry, with whom he had campaigned during the Ghost Dance troubles in North Dakota. With the rest of the 6th, Fechet was now stationed at Fort McKinney, near Buffalo. So Clover rode off to the fort to luxuriate in hot baths and clean sheets and to write dispatches, while the wretched invaders prepared to stand siege for their lives.

They worked all night, and by morning of the eleventh were entrenched behind a very efficient set of fortifications at the TA ranch, where they were virtually impregnable except for a shortage of food supplies. By morning they were besieged by an impromptu army of hornet-mad cowboys and ranchmen, led by Sheriff "Red" Angus of Johnson County. The army numbered over three hundred on the day of surrender.

In Buffalo, churches and schools were turned into headquarters for the steadily arriving recruits; ladies baked cakes to send to Sheriff Angus' command post; the young Methodist preacher, who was possessed of no mean tongue, employed it to denounce this crime of the century. The leading merchant, a venerable Scotsman named Robert Foote, mounted his black horse and, with his long white beard flying in the breeze, dashed up and down the streets, calling the citizens to arms. More impressive still, he threw open his store, inviting them to help themselves to ammunition, slickers, blankets, flour—everything. He was said to be a heavy dealer in rustled beef, and on the invaders' list; but so was almost everyone of importance in Buffalo.

The telegraph wires had been cut repeatedly since the start of the invasion, but on April 12 they were working again momentarily, and a friend in Buffalo got a telegram through to the governor with the first definite word of the invaders' plight. From that time on, all the heavy artillery of influence, from Cheyenne to Washington and on up to the White House, was brought to bear to rescue the cattlemen from the consequences of their act.

Senators Carey and Warren called at the executive mansion late that night and got President Benjamin Harrison out of bed. He was urged to suppress an insurrection in Wyoming, though the question of just who was in insurrection against whom was not clarified. Telegrams flew back and forth. At 12:50 A.M. on April 13, Colonel J. J. Van Horn of the 6th Cavalry wired the commanding general of the Department of the Platte, acknowledging recipt of orders to proceed to the TA ranch.

Two hours later, three troops of the 6th filed out of Fort McKinney in the freezing dark, in a thoroughly disgusted frame of mind because (a) they had just come in that afternoon from chasing a band of marauding Crows back to the reservation and did not relish being ordered out again at three in the morning; and because (b) they were heartily on the side of Johnson County and would rather have left the invaders to their fate.

They reached the TA at daybreak. Inside the beleaguered ranch house Major Wolcott and his men, their food exhausted, were preparing to make a break as soon as it was sufficiently light. They had eaten what they thought would be their last breakfast, and were awaiting the lookout's whistle which would call them to make that last desperate run—like so many Nate Champions—into the ring of hopelessly outnumbering rifles.

But hark! Instead of the suicide signal, a cavalry bugle! Major Wolcott crossed to a window.

"Gentlemen, it is the troops!"

From start to finish the Johnson County story reads like a parody of every Hollywood western ever filmed, and never more so than at this moment. Down the hill swept a line of seven horsemen abreast; between the fluttering pennons rode Colonel Van Horn, Major Fechet, Sheriff Angus; a representative of the governor, who would not have stuck his neck into northern Wyoming at this point for anything; and, of course, Sam T. Clover of the *Chicago Herald*. One of the guidon bearers carried a white handkerchief. An answering flutter of white appeared on the breastworks. Major Wolcott advanced stiffly and saluted Colonel Van Horn.

"I will surrender to you, but to that man"—indicating Sheriff Angus—"never!"

Forty-four prisoners were marched off to the fort, not including the few defectors and two of the Texas mercenaries, who later died of wounds. Of the ringleaders, only one had received so much as a scratch.

"The cattlemen's war" was front-paged all over the nation for some three weeks, with the Boston *Transcript* putting tongue in cheek to remark on the ever-widening activities of Harvard men. Then the rest of the country forgot it. Four days after the surrender, still guarded by unsympathetic troops, the prisoners were removed to Fort Russell, near Cheyenne. Here they were safely away from Johnson County, which had, however, been behaving with remarkable restraint. The weather was worse than ever and the march overland one of the most miserable on record. Apart from that, the killers got off at no heavier cost to themselves than minor inconvenience and some ignominy. They were never brought to justice.

They did, however, pay an admitted $100,000 as the price of the invasion, counting legal expenses and not mentioning the illegal. Of the sordid features of the Johnson County invasion which all but defy comment, the worst was the affair of the trappers. These two simple and unheroic men, who had been with Champion and Nick Ray in the cabin and had the bad luck to witness the KC slaughter, were hustled out of the state under an escort of gunmen in terror of their lives, and thence across Nebraska to

185

Omaha, where they were piled onto a train, still under escort of gunmen and lawyers, and delivered at an eastern destination. The Johnson County authorities and their friends had been trying frantically to get them back, but no subpoenas could be issued because the cattlemen, still protected by the army, were not yet formally charged with anything. Counting bribes to federal officers and judges, legal fees, forfeited bail, and other expenses, it was said to have cost $27,000 to get the witnesses across Nebraska alone. The trappers had been promised a payoff of $2,500 each, and given postdated checks. When presented for cashing, the checks proved to be on a bank that had never existed.

Meanwhile the armor of self-pity remained undented. In their own eyes and those of their friends, the cattlemen were the innocent victims of an outrage. While awaiting a hearing at Fort Russell, they were kept in the lightest of durance, coming and going freely to Cheyenne. Major Wolcott was permitted a trip outside the state. When Fred DeBillier showed signs of cracking under the strain of captivity, raving and uttering strange outcries in the middle of the night, he was tenderly removed, first to a hotel and later to his home in New York, for rest and medical treatment.

Eventually the prisoners were transferred to the state penitentiary at Laramie, where the district judge who ordered the removal assured Governor Amos W. Barber that these important persons would by no means be required to mingle with ordinary convicts. They were then escorted to their new quarters by a guard of honor, which included Wyoming's adjutant general and acting secretary of state.

Public opinion was overwhelmingly against the prisoners, but it was poorly led and ineffective, and public wrath was dissipated into thin air. On their side, however, in the words of a newspaper correspondent, the cattlemen were "backed not only by the Republican machine from President Harrison on down to the state organization, but by at least twenty-five million dollars in invested capital. They have the President, the governor, the courts, their United States Senators, the state legislature and the army at their backs." It was enough.

One sequel to the episode was an attempt to muzzle the press. A small-town editor who criticized the cattlemen too violently was jailed on a charge of criminal libel and held for thirty days—long enough to silence his paper. A second editor was beaten. But the latter, whose name was A. S. Mercer, exacted an eye for an eye in his celebrated chronicle of the invasion, pub-

186

lished two years later and resoundingly entitled: *The Banditti of the Plains, or The Cattlemen's Invasion of Wyoming. The Crowning Infamy of the Ages.*

Thereupon his print shop was burned to the ground, and another subservient judge ordered all copies of the book seized and burned. But while they were awaiting the bonfire, a wagonload of them was removed one night and drawn by galloping horses over the Colorado line. Thereafter copies on library shelves were stolen and mutilated as far away as the Library of Congress until only a few were left. But two new editions have since been published, and so—in the end—Mr. Mercer won.

The same judge who had shown himself so solicitous of the prisoner's comfort granted a change of venue from Johnson County, not to a neutral county but to the cattlemen's own stronghold in Cheyenne. The trial was set for January 2, 1893. Nineteen days later over a thousand veniremen had been examined and there were still only eleven men on the jury. The prolonged financial strain was too much for Johnson County; since there were no witnesses anyway, the prosecution tossed in the towel, and the case was dismissed.

The so-called rustlers came out with the cleaner hands. Good luck had saved them from spilling the blood of the invaders; and while there was one unsolved killing of a cattlemen's adherent afterward, this appears to have been an act of personal grudge, not of community vengeance. The chain reaction of retaliatory murders that could have started never did; and strifetorn Johnson County settled down to peace. The roundups became democratic, with big and little stockmen working side by side. Montagu sons married Capulet daughters; notorious rustlers turned into respectable ranchmen and hobnobbed with their former enemies. One was mentioned for governor, and another rose to high position in—of all things—the Wyoming Stock Growers Association.

Yet, if bitterness has mercifully subsided, a certain remnant of injustice remains. The ghosts of old wrongs unrighted still walk in Buffalo, and, with the law cheated of its due, the pleasant little town with its creek and its cottonwood trees can only wait for the earthly equivalent of the Last Judgment, the verdict of history.

Result of a Miss Deal, Frederick Remington

The Bride Comes to Yellow Sky

STEPHEN CRANE

I

The great Pullman was whirling onward with such dignity of motion that a glance from the window seemed simply to prove that the plains of Texas were pouring eastward. Vast flats of green grass, dull-hued spaces of mesquite and cactus, little groups of frame houses, woods of light and tender trees, all were sweeping into the east, sweeping over the horizon, a precipice.

A newly married pair had boarded this coach at San Antonio. The man's face was reddened from many days in the wind and sun, and a direct result of his new black clothes was that his brick-colored hands were constantly performing in a most conscious fashion. From time to time he looked down respectfully at his attire. He sat with a hand on each knee, like a man waiting in a barber's shop. The glances he devoted to other passengers were furtive and shy.

The bride was not pretty, nor was she very young. She wore a dress of blue cashmere, with small reservations of velvet here and there, and with steel buttons abounding. She continually twisted her head to regard her puff sleeves, very stiff, straight, and high. They embarrassed her. It was quite apparent that she had cooked, and that she expected to cook, dutifully. The blushes caused by the careless scrutiny of some passengers as she had entered the car were strange to see upon this plain, underclass countenance, which was drawn in placid, almost emotionless lines.

They were evidently very happy. "Ever been in a parlor-car before?" he asked, smiling with delight.

"No," she answered; "I never was. It's fine, ain't it?"

"Great! And then after a while we'll go forward to the diner, and get a big lay-out. Finest meal in the world. Charge a dollar."

"Oh, do they?" cried the bride. "Charge a dollar? Why, that's too much—for us—ain't it, Jack?"

"Not this trip, anyhow," he answered bravely. "We're going to go the whole thing."

Later he explained to her about the trains. "You see, it's a thousand miles from one end of Texas to the other; and this train runs right across it, and never stops but four times." He had the pride of an owner. He pointed out to her the dazzling fittings of the coach; and in truth her eyes opened wider as she contemplated the sea-green figured velvet, the shining brass, silver, and glass, the wood that gleamed as darkly brilliant as the surface of a pool of oil. At one end a bronze figure sturdily held a support for a separated chamber, and at convenient places on the ceiling were frescos in olive and silver.

To the minds of the pair, their surroundings reflected the glory of their marriage that morning in San Antonio; this was the environment of their new estate; and the man's face in particular beamed with an elation that made him appear ridiculous to the Negro porter. This individual at times surveyed them from afar with an amused and superior grin. On other occasions he bullied them with skill in ways that did not make it exactly plain to them that they were being bullied. He subtly used all the manners of the most unconquerable kind of snobbery. He oppressed them; but of this oppression they had small knowledge, and they speedily forgot that infrequently a number of travellers covered them with stares of derisive enjoyment. Historically there was supposed to be something infinitely humorous in their situation.

"We are due in Yellow Sky at 3:42," he said, looking tenderly into her eyes.

"Oh, are we?" she said, as if she had not been aware of it. To evince surprise at her husband's statement was part of her wifely amiability. She took from a pocket a little silver watch; and as she held it before her, and stared at it with a frown of attention, the new husband's face shone.

"I bought it in San Anton' from a friend of mine," he told her gleefully.

"It's seventeen minutes past twelve," she said, looking up at him with a kind of shy and clumsy coquetry. A passenger, noting this play, grew excessively sardonic, and winked at himself in one of the numerous mirrors.

At last they went to the dining-car. Two rows of negro waiters, in glowing white suits, surveyed their entrance with interest, and also the equanimity, of men who had been forewarned. The pair fell to the lot of a waiter who happened to feel pleasure in steering them through their meal. He viewed them with the manner of a fatherly pilot, his countenance radiant with benevolence. The patronage, entwined with the ordinary deference,

190

was not plain to them. And yet, as they returned to their coach, they showed in their faces a sense of escape.

To the left, miles down a long purple slope, was a little ribbon of mist where moved the keening Rio Grande. The train was approaching it at an angle, and the apex was Yellow Sky. Presently it was apparent that, as the distance from Yellow Sky grew shorter, the husband became commensurately restless. His brick-red hands were more insistent in their prominence. Occasionally he was even rather absent-minded and far-away when the bride leaned forward and addressed him.

As a matter of truth, Jack Potter was beginning to find the shadow of a deed weigh upon him like a leaden slab. He, the town marshal of Yellow Sky, a man known, liked, and feared in his corner, a prominent person, had gone to San Antonio to meet a girl he believed he loved, and there, after the usual prayers, had actually induced her to marry him, without consulting Yellow Sky for any part of the transaction. He was now bringing his bride before an innocent and unsuspecting community.

Of course people in Yellow Sky married as it pleased them, in accordance with a general custom; but such was Potter's thought of his duty to his friends, or of their idea of his duty, or of an unspoken form which does not control men in these matters, that he felt he was heinous. He had committed an extraordinary crime. Face to face with this girl in San Antonio, and spurred by his sharp impulse, he had gone headlong over all the social hedges. At San Antonio he was like a man hidden in the dark. A knife to sever any friendly duty, any form, was easy to his hand in that remote city. But the hour of Yellow Sky—the hour of daylight—was approaching.

He knew full well that his marriage was an important thing to his town. It could only be exceeded by the burning of the new hotel. His friends could not forgive him. Frequently he had reflected on the advisability of telling them by telegraph, but a new cowardice had been upon him. He feared to do it. And now the train was hurrying him toward a scene of amazement, glee, and reproach. He glanced out of the window at the line of haze swinging slowly in toward the train.

Yellow Sky had a kind brass band, which played painfully, to the delight of the populace. He laughed without heart as he thought of it. If the citizens could dream of his prospective arrival with his bride, they would parade the band at the station and escort them, amid cheers and laughing congratulations, to his adobe home.

He resolved that he would use all the devices of speed and plainscraft in making the journey from the station to his house. Once within that safe citadel, he could issue some sort of vocal bulletin, and then not go among the citizens until they had time to wear off a little of their enthusiasm.

The bride looked anxiously at him. "What's worrying you, Jack?"

He laughed again. "I'm not worrying, girl; I'm only thinking of Yellow Sky."

She flushed in comprehension.

A sense of mutual guilt invaded their minds and developed a finer tenderness. They looked at each other with eyes softly aglow. But Potter often laughed the same nervous laugh; the flush upon the bride's face seemed quite permanent.

The traitor to the feelings of Yellow Sky narrowly watched the speeding landscape. "We're nearly there," he said.

Presently the porter came and announced the proximity of Potter's home. He held a brush in his hand, and, with all his airy superiority gone, he brushed Potter's new clothes as the latter slowly turned this way and that way. Potter fumbled out a coin and gave it to the porter, as he had seen others do. It was a heavy and muscle-bound business, as that of a man shoeing his first horse.

The porter took their bag, and as the train began to slow they moved forward to the hooded platform of the car. Presently the two engines and their long string of coaches rushed into the station of Yellow Sky.

"They have to take water here," said Potter, from a constricted throat and in mournful cadence, as one announcing death. Before the train stopped his eye had swept the length of the platform, and he was glad and astonished to see there was none upon it but the station-agent, who, with a slightly hurried and anxious air, was walking toward the water-tanks. When the train had halted, the porter alighted first, and placed in position a little temporary step.

"Come on, girl," said Potter, hoarsely. As he helped her down they each laughed on a false note. He took the bag from the Negro, and bade his wife cling to his arm. As they slunk rapidly away, his hang-dog glance perceived that they were unloading the two trunks, and also that the station-agent, far ahead near the baggage-car, had turned and was running toward him, making gestures. He laughed, and groaned as he laughed, when he noted the first effect of his marital bliss upon Yellow Sky. He gripped his wife's arm firmly to his side, and they fled. Behind them the porter stood, chuckling fatuously.

II

The California express on the Southern Railway was due at Yellow Sky in twenty-one minutes. There were six men at the bar of the Weary Gentleman saloon. One was a drummer who talked a great deal and rapidly; three were Texans who did not care to talk at that time; and two were Mexican sheepherders, who did not talk as a general practice in the Weary Gentleman saloon. The barkeeper's dog lay on the board walk that crossed in front of the door. His head was on his paws, and he glanced drowsily here and there with the constant vigilance of a dog that is kicked on occasion. Across the sandy street were some vivid green grass-plots, so wonderful in appearance, amid the sands that burned near them in a blazing sun, that they caused a doubt in the mind. They exactly resembled the grass mats used to represent lawns on the stage. At the cooler end of the railway station, a man without a coat sat in a tilted chair and smoked his pipe. The fresh-cut bank of the Rio Grande circled near the town, and there could be seen beyond it a great plum-colored plain of mesquite.

Save for the busy drummer and his companions in the saloon, Yellow Sky was dozing. The newcomer leaned gracefully upon the bar, and recited many tales with the confidence of a bard who has come upon a new field.

"—and at the moment that the old man fell downstairs with the bureau in his arms, the old woman was coming up with two scuttles of coal, and of course—"

The drummer's tale was interrupted by a young man who suddenly appeared in the open door. He cried: "Scratchy Wilson's drunk, and has turned loose with both hands." The two Mexicans at once set down their glasses and faded out of the rear entrance of the saloon.

The drummer, innocent and jocular, answered: "All right, old man. S'pose he has? Come in and have a drink, anyhow."

But the information had made such an obvious cleft in every skull in the room that the drummer was obliged to see its importance. All had become instantly solemn. "Say," said he, mystified, "what is this?" His three companions made the introductory gesture of eloquent speech; but the young man at the door forestalled them.

"It means, my friend," he answered, as he came into the saloon, "that for the next two hours this town won't be a health resort."

The barkeeper went to the door, and locked and barred it; reaching out of the window, he pulled in heavy wooden shutters, and barred them. Immediately a solemn, chapel-like gloom was upon the place. The drummer was looking from one to another.

"But say," he cried, "what is this, anyhow? You don't mean there is going to be a gun-fight?"

"Don't know whether there'll be a fight or not," answered one man, grimly; "but there'll be some shootin'—some good shootin'."

The young man who had warned them waved his hand. "Oh, there'll be a fight fast enough, if any one wants it. Anybody can get a fight out there in the street. There's a fight just waiting."

The drummer seemed to be swayed between the interest of a foreigner and a perception of personal danger.

"What did you say his name was?" he asked.

"Scratchy Wilson," they answered in chorus.

"And will he kill anybody? What are you going to do? Does this happen often? Does he rampage around like this once a week or so? Can he break in that door?"

"No; he can't break down that door," replied the barkeeper. "He's tried it three times. But when he comes you'd better lay down on the floor, stranger. He's dead sure to shoot at it, and a bullet may come through."

Thereafter the drummer kept a strict eye upon the door. The time had not yet been called for him to hug the floor, but, as a minor precaution, he sidled near to the wall. "Will he kill anybody?" he said again.

The men laughed low and scornfully at the question.

"He's out to shoot, and he's out for trouble. Don't see any good in experimentin' with him."

"But what do you do in a case like this? What do you do?"

A man responded: "Why, he and Jack Potter—"

"But," in chorus the other men interrupted, "Jack Potter's in San Anton'."

"Well, who is he? What's he got to do with it?"

"Oh, he's the town marshal. He goes out and fights Scratchy when he gets on one of these tears."

"Wow!" said the drummer, mopping his brow. "Nice job he's got."

The voices had toned away to mere whisperings. The drummer wished to ask further questions, which were born of an increasing anxiety and bewilderment; but when he attempted them, the men merely looked at him in irritation and motioned him to remain silent. A tense waiting hush was upon them. In the deep shadows of the room their eyes shone as they listened for sounds from the street. One man made three gestures at the barkeeper; and the latter, moving like a ghost, handed him a glass and a bottle. The man poured a full glass of whisky, and set down the bottle noiselessly. He gulped the whisky in a swallow, and turned again toward the door in immovable silence. The drummer saw that the barkeeper, without a sound, had taken a Winchester from beneath the bar. Later he saw this individual beckoning to him, so he tiptoed across the room.

"You better come with me back of the bar."

"No, thanks," said the drummer, perspiring; "I'd rather be where I can make a break for the back door."

Whereupon the man of bottles made a kindly but peremptory gesture. The drummer obeyed it, and, finding himself seated on a box with his head below the level of the bar, balm was laid upon his soul at sight of various zinc and copper fittings that bore a resemblance to armor-plate. The barkeeper took a seat comfortably upon an adjacent box.

"You see," he whispered, "this here Scratchy Wilson is a wonder with a gun—a perfect wonder; and when he goes on the war-trail, we hunt our holes—naturally. He's about the last one of the old gang that used to hang out along the river here. He's a terror when he's drunk. When he's sober he's all right—kind of simple—wouldn't hurt a fly—nicest fellow in town. But when he's drunk—whoo!"

There were periods of stillness. "I wish Jack Potter was back from San Anton'," said the barkeeper. "He shot Wilson up once in the leg—and he would sail in and pull out the kinks in this thing."

Presently they heard from a distance the sound of a shot, followed by three wild yowls. It instantly removed a bond from the men in the darkened saloon. There was a shuffling of feet. They looked at each other. "Here he comes," they said.

III

A man in a maroon-colored flannel shirt, which had been purchased for purposes of decoration, and made principally by some Jewish women on the East Side of New York, rounded a corner and walked into the middle of the main street of Yellow Sky. In either hand the man held a long, heavy, blue-black revolver. Often he yelled, and these cries rang through a semblance of a deserted village, shrilly flying over the roofs in a volume that seemed to have no relation to the ordinary vocal strength of a man. It was as if the surrounding stillness formed the arch of a tomb over him. These cries of ferocious challenge rang against the walls of silence. And his boots had red tops with gilded imprints, of the kind beloved in winter by little sledding boys on the hillsides of New England.

The man's face flamed in a rage begot of whisky. His eyes, rolling, and yet keen for ambush, hunted the still doorways and windows. He walked with the creeping movement of the midnight cat. As it occurred to him, he roared menacing information. The long revolvers in his hands were as easy as straws; they were moved with an electric swiftness. The little fingers of each hand played sometimes in a musician's way. Plain from the low collar of the shirt, the cords of his neck straightened and sank, straightened and sank, as passion moved him. The only sounds were his terrible invitations. The calm adobes preserved their demeanor at the passing of this small thing in the middle of the street.

There was no offer of fight—no offer of fight. The man called to the sky. There were no attractions. He bellowed and fumed and swayed his revolvers here and everywhere.

The dog of the barkeeper of the Weary Gentleman saloon had not appreciated the advance of events. He yet lay dozing in front of his master's door. At sight of the dog, the man paused and raised his revolver humorously. At sight of the man, the dog sprang up and walked diagonally away, with a sullen head, and growling. The man yelled, and the dog broke into a gallop. As it was about to enter an alley, there was a loud noise, a whistling, and something spat the ground directly before it. The dog screamed, and, wheeling in terror, galloped headlong in a new direction. Again there was a noise, a whistling, and sand was kicked viciously before it. Fear-stricken, the dog turned and flurried like an animal in a pen. The man stood laughing, his weapons at his hips.

Ultimately the man was attracted by the closed door of the Weary Gentleman saloon. He went to it and, hammering with a revolver, demanded drink.

The door remaining imperturbable, he picked a bit of paper from the walk, and nailed it to the framework with a knife. He then turned his back contemptuously upon this popular resort and, walking to the opposite side of the street and spinning there on his heel quickly and lithely, fired at the bit of paper. He missed it by a half-inch. He swore at himself, and went away. Later he comfortably fusilladed the windows of his most intimate friend. The man was playing with this town; it was a toy for him.

But still there was no offer of fight. The name of Jack Potter, his ancient antagonist, entered his mind, and he concluded that it would be a glad thing if he should go to Potter's house, and by bombardment induce him to come out and fight. He moved in the direction of his desire, chanting Apache scalp-music.

When he arrived at it, Potter's house presented the same still front as had the other adobes. Taking up a strategic position, the man howled a challenge. But this house regarded him as might a great stone god. It gave no sign. After a decent wait, the man howled further challenges, mingling with them wonderful epithets.

Presently there came the spectacle of a man churning himself into deepest rage over the immobility of a house. He fumed at it as the winter wind attacks a prairie cabin in the North. To the distance there should have gone the sound of a tumult like the fighting of two hundred Mexicans. As necessity bade him, he paused for breath or to reload his revolvers.

IV

Potter and his bride walked sheepishly and with speed. Sometimes they laughed together shamefacedly and low.

"Next corner, dear," he said finally.

They put forth the efforts of a pair walking bowed against a strong wind. Potter was about to raise a finger to point the first appearance of the new home when, as they circled the corner, they came face to face with a man in a maroon-colored shirt, who was feverishly pushing cartridges into a large revolver. Upon the instant the man dropped his revolver to the ground and, like lightning, whipped another from its holster. The second weapon was aimed at the bridegroom's chest.

There was a silence. Potter's mouth seemed to be merely a grave for his tongue. He exhibited an instinct to at once loosen his arm from the woman's grip, and he dropped the bag to the sand. As for the bride, her face had gone as yellow as old cloth. She was a slave to hideous rites, gazing at the apparitional snake.

The two men faced each other at a distance of three paces. He of the revolver smiled with a new and quiet ferocity.

"Tried to sneak up on me," he said. "Tried to sneak up on me!" His eyes grew more baleful. As Potter made a slight movement, the man thrust his revolver venomously forward. "No; don't you do it, Jack Potter. Don't you move a finger toward a gun just yet. Don't you move an eyelash. The time has come for me to settle with you, and I'm goin' to do it my own way, and loaf along with no interferin'. So if you don't want a gun bent on you, just mind what I tell you."

Potter looked at his enemy. "I ain't got a gun on me, Scratchy," he said. "Honest, I ain't." He was stiffening and steadying, but yet somewhere at the back of his mind a vision of the Pullman floated: the sea-green figured velvet, the shining brass, silver, and glass, the wood that gleamed as darkly brilliant as the surface of a pool of oil—all the glory of the marriage, the environment of the new estate. "You know I fight when it comes to fighting, Scratchy Wilson; but I ain't got a gun on me. You'll have to do all the shootin' yourself."

His enemy's face went livid. He stepped forward, and lashed his weapon to and fro before Potter's chest. "Don't you tell me you ain't got no gun on you, you whelp. Don't tell me no lie like that. There ain't a man in Texas ever seen you without no gun. Don't take me for no kid." His eyes blazed with light, and his throat worked like a pump.

"I ain't takin' you for no kid," answered Potter. His heels had not moved an inch backward. "I'm takin' you for a damn fool. I tell you I ain't got a gun, and I ain't. If you're goin' to shoot me up, you better begin now; you'll never get a chance like this again."

So much enforced reasoning had told on Wilson's rage; he was calmer. "If you ain't got a gun, why ain't you got a gun?" he sneered. "Been to Sunday-school?"

"I ain't got a gun because I've just come from San Anton' with my wife. I'm married," said Potter. "And if I'd thought there was going to be any galoots like you prowling around when I brought my wife home, I'd had a gun, and don't you forget it."

"Married!" said Scratchy, not at all comprehending.

"Yes, married. I'm married," said Potter, distinctly.

198

"Married?" said Scratchy. Seemingly for the first time, he saw the drooping, drowning woman at the other man's side. "No!" he said. He was like a creature allowed a glimpse of another world. He moved a pace backward, and his arm, with the revolver, dropped to his side. "Is this the lady?" he asked.

"Yes; this is the lady," answered Potter.

There was another period of silence.

"Well," said Wilson at last, slowly, "I s'pose it's all off now."

"It's all off if you say so, Scratchy. You know I didn't make the trouble." Potter lifted his valise.

"Well, I 'low it's off, Jack," said Wilson. He was looking at the ground. "Married!" He was not a student of chivalry; it was merely that in the presence of this foreign condition he was a simple child of the earlier plains. He picked up his starboard revolver, and, placing both weapons in their holsters, he went away. His feet made funnel-shaped tracks in the heavy sand.

In Without Knocking, Charles M. Russell

Wild West

ROBERT BOYLAN

Now let us speak of cowboys who on swift
White horses over blue-black deserts sped,
Their pistols blazing and their proud blood shed
In paint-flecked shanties on the haunted cliffs
Or in the bars of ghost-towns. Let us tell
The legends of fierce heroes motherless,
Not Indians, not Easterners, whose quests
And daring deeds inscribed their names in hell.
Bravely they shot it out, did Wyatt Earp,
Billy the Kid, Bill Hickok, Jesse James.
Now what remains but moving-picture dreams
Of all that fury and fast villainy?
Lone cactuses where bullets spit and ripped
The courage of the eyelid from the eye?
A rusting stirrup and a rowel thrust
Up from the calcifying sun-baked dust
Where some unknown avenger fell to sleep?
A wind-blown piece of buckskin that looked grand
When it was stretched upon the living hip
Of him who lies now six feet under ground?
Cowboys were not immortal. All they did,
Guzzling and gunning, ended when they died.

John Wayne: A Love Song

JOAN DIDION

In the summer of 1943 I was eight, and my father and mother and small brother and I were at Peterson Field in Colorado Springs. A hot wind blew through that summer, blew until it seemed that before August broke, all the dust in Kansas would be in Colorado, would have drifted over the tar-paper barracks and the temporary strip and stopped only when it hit Pikes Peak. There was not much to do, a summer like that: there was the day they brought in the first B-29, an event to remember but scarcely a vacation program. There was an Officers' Club, but no swimming pool; all the Officers' Club had of interest was artificial blue rain behind the bar. The rain interested me a good deal, but I could not spend the summer watching it, and so we went, my brother and I, to the movies.

We went three and four afternoons a week, sat on folding chairs in the darkened Quonset hut which served as a theater, and it was there, that summer of 1943 while the hot wind blew outside, that I first saw John Wayne. Saw the walk, heard the voice. Heard him tell the girl in a picture called *War of the Wildcats* that he would build her a house, "at the bend in the river where the cottonwoods grow." As it happened I did not grow up to be the kind of woman who is the heroine in a Western, and although the men I have known have had many virtues and have taken me to live in many places I have come to love, they have never been John Wayne, and they have never taken me to that bend in the river where the cottonwoods grow. Deep in that part of my heart where the artificial rain forever falls, that is still the line I wait to hear.

I tell you this neither in a spirit of self-revelation nor as an exercise in total recall, but simply to demonstrate that when John Wayne rode through my childhood, and perhaps through yours, he determined forever the shape of certain of our dreams. It did not seem possible that such a man could fall ill, could carry within him that most inexplicable and ungovernable of diseases. The rumor struck some obscure anxiety, threw our very childhoods

202

into question. In John Wayne's world, John Wayne was supposed to give the orders. "Let's ride," he said, and "Saddle up." "Forward *ho,*" and "A man's gotta do what he's got to do." "Hello, there," he said when he first saw the girl, in a construction camp or on a train or just standing around on the front porch waiting for somebody to ride up through the tall grass. When John Wayne spoke, there was no mistaking his intentions; he had a sexual authority so strong that even a child could perceive it. And in a world we understood early to be characterized by venality and doubt and paralyzing ambiguities, he suggested another world, one which may or may not have existed ever but in any case existed no more: a place where a man could move free, could make his own code and live by it; a world in which, if a man did what he had to do, he could one day take the girl and go riding through the draw and find himself home free, not in a hospital with something going wrong inside, not in a high bed with the flowers and the drugs and the forced smiles, but there at the bend in the bright river, the cottonwoods shimmering in the early morning sun.

"Hello, there." Where did he come from, before the tall grass? Even his history seemed right, for it was no history at all, nothing to intrude upon the dream. Born Marion Morrison in Wintereset, Iowa, the son of a druggist. Moved as a child to Lancaster, California, part of the migration to that promised land sometimes called "the west coast of Iowa." Not that Lancaster was the promise fulfilled; Lancaster was a town on the Mojave where the dust blew through. But Lancaster was still California, and it was only a year from there to Glendale, where desolation had a different flavor: antimacassars among the orange groves, a middle-class prelude to Forest Lawn. Imagine Marion Morrison in Glendale. A Boy Scout, then a student at Glendale High. A tackle for U.S.C., a Sigma Chi. Summer vacations, a job moving props on the old Fox lot. There, a meeting with John Ford, one of the several directors who were to sense that into this perfect mold might be poured the inarticulate longings of a nation wondering at just what pass the trail had been lost. "Dammit," said Raoul Walsh later, "the son of a bitch looked like a man." And so after a while the boy from Glendale became a star. He did not become an actor, as he has always been careful to point out to interviewers ("How many times do I gotta tell you, I don't act at all, I *re*-act"), but a star, and the star called John Wayne would spend most of the rest of his life with one or another of those directors, out on some forsaken location, in search of the dream.

Out where the skies are a trifle bluer
Out where friendship's a little truer
That's where the West begins.

Nothing very bad could happen in the dream, nothing a man could not face down. But something did. There it was, the rumor, and after a while the headlines. "I licked the Big C," John Wayne announced, as John Wayne would, reducing those outlaw cells to the level of any other outlaws, but even so we all sensed that this would be the one unpredictable confrontation, the one shoot-out Wayne could lose. I have as much trouble as the next person with illusion and reality, and I did not much want to see John Wayne when he must be (or so I thought) having some trouble with it himself, but I did, and it was down in Mexico when he was making the picture his illness had so long delayed, down in the very country of the dream.

It was John Wayne's 165th picture. It was Henry Hathaway's 84th. It was number 34 for Dean Martin, who was working off an old contract to Hal Wallis, for whom it was independent production number 65. It was called *The Sons of Katie Elder*, and it was a Western, and after the three-month delay they had finally shot the exteriors up in Durango, and now they were in the waning days of interior shooting at Estudio Churubusco outside Mexico City, and the sun was hot and the air was clear and it was lunchtime. Out under the pepper trees the boys from the Mexican crew sat around sucking caramels, and down the road some of the technical men sat around a place which served a stuffed lobster and a glass of tequila for one dollar American, but it was inside the cavernous empty commissary where the talent sat around, the reasons for the exercise, all sitting around the big table picking at *huevos con queso* and Carta Blanca beer. Dean Martin, unshaven. Mack Gray, who goes where Martin goes. Bob Goodfried, who was in charge of Paramount publicity and who had flown down to arrange for a trailer and who had a delicate stomach. "Tea and toast," he warned repeatedly. "That's the ticket. You can't trust the lettuce." And Henry Hathaway, the director, who did not seem to be listening to Goodfried. And John Wayne, who did not seem to be listening to anyone.
"This week's gone slow," Dean Martin said, for the third time.
"How can you say that?" Mack Gray demanded.
"*This . . . week's . . . gone . . . slow*, that's how I can say it."

"You don't mean you want it to end."

"I'll say it right out, Mack, I want it to *end*. Tomorrow night I shave this beard, I head for the airport, I say *adiós amigos!* Bye-bye *muchachos!*"

Henry Hathaway lit a cigar and patted Martin's arm fondly. "Not tomorrow, Dino."

"Henry, what are you planning to add? A World War?"

Hathaway patted Martin's arm again and gazed into the middle distance. At the end of the table someone mentioned a man who, some years before, had tried unsuccessfully to blow up an airplane.

"He's still in jail," Hathaway said suddenly.

"In jail?" Martin was momentarily distracted from the question whether to send his golf clubs back with Bob Goodfried or consign them to Mack Gray. "What's he in jail for if nobody got killed?"

"Attempted murder, Dino," Hathaway said gently. "A felony."

"You mean some guy just *tried* to kill me he'd end up in jail?"

Hathaway removed the cigar from his mouth and looked across the table. "Some guy just tried to kill *me* he wouldn't end up in jail. How about you, Duke?"

Very slowly, the object of Hathaway's query wiped his mouth, pushed back his chair, and stood up. It was the real thing, the authentic article, the move which had climaxed a thousand scenes on 165 flickering frontiers and phantasmagoric battlefields before, and it was about to climax this one, in the commissary at Estudio Churubusco outside Mexico City. "Right," John Wayne drawled. "I'd kill him."

Almost all the cast of *Katie Elder* had gone home, that last week; only the principals were left, Wayne, and Martin, and Earl Holliman, and Michael Anderson, Jr., and Martha Hyer. Martha Hyer was not around much, but every now and then someone referred to her, usually as "the girl." They had all been together nine weeks, six of them in Durango. Mexico City was not quite Durango; wives like to come along to places like Mexico City, like to shop for handbags, go to parties at Merle Oberon Pagliai's, like to look at her paintings. But Durango. The very name hallucinates. Man's country. Out where the West begins. There had been ahuehuete trees in Durango; a waterfall, rattlesnakes. There had been weather, nights so cold that they had postponed one or two exteriors until they could shoot inside at Churubusco. "It was the girl," they explained. "You couldn't keep the girl out in cold like that." Henry Hathaway had cooked in Durango, *gazpacho* and ribs and the steaks that Dean Martin had ordered flown down from the Sands; he had wanted to cook in Mexico City, but the management of the Hotel Bamer refused to let him set up a brick barbecue in his room. "You really missed something, *Durango*," they would say, sometimes joking and sometimes not, until it became a refrain, Eden lost.

But if Mexico City was not Durango, neither was it Beverly Hills. No one else was using Churubusco that week, and there inside the big sound stage that said LOS HIJOS DE KATIE ELDER on the door, there with the pepper trees and the bright sun outside, they could still, for just so long as the picture lasted, maintain a world peculiar to men who like to make Westerns, a world of loyalties and fond raillery, of sentiment and shared cigars, of interminable desultory recollections; campfire talk, its only point to keep a human voice raised against the night, the wind, the rustlings in the brush.

"Stuntman got hit accidentally on a picture of mine once," Hathaway would say between takes of an elaborately choreographed fight scene. "What was his name, married Estelle Taylor, met her down in Arizona."

The circle would close around him, the cigars would be fingered. The delicate art of the staged fight was to be contemplated.

"I only hit one guy in my life," Wayne would say. "Accidentally, I mean. That was Mike Mazurki."

"Some guy. Hey, Duke says he only hit one guy in his life, Mike Mazurki."

"Some choice." Murmurings, assent.

"It wasn't a choice, it was an accident."

"I can believe it."

"You bet."

"Oh boy. Mike Mazurki."

And so it would go. There was Web Overlander, Wayne's makeup man for twenty years, hunched in a blue Windbreaker, passing out sticks of Juicy Fruit. "*Insect spray*," he would say. "Don't tell us about insect spray. We saw insect spray in Africa, all right. Remember Africa?" Or, "*Steamer* clams. Don't tell us about steamer clams. We got our fill of steamer clams all right, on the *Hatari!* appearance tour. Remember Bookbinder's?" There was Ralph Volkie, Wayne's trainer for eleven years, wearing a red baseball cap and carrying around a clipping from Hedda Hopper, a tribute to Wayne. "This Hopper's some lady," he would say again and again. "Not like some of these guys, all they write is sick, sick, sick, how can you call that guy *sick*, when he's got pains, coughs, works all day, *never complains.* That guy's got the best hook since Dempsey, not *sick.*"

And there was Wayne himself, fighting through number 165. There was Wayne, in his thirty-three-year-old spurs, his dusty neckerchief, his blue shirt. "You don't have too many worries about what to wear in these things," he said. "You can wear a blue shirt, or, if you're down in Monument Valley, you can wear a yellow shirt." There was Wayne, in a relatively new hat, a hat which made him look curiously like William S. Hart. "I had this old cavalry hat I loved, but I lent it to Sammy Davis. I got it back, it was unwearable. I think they all pushed it down on his head and said *O.K., John Wayne*—you know, a joke."

There was Wayne, working too soon, finishing the picture with a bad cold and a racking cough, so tired by late afternoon that he kept an oxygen inhalator on the set. And still nothing mattered but the Code. "That guy," he muttered of a reporter who had incurred his displeasure. "I admit I'm balding. I admit I got a tire around my middle. What man fifty-seven doesn't? Big news. Anyway, that guy."

He paused, about to expose the heart of the matter, the root of the distaste, the fracture of the rules that bothered him more than the alleged misquotations, more than the intimation that he was no longer the Ringo Kid. "He comes down, uninvited, but I ask him over anyway. So we're sitting around drinking mescal out of a water jug."

He paused again and looked meaningfully at Hathaway, readying him for the unthinkable denouement. "He had to be *assisted* to his room."

They argued about the virtues of various prizefighters, they argued about the price of J & B in pesos. They argued about dialogue.

"As rough a guy as he is, Henry, I still don't think he'd raffle off his mother's *Bible.*"

"I like a shocker, Duke."

They exchanged endless training-table jokes. "You know why they call this memory sauce?" Martin asked, holding up a bowl of chili.

"Why?"

"Because you *remember it in the morning.*"

"Hear that, Duke? Hear why they call this memory sauce?"

They delighted one another by blocking out minute variations in the free-for-all fight which is a set piece in Wayne pictures; motivated or totally

207

gratuitous, the fight sequence has to be in the picture, because they so enjoy making it. "Listen—this'll really be funny. Duke picks up the kid, see, and then it takes both Dino and Earl to throw him out the door—*how's that?*"

They communicated by sharing old jokes; they sealed their camaraderie by making gentle, old-fashioned fun of wives, those civilizers, those tamers. "So Señora Wayne takes it into her head to stay up and have one brandy. So for the rest of the night it's 'Yes, Pilar, you're right, dear. I'm a bully, Pilar, you're right, I'm impossible.' "

"You hear that? Duke says Pilar threw a table at him."

"Hey, Duke, here's something funny. That finger you hurt today, get the Doc to bandage it up, go home tonight, show it to Pilar, tell her she did it when she threw the table. You know, make her think she was really cutting up."

They treated the oldest among them respectfully; they treated the youngest fondly. "You see that kid?" they said of Michael Anderson, Jr. "What a kid."

"He don't act, it's right from the heart," said Hathaway, patting his heart.

"Hey kid," Martin said. "You're gonna be in my next picture. We'll have the whole thing, no beards. The striped shirts, the girls, the hi-fi, the eye lights."

They ordered Michael Anderson his own chair, with "BIG MIKE" tooled on the back. When it arrived on the set, Hathaway hugged him. "You see that?" Anderson asked Wayne, suddenly too shy to look him in the eye. Wayne gave him the smile, the nod, the final accolade. "I saw it, kid."

On the morning of the day they were to finish *Katie Elder*, Web Overlander showed up not in his Windbreaker but in a blue blazer. "Home, Mama," he said, passing out the last of his Juicy Fruit. "I got on my getaway clothes." But he was subdued. At noon, Henry Hathaway's wife dropped by the commissary to tell him that she might fly over to Acapulco. "Go ahead," he told her. "I get through here, all I'm gonna do is take Seconal to a point just this side of suicide." They were all subdued. After Mrs. Hathaway left, there were desultory attempts at reminiscing, but man's country was receding fast; they were already halfway home, and all they could call up was the

1961 Bel Air fire, during which Henry Hathaway had ordered the Los Angeles Fire Department off his property and saved the place himself by, among other measures, throwing everything flammable into the swimming pool. "Those fire guys might've just given it up," Wayne said. "Just let it burn." In fact this was a good story, and one incorporating several of their favorite themes, but a Bel Air story was still not a Durango story.

In the early afternoon they began the last scene, and although they spent as much time as possible setting it up, the moment finally came when there was nothing to do but shoot it. "Second team out, first team in, *doors closed*," the assistant director shouted one last time. The stand-ins walked off the set, John Wayne and Martha Hyer walked on. "All right, boys, *silencio*, this is a picture." They took it twice. Twice the girl offered John Wayne the tattered Bible. Twice John Wayne told her that "there's a lot of places I go where that wouldn't fit in." Everyone was very still. And at 2:30 that Friday afternoon Henry Hathaway turned away from the camera, and in the hush that followed he ground out his cigar in a sand bucket. "O.K.," he said. "That's it."

Since that summer of 1943 I had thought of John Wayne in a number of ways. I had thought of him driving cattle up from Texas, and bringing airplanes in on a single engine, thought of him telling the girl at the Alamo that "Republic is a beautiful word." I had never thought of him having dinner with his family and with me and my husband in an expensive restaurant in Chapultepec Park, but time brings odd mutations, and there we were, one night that last week in Mexico. For a while it was only a nice evening, an evening anywhere. We had a lot of drinks and I lost the sense that the face across the table was in certain ways more familiar than my husband's.

And then something happened. Suddenly the room seemed suffused with the dream, and I could not think why. Three men appeared out of nowhere, playing guitars. Pilar Wayne leaned slightly forward, and John Wayne lifted his glass almost imperceptibly toward her. "We'll need some Pouilly-Fuissé for the rest of the table," he said, "and some red Bordeaux for the Duke." We all smiled, and drank the Pouilly-Fuissé for the rest of the table and the red Bordeaux for the Duke, and all the while the men with the guitars kept playing, until finally I realized what they were playing, what they had been playing all along: "The Red River Valley" and the theme from *The High and the Mighty*. They did not quite get the beat right, but even now I can hear them, in another country and a long time later, even as I tell you this.

California Dreaming

*Know that on the right hand of the Indies there is an island
called California, very near to the terrestrial paradise.*
—GARCIA ORDONEZ DE MONTALVO

California from the start promised special abundance. The pas-
toral society developed by the Mexicans appeared to all early travelers both hospitable and romantic, allowing for predictable Yankee
grumbling about sanitation. Before the discovery of gold, reports
spoke of a golden land, golden days, and golden opportunities. Even
after most of the Forty-Niners and succeeding waves of migrants
found that their dreams of new beginnings ended in disappoint-
ment, the unofficial dream persisted. Millions followed and still pursue the myth of its golden shores.

Climate in this sun-drenched state always embraced more than
weather. Early and late, promoters sold the riches of the land: agri-
culture, timber, water, real estate. Economy as well as population
grew phenomenally, transforming the scene into a booster's paradise
and attracting job-seekers, sun-seekers, fun-seekers. Somewhere between Beverly Hills and *Sunset* magazine, a pioneering contractor
discovered that patios and swimming pools were natural extensions
of the family dwelling, and luxury became standardized. Along with
employment, newcomers discovered the advantages of a society less
fixed, more open and mobile. In a few more tolerant communities,
an array of visionaries found room to experiment with dreams and
invent lifestyles, attracting all species of true-believers to the cor-
nucopia and carnival on the continent's edge.

If the rate of development was explosive, the toll was impressive, too. California society was more restless, rootless; its cities and highways represented monuments to unplanned and ill-planned growth; its rivers, dammed and diverted, barely supplied the expanding population; its remaining natural beauty was dimmed by smog and jammed by vacationing hordes; its politics (in the comic opera tradition of the Bear Flag Republic) were unpredictable. Like Hollywood, the entire business might have been founded on vanity, greed, and pure illusion.

The California dream is based on the premise of perpetual growth, limitless resources, endless space, with leisure and pleasure for all who can afford it. As befits a legendary place, rumors persist. Ambrose Bierce's theory that when somehow the continent tipped, everything not fixed firmly in place rolled westward is no longer credited. However, beneath the glamor and confidence, what Mark Twain saw in the gold camps might still apply today—a life "wild, free, disorderly, grotesque." Whether the scene previews an exaggerated version of America's future, as some observers fear, whether the spectacle inspires enthusiasm or revulsion, California provides a catalyst in which social changes visibly take shape. Certainly the search for a better life and the pursuit of happiness are full-time occupations of many natives. Certainly believers in tomorrow flock and thrive in the climate of tolerance that, again taking a cue from Hollywood, may be the stuff of fable or a simple absence of tradition. In any event, California epitomizes a state of being, a state of mind, a state of excitement where excess may be the norm and where the clichés turn out not only to be true but may be the whole truth.

A Page from a Californian Almanac

MARK TWAIN

At the instance of several friends who feel a boding anxiety to know beforehand what sort of phenomena we may expect the elements to exhibit during the next month or two, and who have lost all confidence in the various patent medicine almanacs, because of the unaccountable reticence of those works concerning the extraordinary event of the 8th inst., I have compiled the following almanac expressly for the latitude of San Francisco:

Oct. 17   Weather hazy; atmosphere murky and dense. An expression of profound melancholy will be observable upon most countenances.

Oct. 18   Slight earthquake. Countenances grow more melancholy.

Oct. 19   Look out for rain. It would be absurd to look in for it. The general depression of spirits increased.

Oct. 20   More weather.

Oct. 21   Same.

Oct. 22   Light winds, perhaps. If they blow, it will be from the "east'ard, or the nor'ard, or the west'ard, or the suth'ard," or from some general direction approximating more or less to these points of the compass or otherwise. Winds are uncertain—more especially when they blow from whence they cometh and whither they listeth. N.B.—Such is the nature of winds.

Oct. 23   Mild, balmy earthquakes.

Oct. 24   Shaky.

Oct. 25   Occasional shakes, followed by light showers of bricks and plastering. N.B.—Stand from under!

Oct. 26   Considerable phenomenal atmospheric foolishness. About this time expect more earthquakes; but do not look for them, on account of the bricks.

Oct. 27   Universal despondency, indicative of approaching disaster. Abstain from smiling, or indulgence in humorous conversation, or exasperating jokes.

Oct. 28   Misery, dismal forebodings, and despair. Beware of all light discourse—a joke uttered at this time would produce a popular outbreak.

Oct. 29   Beware!

Oct. 30   Keep dark!

Oct. 31   Go slow!

Nov. 1   Terrific earthquake. This is the great earthquake month. More stars fall and more worlds are slathered around carelessly and destroyed in November than in any other month of the twelve.

Nov. 2   Spasmodic but exhilarating earthquakes, accompanied by occasional showers of rain and churches and things.

Nov. 3   Make your will.

Nov. 4   Sell out.

Nov. 5   Select your "last words." Those of John Quincy Adams will do, with the addition of a syllable, thus: "This is the last of earthquakes."

Nov. 6   Prepare to shed this mortal coil.

Nov. 7   Shed!

Nov. 8   The sun will rise as usual, perhaps; but if he does, he will doubtless be staggered some to find nothing but a large round hole
eight thousand miles in diameter in the place where he saw this
world serenely spinning the day before.

The Leader of the People

JOHN STEINBECK

On Saturday afternoon Billy Buck, the ranch-hand, raked together the last of the old year's haystack and pitched small forkfuls over the wire fence to a few mildly interested cattle. High in the air small clouds like puffs of cannon smoke were driven eastward by the March wind. The wind could be heard whishing in the brush on the ridge crests, but no breath of it penetrated down into the ranchcup.

The little boy, Jody, emerged from the house eating a thick piece of buttered bread. He saw Billy working on the last of the haystack. Jody tramped down scuffing his shoes in a way he had been told was destructive to good shoe-leather. A flock of white pigeons flew out of the black cypress tree as Jody passed, and circled the tree and landed again. A half-grown tortoise-shell cat leaped from the bunkhouse porch, galloped on stiff legs across the road, whirled and galloped back again. Jody picked up a stone to help the game along, but he was too late, for the cat was under the porch before the stone could be discharged. He threw the stone into the cypress tree and started the white pigeons on another whirling flight.

Arriving at the used-up haystack, the boy leaned against the barbed wire fence. "Will that be all of it, do you think?" he asked.

The middle-aged ranch-hand stopped his careful raking and stuck his fork into the ground. He took off his black hat and smoothed down his hair. "Nothing left of it that isn't soggy from ground moisture," he said. He replaced his hat and rubbed his dry leathery hands together.

"Ought to be plenty mice," Jody suggested.

"Lousy with them," said Billy. "Just crawling with mice."

"Well, maybe, when you get all through, I could call the dogs and hunt the mice."

"Sure, I guess you could," said Billy Buck. He lifted a forkful of the damp ground-hay and threw it into the air. Instantly three mice leaped out and burrowed frantically under the hay again.

216

Jody sighed with satisfaction. Those plump, sleek, arrogant mice were doomed. For eight months they had lived and multiplied in the haystack. They had been immune from cats, from traps, from poison, and from Jody. They had grown smug in their security, overbearing and fat. Now the time of disaster had come; they would not survive another day.

Billy looked up at the top of the hills that surrounded the ranch. "Maybe you better ask your father before you do it," he suggested.

"Well, where is he? I'll ask him now."

"He rode up to the ridge ranch after dinner. He'll be back pretty soon."

Jody slumped against the fence post. "I don't think he'd care."

As Billy went back to his work he said ominously, "You'd better ask him anyway. You know how he is."

Jody did know. His father, Carl Tiflin, insisted upon giving permission for anything that was done on the ranch, whether it was important or not. Jody sagged farther against the post until he was sitting on the ground. He looked up at the little puffs of wind-driven cloud. "Is it like to rain, Billy?"

"It might. The wind's good for it, but not strong enough."

"Well, I hope it don't rain until after I kill those damn mice." He looked over his shoulder to see whether Billy had noticed the mature profanity. Billy worked on without comment.

Jody turned back and looked at the side-hill where the road from the outside world came down. The hill was washed with lean March sunshine. Silver thistles, blue lupins and a few poppies bloomed among the sage bushes. Halfway up the hill Jody could see Doubletree Mutt, the black dog, digging in a squirrel hole. He paddled for a while and then paused to kick bursts of dirt out between his hind legs, and he dug with an earnestness which belied the knowledge he must have had that no dog had ever caught a squirrel by digging in a hole.

Suddenly, while Jody watched, the black dog stiffened, and backed out of the hole and looked up the hill toward the cleft in the ridge where the road came through. Jody looked up too. For a moment Carl Tiflin on horseback stood out against the pale sky and then he moved down the road toward the house. He carried something white in his hand.

The boy started to his feet. "He's got a letter," Jody cried. He trotted away toward the ranch house, for the letter would probably be read aloud and he wanted to be there. He reached the house before his father did, and ran in. He heard Carl dismount from his creaking saddle and slap the horse on the side to send it to the barn where Billy would unsaddle it and turn it out.

Jody ran into the kitchen. "We got a letter!" he cried.

His mother looked up from a pan of beans. "Who has?"

"Father has. I saw it in his hand."

Carl strode into the kitchen then, and Jody's mother asked, "Who's the letter from, Carl?"

He frowned quickly. "How did you know there was a letter?"

She nodded her head in the boy's direction. "Big-Britches Jody told me."

Jody was embarrassed.

His father looked down at him contemptuously. "He is getting to be a Big-Britches." Carl said. "He's minding everybody's business but his own. Got his big nose into everything."

Mrs. Tiflin relented a little. "Well, he hasn't enough to keep him busy. Who's the letter from?"

Carl still frowned on Jody. "I'll keep him busy if he isn't careful." He held out a sealed letter. "I guess it's from your father."

Mrs. Tiflin took a hairpin from her head and slit open the flap. Her lips pursed judiciously. Jody saw her eyes snap back and forth over the lines. "He says," she translated, "he says he's going to drive out Saturday to stay for a little while. Why, this is Saturday. The letter must have been delayed." She looked at the postmark. "This was mailed day before yesterday. It should have been here yesterday." She looked questioningly at her husband, and then her face darkened angrily. "Now what have you got that look on you for? He doesn't come often."

Carl turned his eyes away from her anger. He could be stern with her most of the time, but when occasionally her temper arose, he could not combat it.

"What's the matter with you?" she demanded again.

In his explanation there was a tone of apology Jody himself might have used. "It's just that he talks," Carl said lamely. "Just talks."

"Well, what of it? You talk yourself."

"Sure I do. But your father only talks about one thing."

"Indians!" Jody broke in excitedly. "Indians and crossing the plains!"

218

Carl turned fiercely on him. "You get out, Mr. Big-Britches! Go on, now! Get out!"

Jody went miserably out the back door and closed the screen with elaborate quietness. Under the kitchen window his shamed, downcast eyes fell upon a curiously shaped stone, a stone of such fascination that he squatted down and picked it up and turned it over in his hands.

The voice came clearly to him through the open kitchen window. "Jody's damn well right," he heard his father say. "Just Indians and crossing the plains. I've heard that story about how the horses got driven off about a thousand times. He just goes on and on, and he never changes a word in the things he tells."

When Mrs. Tiflin answered her tone was so changed that Jody, outside the window, looked up from his study of the stone. Her voice had become soft and explanatory. Jody knew how her face would have changed to match the tone. She said quietly, "Look at it this way, Carl. That was the big thing in my father's life. He led a wagon train clear across the plains to the coast, and when it was finished, his life was done. It was a big thing to do, but it didn't last long enough. Look!" she continued, "it's as though he was born to do that, and after he finished it, there wasn't anything more for him to do but think about it and talk about it. If there'd been any farther west to go, he'd have gone. He's told me so himself. But at last there was the ocean. He lives right by the ocean where he had to stop."

She had caught Carl, caught him and entangled him in her soft tone.

"I've seen him," he agreed quietly. "He goes down and stares off west over the ocean." His voice sharpened a little. "And then he goes up to the Horseshoe Club in Pacific Grove, and he tells people how the Indians drove off the horses."

She tried to catch him again. "Well, it's everything to him. You might be patient with him and pretend to listen."

Carl turned impatiently away. "Well, if it gets too bad, I can always go down to the bunkhouse and sit with Billy," he said irritably. He walked through the house and slammed the front door after him.

Jody ran to his chores. He dumped the grain to the chickens without chasing any of them. He gathered the eggs from the nests. He trotted into the house with the wood and interlaced it so carefully in the wood-box that two armloads seemed to fill it to overflowing.

His mother had finished the beans by now. She stirred up the fire and brushed off the stove-top with a turkey wing. Jody peered cautiously at her to see whether any rancor toward him remained. "Is he coming today?" Jody asked.

"That's what his letter said."

"Maybe I better walk up the road to meet him."

Mrs. Tiflin clanged the stove-lid shut. "That would be nice," she said. "He'd probably like to be met."

"I guess I'll just do it then."

Outside, Jody whistled shrilly to the dogs. "Come on up the hill," he commanded. The two dogs waved their tails and ran ahead. Along the roadside the sage had tender new tips. Jody tore off some pieces and rubbed them on his hands until the air was filled with the sharp wild smell. With a rush the dogs leaped from the road and yapped into the brush after a rabbit. That was the last Jody saw of them, for when they failed to catch the rabbit, they went back home.

Jody plodded on up the hill toward the ridge top. When he reached the little cleft where the road came through, the afternoon wind struck him and blew up his hair and ruffled his shirt. He looked down on the little hills and ridges below and then out at the huge green Salinas Valley. He could see the white town of Salinas far out in the flat and the flash of its windows under the waning sun. Directly below him, in an oak tree, a crow congress had convened. The tree was black with crows all cawing at once.

Then Jody's eyes followed the wagon road down from the ridge where he stood, and lost it behind a hill, and picked it up again on the other side. On that distant stretch he saw a cart slowly pulled by a bay horse. It disappeared behind the hill. Jody sat down on the ground and watched the place where the cart would reappear again. The wind sang on the hilltops and the puff-ball clouds hurried eastward.

Then the cart came into sight and stopped. A man dressed in black dismounted from the seat and walked to the horse's head. Although it was so far away, Jody knew he had unhooked the check-rein, for the horse's head dropped forward. The horse moved on, and the man walked slowly up the hill beside it. Jody gave a glad cry and ran down the road toward them. The squirrels bumped along off the road, and a road-runner flirted its tail and raced over the edge of the hill and sailed out like a glider.

Jody tried to leap into the middle of his shadow at every step. A stone rolled under his foot and he went down. Around a little bend he raced, and there, a short distance ahead, were his grandfather and the cart. The boy dropped from his unseemly running and approached at a dignified walk.

The horse plodded stumble-footedly up the hill and the old man walked beside it. In the lowering sun their giant shadows flickered darkly behind them. The grandfather was dressed in a black broadcloth suit and he wore kid congress gaiters and a black tie on a short, hard collar. He carried his black slouch hat in his hand. His white beard was cropped close and his white eyebrows overhung his eyes like moustaches. The blue eyes were sternly merry. About the whole face and figure there was a granite dignity, so that every motion seemed an impossible thing. Once at rest, it seemed the old man would be stone, would never move again. His steps were slow and certain. Once made, no step could ever be retraced; once headed in a direction, the path would never bend nor the pace increase nor slow.

When Jody appeared around the bend, Grandfather waved his hat slowly in welcome, and he called, "Why, Jody! Come down to meet me, have you?"

Jody sidled near and turned and matched his step to the old man's step and stiffened his body and dragged his heels a little. "Yes, sir," he said. "We got your letter only today."

"Should have been here yesterday," said Grandfather. "It certainly should. How are all the folks?"

"They're fine, sir." He hesitated and then suggested shyly, "Would you like to come on a mouse hunt tomorrow, sir?"

"Mouse hunt, Jody?" Grandfather chuckled. "Have the people of this generation come down to hunting mice? They aren't very strong, the new people, but I hardly thought mice would be game for them."

"No, sir. It's just play. The haystack's gone. I'm going to drive out the mice to the dogs. And you can watch, or even beat the hay a little."

The stern, merry eyes turned down on him. "I see. You don't eat them, then. You haven't come to that yet."

Jody explained, "The dogs eat them, sir. It wouldn't be much like hunting Indians, I guess."

"No, not much—but then later, when the troops were hunting Indians and shooting children and burning teepees, it wasn't much different from your mouse hunt."

They topped the rise and started down into the ranch cup, and they lost the sun from their shoulders. "You've grown," Grandfather said. "Nearly an inch, I should say."

"More," Jody boasted. "Where they mark me on the door, I'm up more than an inch since Thanksgiving even."

Grandfather's rich throaty voice said, "Maybe you're getting too much water and turning to pith and stalk. Wait until you head out, and then we'll see."

Jody looked quickly into the old man's face to see whether his feelings should be hurt, but there was no will to injure, no punishment nor putting-in-your-place light in the keen blue eyes. "We might kill a pig," Jody suggested.

"Oh, no! I couldn't let you do that. You're just humoring me. It isn't the time and you know it."

"You know Riley, the big boar, sir?"

"Yes. I remember Riley well."

"Well, Riley ate a hole into that same haystack, and it fell down on him and smothered him."

"Pigs do that when they can," said Grandfather.

"Riley was a nice pig, for a boar, sir. I rode him sometimes, and he didn't mind."

A door slammed at the house below them, and they saw Jody's mother standing on the porch waving her apron in welcome. And they saw Carl Tiflin walking up from the barn to be at the house for the arrival.

The sun had disappeared from the hills by now. The blue smoke from the house chimney hung in flat layers in the purpling ranchcup. The puff-ball clouds, dropped by the falling wind, hung listlessly in the sky.

Billy Buck came out of the bunkhouse and flung a wash basin of soapy water on the ground. He had been shaving in mid-week, for Billy held Grandfather in reverence, and Grandfather said that Billy was one of the few men of the new generation who had not gone soft. Although Billy was in middle age, Grandfather considered him a boy. Now Billy was hurrying toward the house too.

When Jody and Grandfather arrived, the three were waiting for them in front of the yard gate.

Carl said, "Hello, sir. We've been looking for you."

Mrs. Tiflin kissed Grandfather on the side of his beard, and stood still while his big hand patted her shoulder. Billy shook hands solemnly, grinning under his straw moustache. "I'll put up your horse," said Billy, and he led the rig away.

Grandfather watched him go, and then, turning back to the group, he said as he had said a hundred times before, "There's a good boy. I knew his father, old Mule-tail Buck. I never knew why they called him Mule-tail except he packed mules."

Mrs. Tiflin turned and led the way into the house. "How long are you going to stay, Father? Your letter didn't say."

"Well, I don't know. I thought I'd stay about two weeks. But I never stay as long as I think I'm going to."

In a short while they were sitting at the white oilcloth table eating their supper. The lamp with the tin reflector hung over the table. Outside the dining-room windows the big moths battered softly against the glass.

Grandfather cut his steak into tiny pieces and chewed slowly. "I'm hungry," he said. "Driving out here got my appetite up. It's like when we were crossing. We all got so hungry every night we could hardly wait to let the meat get done. I could eat about five pounds of buffalo meat every night."

"It's moving around does it," said Billy. "My father was a government packer. I helped him when I was a kid. Just the two of us could clean up a deer's ham."

"I knew your father, Billy," said Grandfather. "A fine man he was. They called him Mule-tail Buck. I don't know why except he packed mules."

"That was it," Billy agreed. "He packed mules."

Grandfather put down his knife and fork and looked around the table. "I remember one time we ran out of meat—" His voice dropped to a curious low sing-song, dropped into a tonal groove the story had worn for itself. "There was no buffalo, no antelope, not even rabbits. The hunters couldn't even shoot a coyote. That was the time for the leader to be on the watch. I was the leader, and I kept my eyes open. Know why? Well, just the minute the people began to get hungry they'd start slaughtering the team oxen. Do you believe that? I've heard of parties that just ate up their draft cattle. Started from the middle and worked towards the ends. Finally they'd eat the lead pair, and then the wheelers. The leader of a party had to keep them from doing that."

In some manner a big moth got into the room and circled the hanging kerosene lamp. Billy got up and tried to clap it between his hands. Carl

223

struck with a cupped palm and caught the moth and broke it. He walked to the window and dropped it out.

"As I was saying," Grandfather began again, but Carl interrupted him. "You'd better eat some more meat. All the rest of us are ready for our pudding."

Jody saw a flash of anger in his mother's eyes. Grandfather picked up his knife and fork. "I'm pretty hungry, all right," he said. "I'll tell you about that later."

When supper was over, when the family and Billy Buck sat in front of the fireplace in the other room, Jody anxiously watched Grandfather. He saw the signs he knew. The bearded head leaned forward; the eyes lost their sternness and looked wonderingly into the fire; the big lean fingers laced themselves on the black knees. "I wonder," he began, "I just wonder whether I ever told you how those thieving Piutes drove off thirty-five of our horses."

"I think you did," Carl interrupted. "Wasn't it just before you went up into the Tahoe country?"

Grandfather turned quickly toward his son-in-law. "That's right. I guess I must have told you that story."

"Lots of times," Carl said cruelly, and he avoided his wife's eyes. But he felt the angry eyes on him, and he said, " 'Course I'd like to hear it again."

Grandfather looked back at the fire. His fingers unlaced and laced again. Jody knew how he felt, how his insides were collapsed and empty. Hadn't Jody been called a Big-Britches that very afternoon? He arose to heroism and opened himself to the term Big-Britches again. "Tell about Indians," he said softly.

Grandfather's eyes grew stern again. "Boys always want to hear about Indians. It was a job for men, but boys want to hear about it. Well, let's see. Did I ever tell you how I wanted each wagon to carry a long iron plate?"

Everyone but Jody remained silent. Jody said, "No. You didn't."

"Well, when the Indians attacked, we always put the wagons in a circle and fought from between the wheels. I thought that if every wagon carried a long plate with rifle holes, the men could stand the plates on the outside of the wheels when the wagons were in the circle and they would be protected. It would save lives and that would make up for the extra weight of the iron. But of course the party wouldn't do it. No party had done it before

224

and they couldn't see why they should go to the expense. They lived to regret it, too."

Jody looked at his mother, and knew from her expression that she was not listening at all. Carl picked at a callus on his thumb and Billy Buck watched a spider crawling up the wall.

Grandfather's tone dropped into its narrative groove again. Jody knew in advance exactly what words would fall. The story droned on, speeded up for the attack, grew sad over the wounds, struck a dirge at the burials on the great plains. Jody sat quietly watching Grandfather. The stern blue eyes were detached. He looked as though he were not very interested in the story himself.

When it was finished, when the pause had been politely respected as the frontier of the story, Billy Buck stood up and stretched and hitched his trousers. "I guess I'll turn in," he said. Then he faced Grandfather. "I've got an old powder horn and a cap and ball pistol down to the bunkhouse. Did I ever show them to you?"

Grandfather nodded slowly. "Yes, I think you did, Billy. Reminds me of a pistol I had when I was leading the people across." Billy stood politely until the little story was done, and then he said, "Good night," and went out of the house.

Carl Tiflin tried to turn the conversation then. "How's the country between here and Monterey? I've heard it's pretty dry."

"It is dry," said Grandfather. "There's not a drop of water in the Laguna Seca. But it's a long pull from '87. The whole country was powder then, and in '61 I believe all the coyotes starved to death. We had fifteen inches of rain this year."

"Yes, but it all came too early. We could do with some now." Carl's eye fell on Jody. "Hadn't you better be getting to bed?"

Jody stood up obediently. "Can I kill the mice in the old haystack, sir?"

"Mice? Oh! Sure, kill them all off. Billy said there isn't any good hay left."

Jody exchanged a secret and satisfying look with Grandfather. "I'll kill every one tomorrow," he promised.

Jody lay in his bed and thought of the impossible world of Indians and buffaloes, a world that had ceased to be forever. He wished he could have been living in the heroic time, but he knew he was not of heroic timber. No one living now, save possibly Billy Buck, was worthy to do the things that had been done. A race of giants had lived then, fearless men, men of a staunchness unknown in this day. Jody thought of the wide plains and of the wagons moving across like centipedes. He thought of Grandfather on a huge white horse, marshaling the people. Across his mind marched the great phantoms, and they marched off the earth and they were gone.

He came back to the ranch for a moment, then. He heard the dull rushing sound that space and silence make. He heard one of the dogs, out in the doghouse, scratching a flea and bumping his elbow against the floor with every stroke. Then the wind arose again and the black cypress groaned and Jody went to sleep.

He was up half an hour before the triangle sounded for breakfast. His mother was rattling the stove to make the flames roar when Jody went through the kitchen. "You're up early," she said. "Where are you going?"

"Out to get a good stick. We're going to kill the mice today."

"Who is 'we'?"

"Why, Grandfather and I."

"So you've got him in it. You always like to have someone in with you in case there's blame to share."

"I'll be right back," said Jody. "I just want to have a good stick ready for after breakfast."

He closed the screen door after him and went out into the cool blue morning. The birds were noisy in the dawn and the ranch cats came down from the hill like blunt snakes. They had been hunting gophers in the dark, and although the four cats were full of gopher meat, they sat in a semi-circle at the back door and mewed piteously for milk. Doubletree Mutt and Smasher moved sniffing along the edge of the brush, performing the duty with rigid ceremony, but when Jody whistled, their heads jerked up and their tails waved. They plunged down to him, wriggling their skins and yawning. Jody patted their heads seriously, and moved on to the weathered scrap pile. He selected an old broom handle and a short piece of inch-square scrap wood. From his pocket he took a shoelace and tied the ends of the sticks loosely together to make a flail. He whistled his new weapon through the air and struck the ground experimentally, while the dogs leaped aside and whined with apprehension.

Jody turned and started down past the house toward the old haystack ground to look over the field of slaughter, but Billy Buck, sitting patiently on the back steps, called to him, "You better come back. It's only a couple of minutes till breakfast."

Jody changed his course and moved toward the house. He leaned his flail against the steps. "That's to drive the mice out," he said. "I'll bet they're fat. I'll bet they don't know what's going to happen to them today."

"No, nor you either," Billy remarked philosophically, "nor me, nor anyone."

Jody was staggered by this thought. He knew it was true. His imagination twitched away from the mouse hunt. Then his mother came out on the back porch and struck the triangle, and all thoughts fell in a heap.

Grandfather hadn't appeared at the table when they sat down. Billy nodded at his empty chair. "He's all right? He isn't sick?"

"He takes a long time to dress," said Mrs. Tiflin. "He combs his whiskers and rubs up his shoes and brushes his clothes."

Carl scattered sugar on his mush. "A man that's led a wagon train across the plains has got to be pretty careful how he dresses."

Mrs. Tiflin turned on him. "Don't do that, Carl! Please don't!" there was more of threat than of request in her tone. And the threat irritated Carl.

"Well, how many times do I have to listen to the story of the iron plates, and the thirty-five horses? That time's done. Why can't he forget it, now it's done?" He grew angrier while he talked, and his voice rose. "Why does he have to tell them over and over? He came across the plains. All right! Now it's finished. Nobody wants to hear about it over and over."

The door into the kitchen closed softly. The four at the table sat frozen. Carl laid his mush spoon on the table and touched his chin with his fingers.

Then the kitchen door opened and Grandfather walked in. His mouth smiled tightly and his eyes were squinted. "Good morning," he said, and he sat down and looked at his mush dish.

Carl could not leave it there. "Did did you hear what I said?"

Grandfather jerked a little nod.

"I don't know what got into me, sir. I didn't mean it. I was just being funny."

Jody glanced in shame at his mother, and he saw that she was looking at Carl, and that she wasn't breathing. It was an awful thing that he was doing. He was tearing himself to pieces to talk like that. It was a terrible thing to him to retract a word, but to retrace it in shame was infinitely worse.

Grandfather looked sidewise. "I'm trying to get right side up," he said gently. "I'm not being mad. I don't mind what you said, but it might be true, and I would mind that."

"It isn't true," said Carl. "I'm not feeling well this morning. I'm sorry I said it."

"Don't be sorry, Carl. An old man doesn't see things sometimes. Maybe you're right. The crossing is finished. Maybe it should be forgotten, now it's done."

Carl got up from the table. "I've had enough to eat. I'm going to work. Take your time, Billy!" He walked quickly out of the diningroom. Billy gulped the rest of his food and followed soon after. But Jody could not leave his chair.

"Won't you tell any more stories?" Jody asked.

"Why, sure I'll tell them, but only when—I'm sure people want to hear them."

"I like to hear them, sir."

"Oh! Of course you do, but you're a little boy. It was a job for men, but only little boys like to hear about it."

Jody got up from his place. "I'll wait outside for you, sir. I've got a good stick for those mice."

He waited by the gate until the old man came out on the porch. "Let's go down and kill the mice now," Jody called.

"I think I'll just sit in the sun, Jody. You go kill the mice."

"You can use my stick if you like."

"No, I'll just sit here a while."

Jody turned disconsolately away, and walked down toward the old haystack. He tried to whip up his enthusiasm with thoughts of the fat juicy mice. He beat the ground with his flail. The dogs coaxed and whined about him, but he could not go. Back at the house he could see Grandfather sitting on the porch, looking small and thin and black.

Jody gave up and went to sit on the steps at the old man's feet.

"Back already? Did you kill the mice?"

"No, sir. I'll kill them some other day."

The morning flies buzzed close to the ground and the ants dashed about in front of the steps. The heavy smell of sage slipped down the hill. The porch boards grew warm in the sunshine.

Jody hardly knew when Grandfather started to talk. "I shouldn't stay here, feeling the way I do." He examined his strong old hands. "I feel as though the crossing wasn't worth doing." His eyes moved up the side-hill and stopped on a motionless hawk perched on a dead limb. "I tell those old stories, but they're not what I want to tell. I only know how I want people to feel when I tell them.

"It wasn't Indians that were important, nor adventures, nor even getting out here. It was a whole bunch of people made into one big crawling beast. And I was the head. It was westering and westering. Every man wanted something for himself, but the big beast that was all of them wanted only westering. I was the leader, but if I hadn't been there, someone else would have been the head. The thing had to have a head.

"Under the little bushes the shadows were black at white noonday. When we saw the mountains at last, we cried—all of us. But it wasn't getting here that mattered, it was movement and westering.

"We carried life out here and set it down the way those ants carry eggs. And I was the leader. The westering was as big as God, and the slow steps that made the movement piled up and piled up until the continent was crossed.

"Then we came down to the sea, and it was done." He stopped and wiped his eyes until the rims were red. "That's what I should be telling instead of stories."

When Jody spoke, Grandfather started and looked down at him. "Maybe I could lead the people some day," Jody said.

The old man smiled. "There's no place to go. There's the ocean to stop you. There's a line of old men along the shore hating the ocean because it stopped them."

"In boats I might, sir."

"No place to go, Jody. Every place is taken. But that's not the worst—no, not the worst. Westering has died out of the people. Westering isn't a hunger any more. It's all done. Your father is right. It is finished." He laced his fingers on his knees and looked at them.

Jody felt very sad. "If you'd like a glass of lemonade I could make it for you."

Grandfather was about to refuse, and then he saw Jody's face. "That would be nice," he said. "Yes, it would be nice to drink a lemonade."

Jody ran into the kitchen where his mother was wiping the last of the breakfast dishes. "Can I have a lemon to make a lemonade for Grandfather?"

His mother mimicked—"And another lemon to make a lemonade for you."

"No, ma'am. I don't want one."

"Jody! You're sick!" Then she stopped suddenly. "Take a lemon out of the cooler," she said softly. "Here, I'll reach the squeezer down to you."

Migrant Mother, Nipomo, California, Dorothea Lange

Western Addition

MAYA ANGELOU

In the early months of World War II, San Francisco's Fillmore district, or the Western Addition, experienced a visible revolution. On the surface it appeared to be totally peaceful and almost a refutation of the term "revolution." The Yakamoto Sea Food Market quietly became Sammy's Shoe Shine Parlor and Smoke Shop. Yashigira's Hardware metamorphosed into La Salon de Beauté owned by Miss Clorinda Jackson. The Japanese shops which sold products to Nisei customers were taken over by enterprising Negro businessmen, and in less than a year became permanent homes away from home for the newly arrived Southern Blacks. Where the odors of tempura, raw fish and *cha* had dominated, the aroma of chitlings, greens and ham hocks now prevailed.

The Asian population dwindled before my eyes. I was unable to tell the Japanese from the Chinese and as yet found no real difference in the national origin of such sounds as Ching and Chan or Moto and Kano.

As the Japanese disappeared, soundlessly and without protest, the Negroes entered with their loud jukeboxes, their just-released animosities and the relief of escape from Southern bonds. The Japanese area became San Francisco's Harlem in a matter of months.

A person unaware of all the factors that make up oppression might have expected sympathy or even support from the Negro newcomers for the dislodged Japanese. Especially in view of the fact that they (the Blacks) had themselves undergone concentration-camp living for centuries in slavery's plantations and later in sharecroppers' cabins. But the sensations of common relationship were missing.

The Black newcomer had been recruited on the dessicated farm lands of Georgia and Mississippi by war-plant labor scouts. The chance to live in two- or three-story apartment buildings (which became instant slums), and to earn two- and even three-figured weekly checks, was blinding. For the first time he could think of himself as a Boss, a Spender. He was able to pay

232

other people to work for him, i.e. the dry cleaners, taxi drivers, waitresses, etc. The shipyards and ammunition plants brought to booming life by the war let him know that he was needed and even appreciated. A completely alien yet very pleasant position for him to experience. Who could expect this man to share his new and dizzying importance with concern for a race that he had never known to exist?

Another reason for his indifference to the Japanese removal was more subtle but was more profoundly felt. The Japanese were not whitefolks. Their eyes, language and customs belied the white skin and proved to their dark successors that since they didn't have to be feared, neither did they have to be considered. All this was decided unconsciously.

No member of my family and none of the family friends ever mentioned the absent Japanese. It was as if they had never owned or lived in the houses we inhabited. On Post Street, where our house was, the hill skidded slowly down to Fillmore, the market heart of our district. In the two short blocks before it reached its destination, the street housed two day-and-night restaurants, two pool halls, four Chinese restaurants, two gambling houses, plus diners, shoeshine shops, beauty salons, barber shops and at least four churches. To fully grasp the never-ending activity in San Francisco's Negro neighborhood during the war, one need only know that the two blocks described were side streets that were duplicated many times over in the eight- to ten-square-block area.

The air of collective displacement, the impermanence of life in wartime and the gauche personalities of the more recent arrivals tended to dissipate my own sense of not belonging. In San Francisco, for the first time, I perceived myself as part of something. Not that I identified with the new-comers, nor with the rare Black descendants of native San Franciscans, nor with the whites or even the Asians, but rather with the times and the city. I understood the arrogance of the young sailors who marched the streets in marauding gangs, approaching every girl as if she were at best a prostitute and at worst an Axis agent bent on making the U.S.A. lose the war. The un-dertone of fear that San Francisco would be bombed which was abetted by weekly air raid warnings, and civil defense drills in school, heightened my sense of belonging. Hadn't I, always, but ever and ever, thought that life was just one great risk for the living?

Then the city acted in wartime like an intelligent woman under siege. She gave what she couldn't with safety withhold, and secured those things which lay in her reach. The city became for me the ideal of what I wanted to be as a grownup. Friendly but never gushing, cool but not frigid or distant, distinguished without the awful stiffness.

To San Franciscans "the City That Knows How" was the Bay, the fog, Sir Francis Drake Hotel, Top o' the Mark, Chinatown, the Sunset District and so on and so forth and so white. To me, a thirteen-year-old Black girl, stalled by the South and Southern Black life style, the city was a state of beauty and a state of freedom. The fog wasn't simply the steamy vapors off the bay caught and penned in by hills, but a soft breath of anonymity that shrouded and cushioned the bashful traveler. I became dauntless and free of fears, intoxicated by the physical fact of San Francisco. Safe in my protecting arrogance, I was certain that no one loved her as impartially as I. I walked around the Mark Hopkins and gazed at the Top o' the Mark, but (maybe sour grapes) was more impressed by the view of Oakland from the hill than by the tiered building or its fur-draped visitors. For weeks, after the city and I came to terms about my belonging, I haunted the points of interest and found them empty and un-San Francisco. The naval officers with their well-dressed wives and clean white babies inhabited another time-space dimension than I. The well-kept old women in chauffeured cars and blond girls in buckskin shoes and cashmere sweaters might have been San Franciscans, but they were at most gilt on the frame of my portrait of the city.

Pride and Prejudice stalked in tandem the beautiful hills. Native San Franciscans, possessive of the city, had to cope with an influx, not of awed respectful tourists but of raucous unsophisticated provincials. They were also forced to live with skin-deep guilt brought on by the treatment of their former Nisei schoolmates.

Southern white illiterates brought their biases intact to the West from the hills of Arkansas and the swamps of Georgia. The Black ex-farmers had not left their distrust and fear of whites which history had taught them in distressful lessons. These two groups were obliged to work side by side in the war plants, and their animosities festered and opened like boils on the face of the city.

San Franciscans would have sworn on the Golden Gate Bridge that racism was missing from the heart of their air-conditioned city. But they would have been sadly mistaken.

A story went the rounds about a San Franciscan white matron who

234

refused to sit beside a Negro civilian on the streetcar, even after he made room for her on the seat. Her explanation was that she would not sit beside a draft dodger who was a Negro as well. She added that the least he could do was fight for his country the way her son was fighting on Iwo Jima. The story said that the man pulled his body away from the window to show an armless sleeve. He said quietly and with great dignity. "Then ask your son to look around for my arm, which I left over there."

The New Californian

ALISTAIR COOKE

It had been one of those rancid weeks of the Eastern summer, with the temperature in the high nineties, and the streets like ovens, when the sweat gets in your eyes and the newspapers feel like dishcloths. Happily, I had to go to California, to Los Angeles, where they were sympathizing aloud with all those people—and there are not many—who haven't had the sense to move to California. Los Angeles, after all, had invigorating temperatures in the eighties and was stimulated by its healthful smog, a thick steaming yellow layer formed by the sea mists moving in on the industrial smoke of that thriving huge city. It produces a foretaste of the special hell which, a recent survey warns us, will suffocate us all by about 2000 A.D. I expect, myself, to have suffocated in the ordinary course of nature by then. But the young, tanned, long-legged, heedless Californians don't believe in population projections or the existence of hydrocarbons and nitrogen oxides in the air. They have no knowledge and no fear, and perhaps it is the best way to go.

I stayed with a friend who has just built a house on the top of the rim of the mountains that form a bowl in which sits Los Angeles. He himself is just above the smog line, so that on clear days you can see forever; but on most days you can watch, or imagine, the quarter of a million workers on aircraft and space equipment stewing in the San Fernando Valley. He is fairly new to California. So he is, like all such, a professional Californian. They are a particular human breed, much touchier than the oldest resident about the usual complaints—the peaches the size of footballs that have no taste, the roses the size of grapefruit that have no smell. With such a man you do not discuss what is good or bad, what is awful and wonderful about California. It is all miraculous and it will go on forever.

We drove directly from the airport to his house, first whizzing twenty miles along the freeway buckled in our seat belts and slotted in one of the eight lanes of the highway. We came off it and went winding up a two-lane

236

spiral till there was nothing above us but the burned-out shrubbery of the mountains and beyond that the sky and a wheeling buzzard or two. Along the way he talked about what other people might think of as the problems of living in California but which he—a boy from Missouri who had lived most of his life in Chicago—called rather the joy of building his little gray home in the West. "You know something," he said, "there's nothing like it out here. Nothing. You wait and see."

I did not have to wait long. I saw a whole mountainside plowed away, or rather sliced away, and the slice deposited in the valley below and pressed down by an armored battalion to provide a stable bed for a "development" of three hundred new ranch-type "homes," what we used to call bungalows. It was not a pretty sight and he conceded that "we're doing something about these raiders. We've gotten together, one or two of us around here, and formed a protective association. We've done a bit of lobbying in Sacramento and we hope to get the state in on this thing, declare this section a state park or forest or something."

We wheeled around the face of a mountain veined with firebreaks and passed a new firehouse. "That's another of our little projects," he said. "Costs like the devil but it makes you feel a little easier nights." We swung up and down and plunged into a long curving driveway and came to his—I almost said garage—to his carport. (A low bridge in California is not a low bridge; the signs say, "Impaired vertical clearance.") He thinks of shoving this two-car garage back into the mountainside and extending the present patio to provide for a tennis court. Meanwhile, he showed me a small decorative wall high above the house with a carpet of thick vines between it and another wall of the same design—a sort of Regency, Greek-key motif. "Very pretty," I said.

"Hell, that's not décor," he said, "that's protection. Those are fire walls. And the vines, too; they're not very decorative either, but they burn very slow and give off lots of smoke, so you won't be caught napping." This reminded me that I had got up at four a.m. his time and had a five-hour flight, and I was going to suggest a nap but thought better of it.

I met his maid, a smiling German girl, and when she'd gone away he whispered to me that he'd insisted she take driving lessons. Although I've known California for over thirty years I didn't instantly get the connection. But it was very firm to him. "You don't think I want a girl marooned here in the middle of the night—trapped by a forest fire. She doesn't think she's a very good driver but I told her just so she can get out and down the mountain."

We next examined the automatic sprinkler system he has installed in the bushes above the house and around the small garden. "Goes on," he explained, "whenever the ground heat rises above a certain temperature." The sort of precaution that more of us should take. At any rate, he told me I could relax, and anyone who has seen a California fire gobble up the tinder of the mountain brush should be grateful for this reassurance.

"Well," he said with a cheerful change of tone, "how about a dip?" He indicated the kidney-shaped pool and its glimmering turquoise water. I motioned to unbutton a shirt. "Hold it!" he commanded, and just in time. Because there was a pleasant young man walking toward us from the hillside and he had in his hand a long pipe like a giant vacuum cleaner. He started to dip it in the pool. He was filtering the water and clearing off a light scum of leaves. My friend groaned. "I tell you, trying to keep this pool clear. God knows what it costs by now."

By the time the young man had finished his filtering we were pretty burned up by the sun, which you might think is the whole idea of southern California. "No point," said my host, "sitting and sweating out here; let's get inside where we can breathe right." We went in through a glass-paneled door and sat in his large circular living room and breathed right. He walked over to a thermostat on the wall and flicked it with a fingernail. It let off a minute fizzing sound like a small escape of soda water. "That'll be better," he said and indicated that he had set the air conditioning at seventy. It was dry and cool. So now, what? The sun was blazing away but sinking fast. Obviously, it was time to think of a drink. This is always a very delicate moment in the joust known as status seeking. It is entirely possible that Californians by themselves drink nothing but beer or distilled barley juice. But the visitor feels compelled to act for a time like his picture of a "typical Californian." So, even more, do the new Californians. Anywhere else on earth you might say Scotch or a martini. But it is part of the California legend, accepted without question by all Easterners, that Californians change the fashion in drinks about as often as they change their playshirts. I well remember, about ten years ago, when another new Californian casually suggested a "bullshot," and I looked at him as if he had suggested an elk or a buffalo. A bullshot was just then coming in California and would, in the nor-

238

mal course of time (about two years), make its way to such outlying provincial capitals as New York and Washington.

"You honestly don't know what a bullshot is?" my friend asked in amused astonishment. "How about Vietnam?"

"That I've heard of," I said.

He explained, like a doctor telling a small tot how to swallow an aspirin tablet. "Just beef bouillon with a slug of vodka." It is one way of taking soup and getting plastered at the same time. So now my new host made a suggestion or two—"A screwdriver, mountain mule? How about the Thing?"

"How about," I said quickly, "a bullshot?"

"Sure," he said, "why not?" and his expression conveyed that he was not the type to jeer at a maiden aunt who sticks to her gooseberry wine. He made the Thing for himself, and I'm not going to give away *that* recipe, not before it gets served in the White House. He handed me what I would call a tureen but what he assured me was listed in the catalogue as a "party goblet." It contained about a quart of bullshot.

He stretched himself and leaned over to a large jewel box, which might have been a monster cigarette lighter equipped for a man who was going to sit and smoke himself to death without moving. It was a cigarette lighter. It too fizzed and ejected streams of invisible gas, but no light. He picked up a miniature Bible. It was also a cigarette lighter. More fruitless clickings. I thought it was time I did something to restore the prestige of the East. "Remember George Kaufman's line about cigarette lighters?" I yawned.

He was now juggling cigarette lighters the way a Japanese salesman handles transistor radios. "No," he said, "what did Kaufman say?"

"He said that if matches had been invented after lighters they'd be the sensation of the twentieth century."

"A great line," he chortled and went off to the kitchen for a match. At last we sat and sighed and hugged our drinks. "God!" he cried suddenly and quietly, weary beyond telling. He looked across the pool to a fringe of lawn encircled by a short wall which stopped you falling down a bank of vines and the mountain. "Look at that miserable grass! Nobody knows de trouble I seen with that grass."

I peered into the declining sun at the frowzy lawn. "It does look a little beaten up," I said.

"Not beaten up," he snorted, "eaten up."

I was about to ask by whom or what, but at that moment something popped through a hole in the wall, bounced on the lawn, jumped up on the wall, and sat facing out over the valley with its back to us. It looked like one of those gargoyles gazing out over Paris, but knowing a little about the exotic fauna of California I guessed it might be a mongoose or possibly a miniature kangaroo.

"Damn squirrels," muttered my host, "they nibble away everywhere." He reeled off a whole seed catalogue of grasses he'd planted and torn up. "But it does no good, we're just overrun with opossum and skunks and squirrels and muskrat, and the goddam deer come roaming in at night. But gophers. Gophers are the worst. Just look at those holes!"

Through the orange haze of the sunlight I could just see what he meant. It was not so much a lawn as a chewed-up, rudimentary putting green. He marched off into his bedroom and returned with a rifle. He gingerly slid open the glass doors. He sat just inside the room, and while he was loading the rifle he flicked what I thought was another cigarette lighter, but it was something else this time and the television set whooshed on. A sheriff or a rustler was galloping through a canyon and letting off cannonades of rifle fire. My friend lifted the rifle from his lap and looked toward the lawn—an alert, suburban Hemingway. A gopher stuck its head out of a hole. My friend sighted and banged away. From the telly came an answering blast of gunsmoke.

"Yes, sir," said my friend, "it's a great life out here."

"You can say that again," I said. He said it again.

240

Highway Moderne, Marin County, CA, Peter Monahan

A Supermarket in California

ALLEN GINSBERG

What thoughts I have of you tonight, Walt Whitman,
for I walked down the sidestreets under the trees with a
headache self-conscious looking at the full moon.

In my hungry fatigue, and shopping for images, I
went into the neon fruit supermarket, dreaming of your
enumerations!

What peaches and what penumbras! Whole families
shopping at night! Aisles full of husbands! Wives in the
avocados, babies in the tomatoes!—and you, Garcia Lorca,
what were you doing down by the watermelons?

I saw you, Walt Whitman, childless, lonely old
grubber, poking among the meats in the refrigerator
and eyeing the grocery boys.

I heard you asking questions of each: Who killed the
pork chops? What price bananas? Are you my Angel?

I wandered in and out of the brilliant stacks of cans
following you, and followed in my imagination by the
store detective.

We strode down the open corridors together in our
solitary fancy tasting artichokes, possessing every frozen
delicacy, and never passing the cashier.

Where are we going, Walt Whitman? The doors close
in an hour. Which way does your beard point tonight?

(I touch your book and dream of our odyssey in the
supermarket and feel absurd.)

Will we walk all night through solitary streets? The
trees add shade to shade, lights out in the houses, we'll
both be lonely.

Will we stroll dreaming of the lost America of love
past blue automobiles in driveways, home to our silent cottage?
Ah, dear father, graybeard, lonely old courage—teacher,
what America did you have when Charon quit poling
his ferry and you got out on a smoking bank and stood
watching the boat disappear on the black waters of Lethe?

The New West

The West is a country of the mind, and so eternal.
—ARCHIBALD MACLEISH

The end of one of America's greatest novels has Huck turn his back on getting "sivilized" and strike out for "the territory ahead." His youth, innocence, experience, resourcefulness, humor, guile, and courage all incline westward, toward possibilities larger than anything observed on the river. His final act instinctively points toward more adventure, new opportunity, unclaimed land and wealth, a measure of risk balanced against the promise of reward, and the unshakeable conviction that a man could find or make a better life. Twain had the sense not to pursue the matter. Huck remains a boy forever, just as the West remains forever possible in the American mind.

Museums, annual celebrations, and the entertainment industry preserve the Wild West in memory. But legends and legacies die hard, and the heritage survives in towns between the prairies and now crowded Pacific Slope. Despite the recreation boom and the continuing plunder of resources, vast reaches resist development. Mile after mile of the Great American Desert refuses to bloom, despite the dreams of promoters whose optimism has never been limited by the reality of available resources.

Until air transport made all sections of the continent no more distant than a day's travel, isolation was part of the West's psychological as well as geographical experience. Crossing the sparsely settled interior of the region, motorists who stray from the interstate freeways can still encounter a living sense of the past, a breed of self-reliance imposed by distance, a friendliness long vanished in more populous areas.

The western experience still challenges the people who live there with a new set of problems. If the region is to retain its character, its people must assert those baffling virtues ascribed to them by historian Walter Prescott Webb: "They are," he said, "unconventional, because they could not make conventions work, found success only by defying them. They altered everything, would try anything, and were satisfied with nothing. They puzzled their neighbors, one another, and themselves."*

The tremendous growth of population and industry in the last quarter century has brought new forces into direct conflict. Advocates of technology and commerce who believe that continued growth insures a vital economy and guarantees the good life have run into opposition from environmentalists who believe that air and land and water and space must be protected and preserved or lost forever. Courts and legislatures have become battlegrounds for competing interests, where this time public awareness that resources are not infinite has stalled and may avert wholesale, full-scale exploitation.

Power combines have plans to strip mine the deserts of the southwest and range lands of the Rocky Mountains, dam the last tributaries of the Columbia Basin, place nuclear reactors down the Pacific shore, all to supply energy for distant regions. The pollution from generating plants, refineries, and reactors threatens to bring all the advantages of urban murk to remote scenic spaces. In air-conditioned suites, energy planners justify this last great raid on the West's resources by claiming it is the price people must pay to maintain their standard of living. Thus while the legacy of fresh air, clear skies, and open space cannot be exported, it can certainly be

---

*Walter Prescott Webb, "What is 'The West'?" in *This Is the West*, Robert Howard, ed. (Chicago: Rand McNally, 1957), p. 8.

degraded, bringing another kind of democracy to what is left of the frontier: the democracy of blight and clutter.

The integrity of the land as well as the quality of life hang in the balance. Perhaps the last great battle for the West is now in progress. Combines and government agencies have joined the historical parade of opportunists in a race to determine not who gets there first but who gets what is left. The West is up for grabs again, and the exploiters, with technology and politics and tradition on their side, know how to get around or, if necessary, plow under the present natives. We shall see who wins this time.

Some images endure. Homage is still paid to the cowboy legend, particularly by the Western Writers of America, whose three hundred members faithfully churn out horse opera. Its classic stereotypes pace through dust-covered plots to melodramatic showdowns. Both print and screen spin out yarns for an audience much in need of heroes and ready to escape into a mythic nineteenth-century landscape where simple solutions are imaginable. However, perhaps the dominant image of the New West is the four-wheel drive pick-up truck, equipped with wide-track tires, C-B radio, stereo tapedeck, and loaded gun rack. Whether on a ranch or in town, new homes are likely to be earth-tone painted aluminum, mobile and unsightly. But these suit the economics of the New West in hot pursuit of the booming energy and recreation industries.

Westerners, like most Americans, view themselves through a tangle of contradictions. Their country and their destiny are less manifest than they were a century ago, for the westward experience failed to shape a coherent culture. Somewhere between El Paso, Jackson Hole, Salt Lake City, Phoenix, Los Angeles, and Seattle, the people made accommodations with the land, took what opportunities they found, but with the exception of the Mormons built no enduring communities. Geography apart, the various results lack completeness, and the difference between cultural fragmentation and regional diversity depends largely on how one regards the spec-

247

tacle beyond the hundredth meridian. Today the real story of the West can be found in the lives of the people who live there, who in Wallace Stegner's words "confront the real problems of real life in a real region, and have gone some distance toward understanding the conditions of western life."* Despite the myths and mirages of the past, the region still promises a new life in a splendid setting. Despite the stereotypes, people still arrive from everywhere. Despite the mistakes and confusion, the idea of the West still generates excitement.

*Wallace Stegner, "Introduction," *The Sound of Mountain Water* (Garden City, N.Y.: Doubleday, 1969), p. 32.

Night Journey

THEODORE ROETHKE

Now as the train bears west,
Its rhythm rocks the earth,
And from my Pullman berth
I stare into the night
While others take their rest.
Bridges of iron lace,
A suddenness of trees,
A lap of mountain mist
All cross my line of sight,
Then a bleak wasted place,
And a lake below my knees.
Full on my neck I feel
The straining at a curve;
My muscles move with steel,
I wake in every nerve.
I watch a beacon swing
From dark to blazing bright;
We thunder through ravines
And gullies washed with light.
Beyond the mountain pass
Mist deepens on the pane;
We rush into a rain
That rattles double glass.
Wheels shake the roadbed stone,
The pistons jerk and shove,
I stay up half the night
To see the land I love.

Powder Face, Charles M. Russell

The Conservatism of
Charles M. Russell

J. FRANK DOBIE

One cannot imagine Charles M. Russell living in a world without horses. If the wheel had never been devised, he could have lived content. The steamboat had carried traders and trappers up the Missouri River and become a feature in the pageant of the West before he was born; he accepted the steamboat, respected it. When in 1880, at the age of sixteen, he went to Montana, he traveled by the railway to its end and then took the stage. The Far West was at that time still an unfenced and comparatively unoccupied expanse of grass and mountains; he accepted and respected the steam engine as one of its features. As it hauled in plows, barbed wire and people, people, people, he would, had he had the power, have Joshuaed the sun to a permanent standstill.

The Russell genius was averse to change. No single collection of his great art could be regarded as a full document on the evolution of transportation in the West; although in his fertile life span he came close to this. Such a series would include the old Red River cart drawn with such casual care in his *Pen Sketches* (about 1899). Other able drawings and paintings, except that of the Pony Express, focus upon conveyances, progressing from dog travois to railroad train, that stress incident and effect upon human beings rather than the transports themselves.

Including the transports, Russell did document the Old West. Plains Indian or frontiersman dominates countless paintings. Russell never generalized. In any Russell picture of horses, for example, a particular horse at a particular time reponds in a particular way to a particular stimulus; in the same way, his man-made objects are viewed under particular circumstances. Here the steamboat and railway train are interesting through the eyes of the Indians whom they are dooming, very much as in one of Russell's paintings a wagon, unseen, is interesting for the alarm that sight of its tracks over prairie grass gives a band of scouting warriors. He was positively not interested in anything bearing mechanical evolution.

251

C. M. Russell's passionate sympathy for the primitive West welled into antipathy for the forces relegating it—and for him automobiles and tractors expressed those forces. He never glimpsed, much less accepted, "the one increasing purpose" in evolutionary processes that enables the contemporary Texas artist, Tom Lea for example, to comprehend with equanimity and equal sympathy the conquistador riding the first horse upon an isolated continent and the airplane that, more than four hundred years afterwards, bridges continents. Each a distinct man and a distinct artist, Tom Lea is at home in a cosmopolitan world of change, whereas Charlie Russell was at home only in a West that had ceased to exist by the time he arrived at artistic maturity. Tom Lea grapples intellectually with his world, is a thinker; Charlie Russell evaluated life out of instinctive predilections. Vitality, that "one thing needful" to all creative work, shows constantly in the work of both.

Russell's opposition to change was but the obverse of his concentration upon the old. His art can be comprehended only through an understanding of his conservatism. It was not the conservatism of the privileged who resent change because change will take away their privileges. It was the conservatism of love and loyalty.

Before he died in 1926, the airplane was changing the world; he dismissed it as a "flying machine." He was fond of skunks, a family of which he protected at his lodge on Lake McDonald, but his name for the automobile was "skunk wagon." His satisfaction in a cartoon he made showing mounted Indians passing a broken-down skunk wagon is manifest. His forward-looking wife Nancy—to whom Russell's career as a serious artist was largely owing—would say to him, "Charlie, why don't you take an interest in something besides the past?" "She lives for tomorrow and I live for yesterday," he said. For a long time he refused to ride in an automobile; he never did put a hand on a steering wheel. "You can have a car," he often said to Nancy, "but I'll stick to my hoss; we understan' each other better." At the World's Fair, in 1903, at St. Louis, the place of his birth and boyhood, he passed by the exhibitions of twentieth-century progress and found kinship with a caged coyote "who licked my hand like he knew me. I guess I brought the smell of plains with me."

"Invention," he wrote to a friend, "has made it easy for mankind but it has made him no better. Machinery has no branes." He resented the advent

252

of the electric lights as deeply, but not so quietly, as Queen Victoria. He once called the automatic rifle a "God-damned diarrhoea gun"—and I wonder how he would have spelled it. The old-time six-shooter and Winchester rifle were good enough for him. In the physical world he was a fundamentalist. It began going to hell for him about 1889, the year that Montana Territory became a state with ambitions to develop. One time Nancy got him to make a speech at a kind of booster gathering. The toastmaster introduced him as a pioneer.

Charlie began: "I have been called a pioneer. In my book a pioneer is a man who comes to a virgin country, traps off all the fur, kills off all the wild meat, cuts down all the trees, grazes off all the grass, plows the roots up, and strings ten million miles of bob wire. A pioneer destroys things and calls it civilization. I wish to God that this country was just like it was when I first saw it and that none of you folks were here at all."

About this time he realized that he had insulted his audience. He grabbed his hat and, in the boots and desperado sash that he always wore, left the room.

A string of verses that he wrote to Robert Vaughn concludes:

> Here's to hell with the booster,
> The land is no longer free,
> The worst old timer I ever knew
> Looks dam good to me.

Russell's devotion to old times, old ways, the Old West did not come from age. It was congenital. Even in infancy he pictured the West of Indians, spaces and outlanders and knew that he wanted it. Only when he got there did he begin to live. When he was forty-three years old, he looked at the "sayling car lines" (elevated) of New York and set down as a principle of life that the "two miles of railroad track and a ficw hacks" back in Great Falls were "swift enouf" for him. From Chicago in 1916 he wrote his friend and neighbor A. J. Trigg:

> It's about thirty-two years since I first saw this burg. I was armed with a punch pole, a stock car under me loaded with grass eaters. I came from the big out doores and the light, smoke and smell made me lonsum. The hole world has changed since then I have not. I'm no more at home in a big city than I was then an I'm still lonsum.

253

He wanted room; he wanted to be left alone; he believed in other people being left alone. His last request was that his body be carried to the grave behind horses and not by a machine, and that is the way it was carried.

In one respect Charlie Russell was far ahead of his contemporaries, who generally said that the only good Indian was a dead Indian. He had profound sympathy for the Plains Indians. His indignation against sharks greedy for their land was acid. "The land hog is the only animal known that lives without a heart." He hated prohibition laws and all kinds of prohibitors; he hated fervidly white men who debauched Indians with liquor. He painted the women and children as well as warriors of several tribes, always with accuracy in physical detail and recognition of their inherent dignity. "Those Indians have been living in heaven for a thousand years," he said to cowman Teddy Blue [Granville Stuart's son-in-law], "and we took it way from 'em for forty dollars a month." When sometimes he spoke of "my people" he meant the Horseback Indians. He called the white man "Nature's enemy." The Indians harmonized with Nature and had no more desire to "conquer" it or alter any aspect of it than a cottontail rabbit.

Over and over, he pictured schooners, freight wagons, packhorses, Indian buffalo hunters, cowboys, Northwest Mounted Police, horse thieves, cow thieves, stage robbers and other horseback men. Bull-whackers, mule skinners, stage drivers and their contemporaries of the frontier were as congenial to him as "Nature's cattle"—among which the coyote and the tortoise were in as good standing as the elk and the antelope and in better standing than a "cococola soke." "He can tell what's the matter with a ford by the nois it makes but he wouldn't know that a wet cold horse with a hump in his back is dangerous."

The "increasing purpose" of man's development of passenger vehicles has been to achieve more speed. Charlie Russell has often been styled the artist of Wild West action. It is true that his range bulls lock horns and his longhorn cows get on the prod, that his cowboys often shoot, that his cow horses are apt to break in two, that his grizzly bears are hungrier for hot blood than Liver-Eating Johnson; in short, that violence was with him a favorite theme. At the same time, no other picturer of the Old West has so lingered in repose. He likes cow horses resting their hips at hitching racks or standing with bridle reins "tied to the ground"; his masterpiece of range life is a trail boss sitting sideways on his horse watching a long herd stringing up a draw as slowly as "the lowing herd" of milk cows winds "o'er the lea" in Gray's *Elegy*. One of his most dramatic paintings is of shadows. The best thing in his superb story of a stampede, "Longrope's Last Guard," in *Trails Plowed Under*, is the final picture of Longrope wrapped in his blankets and put to bed on the lone prairie. "It sounds lonesome, but he ain't alone, cause these old prairies has cradled many of his kind in their long sleep."

In only some of the great paintings in the large C. M. Russell collection at the Historical Society of Montana, in Helena, does drama reside in fast or violent action. There is drama in all Russell art, but it is the drama of potentiality, of shadowing destiny, of something coming, of something left behind. Russell illustrated a little-known pamphlet entitled *Back Trailing on the Old Frontiers*. He was a great traveler in that direction; he was as cold as a frosted crowbar towards the fever for being merely, no matter how rapidly, transported, as afflicts so many Americans today.

If the Old West was important to itself, Charlie Russell was important also, for he was—in art—its most representative figure.

If the Old West is still important in any way to the modern West, Russell remains equally important. If the Old West is important to faraway lands and peoples, Charles M. Russell is important. He not only knew this West, he felt it. It moved him, motivated him, and gave him articulation, as a strong wind on some barren crag shapes all the trees that try to grow there.

Sometimes Russell lacked perspective on the whole of life. Sometimes he overdid violence and action, particularly that brand demanded by appreciators of calendars. But he never betrayed the West.

When one knows and loves the thousands of little truthful details that Charlie Russell put into the ears of horses, the rumps of antelopes, the nostrils of deer, the eyes of buffaloes, the lifted heads of cattle, the lope of coyotes, the stance of a stage driver, the watching of a shadow of himself by a cowboy, the response of an Indian storyteller, the way of a she-bear with her cub, the you-be-damned independence of a monster grizzly, the ignorance of an ambling terrapin, the lay of grass under a breeze, and a whole catalogue of other speaking details dear to any lover of Western life, then one cherishes all of Charles M. Russell.

The Serpents of Paradise

EDWARD ABBEY

The April mornings are bright, clear and calm. Not until the afternoon does the wind begin to blow, raising dust and sand in funnel-shaped
twisters that spin across the desert briefly, like dancers, and then collapse—
whirlwinds from which issue no voice or word except the forlorn moan of
the elements under stress. After the reconnoitering dust-devils comes the
real the serious wind, the voice of the desert rising to a demented howl and
blotting out sky and sun behind yellow clouds of dust, sand, confusion, embattled birds, last year's scrub-oak leaves, pollen, the husks of locusts, bark
of juniper. . . .

Time of the red eye, the sore and bloody nostril, the sand-pitted wind-
shield, if one is foolish enough to drive his car into such a storm. Time to sit
indoors and continue that letter which is never finished—while the fine dust
forms neat little windrows under the edge of the door and on the window-
sills. Yet the springtime winds are as much a part of the canyon country as
the silence and the glamorous distances; you learn, after a number of years,
to love them also.

The mornings therefore, as I started to say and meant to say, are all the
sweeter in the knowledge of what the afternoon is likely to bring. Before
beginning the morning chores I like to sit on the sill of my doorway, bare
feet planted on the bare ground and a mug of hot coffee in hand, facing the
sunrise. The air is gelid, not far above freezing, but the butane heater inside
the trailer keeps my back warm, the rising sun warms the front, and the coffee warms the interior.

Perhaps this is the loveliest hour of the day, though it's hard to choose.
Much depends on the season. In midsummer the sweetest hour begins at
sundown, after the awful heat of the afternoon. But now, in April, we'll take
the opposite, that hour beginning with the sunrise. The birds, returning from
wherever they go in winter, seem inclined to agree. The pinyon jays are
whirling in garrulous, gregarious flocks from one stunted tree to the next

and back again, erratic exuberant games without any apparent practical function. A few big ravens hang around and croak harsh clanking statements of smug satisfaction from the rimrock, lifting their greasy wings now and then to probe for lice. I can hear but seldom see the canyon wrens singing their distinctive song from somewhere up on the cliffs: a flutelike descent—never ascent—of the whole-tone scale. Staking out new nesting claims, I understand. Also invisible but invariably present at some indefinable distance are the mourning doves whose plaintive call suggests irresistibly a kind of seeking-out, the attempt by separated souls to restore a lost communion:

Hello . . . they seem to cry, *who . . . are . . .you?*

And the reply from a different quarter. *Hello* . . . (pause) *where . . . are . . . you?*

No doubt this line of analogy must be rejected. It's foolish and unfair to impute to the doves, with serious concerns of their own, an interest in questions more appropriate to their human kin. Yet their song, if not a mating call or a warning, must be what it sounds like, a brooding meditation on space, on solitude. The game.

Other birds, silent, which I have not yet learned to identify, are also lurking in the vicinity, watching me. What the ornithologist terms l.g.b.'s—little gray birds—they flit about from point to point on noiseless wings, their origins obscure.

As mentioned before, I share the housetrailer with a number of mice. I don't know how many but apparently only a few, perhaps a single family. They don't disturb me and are welcome to my crumbs and leavings. Where they came from, how they got into the trailer, how they survived before my arrival (for the trailer had been locked up for six months), these are puzzling matters I am not prepared to resolve. My only reservation concerning the mice is that they do attract rattlesnakes.

I'm sitting on my doorstep early one morning, facing the sun as usual, drinking coffee, when I happen to look down and see almost between my bare feet, only a couple of inches to the rear of my heels, the very thing I had in mind. No mistaking that wedgelike head, that tip of horny segmented tail peeping out of the coils. He's under the doorstep and in the shade where the ground and air remain very cold. In his sluggish condition he's not likely to strike unless I rouse him by some careless move of my own.

257

There's a revolver inside the trailer, a huge British Webley .45, loaded, but it's out of reach. Even if I had it in my hands I'd hesitate to blast a fellow creature at such close range, shooting between my own legs at a living target flat on solid rock thirty inches away. It would be like murder; and where would I set my coffee? My cherrywood walking stick leans against the trailerhouse wall only a few feet away but I'm afraid that in leaning over for it I might stir up the rattler or spill some hot coffee on his scales.

Other considerations come to mind. Arches National Monument is meant to be among other things a sanctuary for wildlife—for all forms of wildlife. It is my duty as a park ranger to protect, preserve and defend all living things within the park boundaries, making no exceptions. Even if this were not the case I have personal convictions to uphold. Ideals, you might say. I prefer not to kill animals. I'm a humanist; I'd rather kill a *man* than a snake.

What to do. I drink some more coffee and study the dormant reptile at my heels. It is not after all the mighty diamondback, *Crotalus atrox*, I'm confronted with but a smaller species known locally as the horny rattler or more precisely as the Faded Midget. An insulting name for a rattlesnake, which may explain the Faded Midget's alleged bad temper. But the name is apt: he is small and dusty-looking, with a little knob above each eye—the horns. His bite though temporarily disabling would not likely kill a full-grown man in normal health. Even so I don't really want him around. Am I to be compelled to put on boots or shoes every time I wish to step outside? The scorpions, tarantulas, centipedes, and black widows are nuisance enough.

I finish my coffee, lean back and swing my feet up and inside the doorway of the trailer. At once there is a buzzing sound from below and the rattler lifts his head from the coils, eyes brightening, and extends his narrow black tongue to test the air.

After thawing out my boots over the gas flame I pull them on and come back to the doorway. My visitor is still waiting beneath the doorstep, basking in the sun, fully alert. The trailerhouse has two doors. I leave by the other and get a long-handled spade out of the bed of the government pickup. With this tool I scoop the snake into the open. He strikes; I can hear the click of the fangs against steel, see the stain of venom. He wants to stand and fight, but I am patient; I insist on herding him well away from the trailer. On guard, head aloft—that evil slit-eyed weaving head shaped like

258

the ace of spades—tail whirring, the rattler slithers sideways, retreating slowly before me until he reaches the shelter of a sandstone slab. He backs under it.

You better stay there, cousin, I warn him; if I catch you around the trailer again I'll chop your head off.

A week later he comes back. If not him, his twin brother. I spot him one morning under the trailer near the kitchen drain, waiting for a mouse. I have to keep my promise.

This won't do. If there are midget rattlers in the area there may be diamondbacks too—five, six or seven feet long, thick as a man's wrist, dangerous. I don't want *them* camping under my home. It looks as though I'll have to trap the mice.

However, before being forced to take that step I am lucky enough to capture a gopher snake. Burning garbage one morning at the park dump, I see a long slender yellow-brown snake emerge from a mound of old tin cans and plastic picnic plates and take off down the sandy bed of a gulch. There is a burlap sack in the cab of the truck which I carry when plucking Kleenex flowers from the brush and cactus along the road; I grab that and my stick, run after the snake and corner it beneath the exposed roots of a bush. Making sure it's a gopher snake and not something less useful, I open the neck of the sack and with a great deal of coaxing and prodding get the snake into it. The gopher snake, *Drymarchon corais couperi*, or bull snake, has a reputation as the enemy of rattlesnakes, destroying or driving them away whenever encountered.

Hoping to domesticate this sleek, handsome and docile reptile, I release him inside the trailerhouse and keep him there for several days. Should I attempt to feed him? I decide against it—let him eat mice. What little water he may need can also be extracted from the flesh of his prey.

The gopher snake and I get along nicely. During the day he curls up like a cat in the warm corner behind the heater and at night he goes about his business. The mice, singularly quiet for a change, make themselves scarce. The snake is passive, apparently contented, and makes no resistance when I pick him up with my hands and drape him over an arm or around my neck. When I take him outside into the wind and sunshine his favorite place seems to be inside my shirt, where he wraps himself around my waist and rests on my belt. In this position he sometimes sticks his head out between shirt buttons for a survey of the weather, astonishing and delighting any tourist who may happen to be with me at the time. The scales of a snake are dry and smooth, quite pleasant to the touch. Being a cold-blooded creature, of course, he takes his temperature from that of the immediate environment—in this case my body.

We are compatible. From my point of view, friends. After a week of close association I turn him loose on the warm sandstone at my doorstep and leave for a patrol of the park. At noon when I return he is gone. I search everywhere beneath, nearby and inside the trailerhouse, but my companion has disappeared. Has he left the area entirely or is he hiding somewhere close by? At any rate I am troubled no more by rattlesnakes under the door.

The snake story is not yet ended.

In the middle of May, about a month after the gopher snake's disappearance, in the evening of a very hot day, with all the rosy desert cooling like a griddle with the fire turned off, he reappears. This time with a mate.

I'm in the stifling heat of the trailer opening a can of beer, barefooted, about to go outside and relax after a hard day watching cloud formations. I happen to glance out the little window near the refrigerator and see two gopher snakes on my verandah engaged in what seems to be a kind of ritual dance. Like a living caduceus they wind and unwind about each other in undulant, graceful, perpetual motion, moving slowly across a dome of sandstone. Invisible but tangible as music is the passion which joins them—sexual? combative? both? A shameless *voyeur*, I stare at the lovers, and then to get a closer view run outside and around the trailer to the back. There I get down on hands and knees and creep toward the dancing snakes, not wanting to frighten or disturb them. I crawl to within six feet of them and stop, flat on my belly, watching from the snake's-eye level. Obsessed with their ballet, the serpents seem unaware of my presence.

The two gopher snakes are nearly identical in length and coloring; I cannot be certain that either is actually my former household pet. I cannot even be sure that they are male and female, though their performance resembles so strongly a *pas de deux* by formal lovers. They intertwine and separate, glide side by side in perfect congruence, turn like mirror images of each other and glide back again, wind and unwind again. This is the basic pattern but there is a variation: at regular intervals the snakes elevate their heads, facing one another, as high as they can go, as if each is trying to outreach or overawe the other. Their heads and bodies rise, higher and higher, then topple together and the rite goes on.

I crawl after them, determined to see the whole thing. Suddenly and simultaneously they discover me, prone on my belly a few feet away. The dance stops. After a moment's pause the two snakes come straight toward me, still in flawless unison, straight toward my face, the forked tongues flickering, their intense wild yellow eyes staring directly into my eyes. For an instant I am paralyzed by wonder; then, stung by a fear too ancient and powerful to overcome I scramble back, rising to my knees. The snakes veer and turn and race away from me in parallel motion, their lean elegant bodies making a soft hissing noise as they slide over the sand and stone. I follow them for a short distance, still plagued by curiosity, before remembering my place and the requirements of common courtesy. For godsake let them go in peace, I tell myself. Wish them luck and (if lovers) innumerable offspring, a life of happily ever after. Not for their sake alone but for your own.

In the long hot days and cool evenings to come I will not see the gopher snakes again. Nevertheless I will feel their presence watching over me like totemic deities, keeping the rattlesnakes far back in the brush where I like them best, cropping off the surplus mouse population, maintaining useful connections with the primeval. Sympathy, mutual aid, symbiosis, continuity.

How can I descend to such anthropomorphism? Easily—but is it, in this case, entirely false? Perhaps not. I am not attributing human motives to my snake and bird acquaintances. I recognize that when and where they serve purposes of mine they do so for beautifully selfish reasons of their own. Which is exactly the way it should be. I suggest, however, that it's a foolish, simple-minded rationalism which denies any form of emotion to all animals but man and his dog. This is no more justified than the Moslems are in denying souls to women. It seems to me possible, even probable, that many of the nonhuman undomesticated animals experience emotions unknown to us. What do the coyotes mean when they yodel at the moon? What are the dolphins trying so patiently to tell us? Precisely what did those two enraptured gopher snakes have in mind when they came gliding toward my eyes over the naked sandstone? If I had been as capable of trust as I am susceptible to fear I might have learned something new or some truth so very old we have all forgotten it.

261

They do not sweat and whine about their condition,
They do not lie awake in the dark and weep for their sins. . . .

All men are brothers, we like to say, half-wishing sometimes in secret it were not true. But perhaps it is true. And is the evolutionary line from protozoan to Spinoza any less certain? That also may be true. We are obliged, therefore, to spread the news, painful and bitter though it may be for some to hear, that all living things on earth are kindred.

From Our Album

LAWSON FUSAO INADA

I. "BEFORE THE WAR"

"Before the war"
means Fresno, a hedged-in house,
two dogs in the family.

Blackie, the small one, mine,
lapped at his insides
on the floorboard, on the way to the doctor.

Jimmy, my father's shepherd,
wouldn't eat after the evacuation.
He wouldn't live with another master

and pined away, skin and bone.

With feelings more than pride,
we call him our one-man dog.

II. MUD

Mud in the barracks—
a muddy room, a chamber pot.

Mud in the moats
around each barracks group.

The New West

Mud on the shoes
trudging to the mess hall.

Mud in the swamp
where the men chopped wood.

Mud on the guts
under a loaded wagon—

crushed in the mud by the wheel.

III. DESERT SONGS

1. All That We Gathered

Because there was little else to do,
they led us to the artillery range
for shells, all that we gathered,
and let us dig among dunes
for slugs, when they were through.

Because there was little else to do,
one of them chased a stray
with his tail between his legs
and shot him through the head.

2. Shells

A desert tortoise—
something mute and hard—

something to decorate
a desert Japanese garden;

264

gnarled wood, smooth
artillery shells for a border.

When a guard
smashes one, the shell

cracks open and the muscles ooze.

3. *It Is Only Natural*

The pheasant is an Oriental creature,
so it is only natural
that one should fly into camp

and, famished by rations and cans,
break out in secret, native dance
over a fire, on a black coal stove.

4. *Song of the 442nd*

Caged creatures
have curious moods.

Some of them choose
to be turned

loose in a group,
to take their chances

in the open.

5. *Steers*

Because a dentist
logically drives a butcher truck,

The New West

I rode with my father
to the slaughterhouse on an afternoon.

Not hammers, not bullets,
could make him close his eyes.

6. *He Teaches*

He jerks the eyes
from birds, feet
from lizards,

and punishes
ants with the gaze
of a glass.

And with his sly
gaze, his child's face,
he teaches

what has its place,
and must be
passed on to others.

IV. SONG OF CHICAGO

When the threat lessened,
when we became tame,
my father and friends
took a train to Chicago

for factory work,
for packaging bolts.

266

One grew a mustache
and called himself Carlos.

And they all made a home
with those of their own—

rats, bedbugs, blacks.

Chief Joseph, Nez Percé, Edward S. Curtis

White Man Still Speaks with Forked Tongue

MICHAEL ARLEN

A number of people have spoken to me approvingly about a two-hour special program called *I Will Fight No More Forever*, concerning the Nez Percé Indians and their stirring, ill-fated campaign against the government in 1877. Though I didn't see the program when it was first broadcast, a few weeks ago, by ABC, I was told that it would be shown again in the future, and so I recently arranged to watch it, partly out of interest in the subject and partly because—the levels of ordinary television programming being what they are—it seemed that a special production such as this (which was accompanied by press information stating that the director, Richard Heffron, had amassed "more than 1,000 pounds" of written material during his research) doubtless represented the higher achievement levels of the craft. In fact, I found it a commendable production in many ways. I also found myself thinking that if this was one of the more ambitious exercises of contemporary television, then perhaps it was worth repaying the compliment, so to speak, and treating it with comparable seriousness, or, at least with something beyond the usual commentary one hears or reads about the better type of program: "Fine show . . . sensitive . . . carefully researched . . ." What follows, then, is a brief attempt to consider one of the few serious ventures of current commercial television on the terms that I believe it has set for itself: the historical re-creation of the significant events of one of this country's last notable Indian wars.

The television account, which describes itself as accurate ("This story is true"), opens in June 1877 with a scene of two Nez Percé men hunting an eagle on a ridge above the Wallowa Valley, in northeastern Oregon. The Indians are soon surprised by two surly white settlers and (unjustly, it appears) are accused of horse-stealing. One of the settlers, called Grant, shoots the older Indian, Eagle Robe, in a particularly cowardly and sadistic fashion. When the surviving Nez Percé, Eagle Robe's son, returns to his camp, many of the younger warriors are eager for revenge, but Chief Joseph, the thirty-seven-year-old Nez Percé chief (played with earnest dignity by Ned Romero), restrains them. This sequence of events sets the tone for a meeting that then takes place between Joseph and his Nez Percés and Major General Oliver Otis Howard, the commander of the Department of the Columbia, and an Indian agent, John Monteith. General Howard (played in a grizzled, gruff-but-kindly manner by James Whitmore) is a forty-six-year-old veteran of the Civil War, in which he lost an arm and gained a reputation for soldierly decency in his treatment of freed slaves. Here he is depicted as clearly an apolitical soldier who is personally sympathetic to the Nez Percé position and is a friend of Chief Joseph's. At the beginning of the meeting, Howard and Joseph chat about Joseph's wife and expected child. Howard presents Joseph with a handmade doll as a present for the infant from Mrs. Howard. Then Monteith, the Indian agent, says curtly, "We have all received orders from our government." General Howard adds, compassionately, "I'm sorry it's not favorable to your cause, Joseph." Monteith reads aloud an order from the Secretary of the Interior which, by authority of President Grant, commands the Nez Percés to "give up their land and settle on the reservation within thirty days of this notice."

This far, the story has broadly corresponded with the historical record—at least, in the general sense of showing the hostility between the new Oregon settlers and the Nez Percés, and in pointing out the equally general theme of the government's decision, in 1877, to move the Nez Percés from the Wallowa Valley to a reservation farther north. Still, there are noticeable discrepancies in the television account. Some are minor, and are of what might be called a technical or pedantic nature. For instance, the murder of Eagle Robe by the settler Grant just before the parley with General Howard appears to be at least a partial fabrication, based on the actual but not notably sadistic shooting of Eagle Robe by a settler called Larry Ott, which had taken place two years earlier, in 1875. A more complicated divergence lies in the depiction of General Howard and of his role in the reservation matter. The television account generally presents Howard as a stouthearted military man who has been put in a difficult situation vis-à-vis the Nez Percés by President Grant and Washington bureaucrats. However, the facts seem to show that—though there were undeniably strong pressures on Washington from the Oregon settlers to move the Nez Percés out of the Wallowa Valley—it was actually Howard who forced the issue, at the Indians' expense. Thus, Alvin M. Josephy, Jr., wrote in his excellent history *The Nez Percé Indians and the Opening of the Northwest:*

> Soon afterward [in 1876], Howard's thinking had become settled on the matter. Taking the position . . . that the whites could no longer be ousted, he had decided that the government should end the conflict . . . by extinguishing the Indians' rights to all off-reservation lands through a fair and just purchase of those claims from every band that had not signed the 1863 treaty. . . . Howard, in his future actions, showed that he had totally abandoned his position of 1875, at which time he had said that it had been a mistake to take the Wallowa from the Indians. Now he would take it, by negotiation and payment if possible, but by force if necessary. Moreover, by having the government accept and promptly execute his policy, he would make inevitable an injustice that might have been avoided.

As for the heartwarming scene in which General Howard engages in familial small talk with the Nez Percé chief, this is not totally inconceivable, but it is unlikely to have happened at that time. In fact, at the parley with the Nez Percés which historically preceded this final meeting, Howard had been so alienated from the Indians that he later characterized one of their great war chiefs, old Toohoolhoolzote, as a "large, thick-necked, ugly, obstinate savage of the worst type," and, in a fit of temper, arrested him. The June meeting shown on television (which actually took place on May 14) had thus begun not with gifts of handmade dolls but with the reluctant release by Howard of the furious old chief.

About a month afterward, the Nez Percé war began. In the television account, the Nez Percés return to their camp after the meeting with Howard, and some of the warriors rail angrily at the white men while Joseph counsels that they proceed peacefully to the reservation. That night, three young Nez Percés ride into a nearby settlement, where they find Grant—the killer of Eagle Robe—in a saloon. Grant backs off, reaches for his gun, but a Nez Percé kills him. The three Nez Percés graciously leave the other settlers in the saloon unharmed ("Woman, your white man is not worth killing") and ride back to camp. Joseph is aghast at what they have done. "You have had your revenge," he says. "Now the whites will have theirs!" However, he remains conciliatory. "But if Howard will listen I will speak to him," he says.

271

Again, this is not significantly untrue to the spirit of the historical record, but certain details have been altered or omitted. For instance, after the meeting with Howard the Nez Percés (counseled by Joseph and his brother Ollokot) had promptly accepted the government's summons to the reservation, and had ridden nineteen days north and were camped within a few miles of their destination when two incidents took place. First—taunted by members of his own tribe for cowardice—the son of Eagle Robe, with two reluctant companions, rode into a settlement near Mount Idaho looking for Larry Ott, to avenge the murder of his father, which had taken place two years previously. Ott had since left the territory, but the Nez Percé trio came upon various other settlers, and killed four men and wounded another. Then, in the next few days, other Nez Percés joined the three warriors, and—fueled by alcohol and past resentments—massacred roughly fifteen white settlers in the area of White Bird Canyon. One evening, Joseph and Ollokot and the remaining Nez Percés were briefly counterattacked by a small band of settlers, and Joseph decided that he would have to join with the raiders. From his headquarters, General Howard notified Washington that another Indian war had broken out in the West.

Thus commenced the great saga of the Nez Percé ride of more than sixteen hundred miles—pursued at various times by ten different detachments of the United States Army—from Oregon through the Idaho Territory, across the Bitterroot Mountains, into the Montana Territory, across the Continental Divide, through Yellowstone Park, and eventually, north across the Absaroka range of the Wyoming Territory toward Canada. In most respects, the television account appears faithful to the broad outline of the Nez Percé odyssey, but there are certain changes in detail, some of which merely reflect a perhaps human penchant for casual inaccuracy (which might have been less noticeable if it were not for the repeated assertions of historical truth in the narration), though there are others where the inaccuracies, however casual, contribute to a quite different overall effect. An example of a lesser, technical detail may be a scene of the devastating employment by army troops of a howitzer against the Nez Percé encampment at the Big Hole. The facts seem to be that Colonel John Gibbon's command possessed a howitzer but the gun did not reach the battle until the principal day's fighting was over, and then it was rapidly captured by the Indians and overturned.

A more significant alteration of historical fact or likelihood, however, occurs in the dramatization of the battle of White Bird Canyon. At the beginning (in the television account), Joseph and the Nez Percés are pictured as unsure whether or not they are yet in a state of war with the government. "There will be no attack unless the soldiers shoot," says Joseph. Shortly after that, two companies of cavalry appear, accompanied by several armed settlers. The Indians send out three men carrying a truce flag, presumably to parley with the officer in charge, Captain David Perry, and one of the truce Indians is deliberately shot by a trigger-happy settler, who maliciously remarks, "Boys, I got my Indian. You better get yours." The Nez Percés then return fire, and quickly mount a charge against the soldiers, who are routed. However, according to Merrill D. Beal, another scholarly authority on the Nez Percé war, the Nez Percés were clearly set for battle when Perry's troops arrived—perhaps because in actuality they had lately massacred nearly twenty settlers, not merely a fictitious Grant. Then, though there appears to have been an informal truce team, which was mistakenly fired at by an army scout, Arthur Chapman (Perry, however, makes no mention of the truce team in his dispatch), the truce-team Indians were unharmed and backed away, returning to their lines. What followed next was an exchange of rifle fire between the well-protected Nez Percés and the soldiers, with the result that Perry's command was driven off.

There is one further divergence of fact and tone toward the end of the drama, which is worth mentioning not because the particular scene, as played by Whitmore, Romero, etc., was aesthetically displeasing (on the contrary, it seemed an effective dramatic moment) but as a kind of aside, or footnote, for it seems to me that the actual personalities and events of the Nez Percé war were decidedly more interesting—in the context of their own untidy reality—than were their trimly scripted counterparts (by screenwriters Jeb Rosebrook and Theodore Strauss) as recreated for us today. What happened in history was that when Chief Joseph and roughly 550 remaining Nez Percés escaped a trap set by General Howard on the Clark Fork River and headed north toward Canada, Howard desperately sent couriers to Colonel Nelson Miles, whose command lay more than two hundred miles to the northeast, and asked him to hasten across Montana and intercept the Nez Percés. The television account, while noting Howard's dilemma, implies that the general was still in control of the situation and was thus perpetrating a ruse. ("But we've got to slow the Indians down.

There's only one way to do that. Slow down ourselves.") However, the facts seem to show that by then Howard was already embarrassed militarily and in the national press, and was virtually out of the fight. Indeed, it was Miles—a bellicose and ambitious officer, who had once been Howard's aide-de-camp—who actually caught Joseph and ended the war, and who thereafter took the credit for both deeds. In the television version, doubtless in deference to Whitmore's top-billing portrayal of Howard, Miles has little more than a walk-on role: on the cold, bleak terrain of the Bear Paw Mountains, below the Canadian border, the Second Cavalry makes a surprise attack on the Nez Percés and apparently scores a decisive victory. The next day, General Howard and his troops appear, and, flanked by his aide and Colonel Miles, he receives the Nez Percé surrender from Chief Joseph, who drops his rifle on the ground and delivers his famous speech, which ends with the words "I will fight no more forever." Again, the truth is not completely different, but neither is it quite the same. To begin with, though Colonel Miles took over active pursuit of the Nez Percés, Miles and his command (which included at least two cavalry units and one infantry unit) did not really surprise the Indians, and the battle at the Bear Paws was extremely close, with the army taking many casualties and Miles having to order his men to dig in for a siege. The weather was freezing. Snow had begun to fall. Miles was further worried about the presence of Sitting Bull and about two thousand Sioux some forty miles north, across the Canadian border, and asked to have a conference with Chief Joseph. Joseph came to the army camp to discuss surrender (which Miles seems to have been pressing for), and the colonel ignominiously arrested the Nez Percé chief and held him hostage. Fortunately, the Nez Percés had simultaneously held one of Miles's aides hostage in their camp, and the next day the Indian and the cavalryman were exchanged. Some scattered fighting continued. Nearly six inches of snow lay on the ground. General Howard finally showed up five days later. As Miles wrote in his memoirs, *Personal Recollections of General Nelson A. Miles,* published in 1897: "On the evening of the 4th of October, General Howard came up with an escort of twelve men, and, remaining in our camp over night, was present next morning at the surrender of Chief Joseph and the entire Indian camp." About two o'clock of a bitter-cold afternoon, Joseph and five of his surviving warriors approached the army camp. He handed his rifle to Colonel Miles, who took it. The war was over.

Though this "true" film account of the Nez Percé war, then, is generally faithful to the situation as a whole, and achieves a commendable accuracy in matters of costume and war paint and the like, its value to the audience is, all the same, more likely to be that of entertainment (as in a good historical novel) than that of a filmed historical record—or truth. Some of the film's inaccuracies or discrepancies are incidental in terms of telling a dramatic story; for instance, there are several cozy family scenes between Chief Joseph and his "wife, Toma," but the fact is that he had two wives. On television, it probably makes for a more coherent or a more acceptable narrative if he has one. Other askew details are a result of the unscriptability of nature; for instance, a key element in the Nez Percé escape from General Howard after White Bird Canyon was the flood conditions in June on the Salmon River—whose televised counterpart (in Mexico) is shown to be a gently flowing stream.

But, overall, the most important alterations in detail and texture are in the film account's simplification of the two key roles: General Howard and Chief Joseph. James Whitmore's Howard is a dramatic portrait that has been painted with some praiseworthy realism, but in the end it remains that of a conventional actor-hero, and takes into account neither that Howard had a considerable role in provoking the Nez Percé war through his own reservation policies nor that by the end of the campaign he was not the nobly authoritative figure depicted as receiving Joseph's surrender. Ned Romero's portrayal of Joseph, for its part, seems superficially faithful to the dignity and common sense of this notable Indian, but here, too, the television version created distortions in its simplifications—in this case, of Chief Joseph's actual position among the Nez Percés and in the Nez Percé war. Principally, the television account reinforces a kind of popular myth of the time that Joseph was *the* Nez Percé chief and that he was a great military strategist—beliefs that doubtless derived from the fact that in military dispatches from the Nez Percé war American commanders found it convenient to refer to Joseph's relatively accessible name (his father, Tuekakas, had been baptized Joseph by a Presbyterian missionary and had passed the name on to his son), and also from a certain self-serving ignorance in various memoirists. Thus, Colonel Miles (who, as we saw, arrived late to the war) referred to Joseph in his memoirs, twenty years later, as "the Indian Napoleon." Similarly, in the television version General Howard (who had fought

275

against General Robert E. Lee in the Civil War) remarks, "I've never fought a better general." The facts seem to be that though Joseph's sagacity and diplomacy eventually came to carry dominant influence in Nez Percé councils—especially after the Nez Percés had lost the war and were taken to the reservation—during most of the fighting on the long march Joseph had been but one of several chiefs (such as White Bird, Looking Glass, and old Toohoolhoolzote) and by no means the most militarily adept among them. As the historian L. V. McWhorter wrote in *Hear Me, My Chiefs!*, "Joseph, the war chief, is a creature of legend; Joseph, the Indian Napoleon, does not emerge from the Nez Percé chronicles of their great fight for freedom." In a more even-handed approach, Alvin Josephy, Jr., has written:

> The fact that neither Joseph nor any other individual chief had been responsible for the outstanding strategy and masterful success of the campaign is irrelevant. The surrender speech, taken down by Howard's adjutant and published soon afterwards, confirmed Joseph in the public's mind as the symbol of the Nez Percés' heroic, fighting retreat.

Perhaps it is a fine point that would have mattered only to the Nez Percés—though, being uncommonly democratic, they would probably not have pushed it.

It would be unfortunate if these comments dissuaded anyone from watching *I Will Fight No More Forever* when it is next shown on television, for it is certainly an entertaining and interesting rendering of an exceptional saga, and it has been translated into telefilm with a greater concern for the Indian position than has been shown by most filmmakers in the past. All the same, it raises questions of accuracy and truth which I suspect may become more common as the public's longing for reality, or at least dramatized reality, becomes more widespread. After watching the television film, I mentioned my doubts about some of the film's depictions—notably of General Howard—and about the "political" highlighting of white brutality and avoidance of Indian brutality to a television producer, who replied: "The point is that the public gets to see a relatively honest film on a subject that it otherwise mightn't have looked at." I am sure that this is true, and it is an argument based on apparent benefit to the general audience, but I think the questions remain. For instance, what is "relative honesty" when it comes to portraying actual lives and events? Admittedly, our notion of history may be an arrogant impossibility, since each move a person makes is precisely *that* move, so that even the common events of a lifetime become an almost mathematical complex of "moves": a vast molecular network of precise, interlocking factors of event and personality which we peer at from a distance, usually with only the most inadequate equipment for examining the whole structure. All the same, despite what we do with it and to it, there remains something noble and important about truth, and maybe especially about the so-called simple truths of a man's or a woman's life. And possibly this is one of the reasons that until recently imaginative artists have shied away from putting actual people into their fabrications—those tales and novels that are invariably fabricated from the events and personalities of actual people. Lately, the line that separates our ways of looking at life has become more and more blurred—with history, journalism, and storytelling seemingly mixed together as in a stewpot. The tendency derives, one is told, from our less compartmentalized times. "This story is true," asserts the prologue to the television film about the Nez Percé war. Alas, it is not quite true; it is somewhat true; it is nearly true. Much of the genial haziness of our historical perceptions certainly lies in our restless, modern tampering with reality in the guise of providing attractive "information," or even of righting past wrongs: thus, if Indians were once mis-shown as savages, we will now presumably assist the Indian by mis-showing the settlers as brutes. At any rate, the entertainment public appears to be the gainer, and there is merit in that. Moreover, if it happens that there are imperfections in this historical entertainment, with details of fact or character not fully portrayed, or else distorted, perhaps it will also happen that *I Will Fight No More Forever* may encourage some in its audience to pursue the story further, into history and the considerable literature on the subject—and that itself would be no small achievement. But as for larger questions of truth and accuracy, it is surely worth making a distinction between the relativity of truth and the relative care or seriousness with which many nowadays try to approach it. Absolute truth may be as elusive or as distant as the boundaries of the universe, but a commitment to sighting it is what counts; else the alternative is to slide sideways into the propagandizing and counter-propagandizing tendencies of our times. In the end, those surviving primitive peoples who even today direct their quaintly naïve gestures at photographers for fear of

277

losing their souls may be closer to a conception of truth than we are, who ceaselessly dabble with it. After all, how better, finally, to steal someone's soul than by re-creating him on paper or canvas, or stone, bronze, wood or film, with good will and fine intentions and a certain regard for technical accuracy—but *not quite right?*

Plans for Altering the River

RICHARD HUGO

Those who favor our plan to alter the river
raise your hand. Thank you for your vote.
Last week, you'll recall, I spoke about how water
never complains. How it runs where you tell it,
seemingly at home, flooding grain or pinched
by geometric banks like those in this graphic
depiction of our plan. We ask for power:
a river boils or falls to turn our turbines.
The river approves our plans to alter the river.

Due to a shipwreck downstream, I'm sad to report
our project is not on schedule. The boat
was carrying cement for our concrete rip rap
balustrade that will force the river to run
east of the factory site through the state-owned
grove of cedar. Then, the uncooperative
carpenters union went on strike. When we get
that settled, and the concrete, given good weather
we can go ahead with our plan to alter the river.

We have the injunction. We silenced the opposition.
The workers are back. The materials arrived
and everything's humming. I thank you
for this award, this handsome plaque I'll keep
forever above my mantle, and I'll read
the inscription often aloud to remind me
how with your courageous backing I fought
our battle and won. I'll always remember
this banquet this day we started to alter the river.

The New West

Flowers on the bank? A park on Forgotten Island?
Return of cedar and salmon? Who are these men?
These Johnnys-come-lately with plans to alter the river?
What's this wild festival in May
celebrating the runoff, display floats on fire
at night and a forest dance under the stars?
Children sing through my locked door, 'Old stranger,
we're going to alter, to alter, alter the river.'
Just when the water was settled and at home.

Real Losses, Imaginary Gains

WRIGHT MORRIS

On the firm's stationery, the loose pages in disorder, sent off to me by regular mail to a previous address, my cousin Daniel writes me that our Aunt Winona has passed away. A blow to us all. A loss that found him unprepared. Among her meager effects, stored away in its box, he found the silk kimono he had brought her from Hong Kong. Money given to her she sent to missionaries. He writes me in longhand, filling the margins, using both sides of the paper, giving vent to his affection, his frustration, his help-lessness. In the past he only wrote such letters to her.

I see by the date it is more than three weeks since she passed away. My father's people, protesting but resigned, still reluctantly die, or go to their reward, but my mother's four sisters have all passed away. The phrase is ac-curate, and I use it out of respect for the facts.

Last summer we stopped in Boise to see her, the house both crushed and supported by huge bushes of lilacs. When I put my arms around her she said, "There's nothing much to me, is there?" One day she would say, "Let me just rest a moment," and pass away.

My aunt's couch faced the door, which stood open, the view given a sepia tone by the rusted screen. At the bottom, where children sometimes leaned, it bulged inward to shape a small hole. The view framed by the door was narrow if seen from the couch. Lying there, my aunt took in only what was passing: she did not see what approached, or how it slipped away. On the steps of the bungalow across the street children often crouched, listen-ing to summer. In the yard a knotted rope dangled a tire swing to where it had swept away the grass. A car passed, a stroller passed, music from some-where hovered and passed, hours and days, weeks and months, spring to winter and back to spring, war and peace, affluence and depression, loved ones, old ones, good ones and bad ones, all passed away.

"Who is that?" she asked, as the picture framed by the door altered. My aunt lay on the couch, I was seated on the ottoman at her side. We were

281

able to share the sunlit picture and the wavering shadow it cast toward the porch. The glare of light penetrated the sleeves of an elderly lady's blouse, and took an X-ray impression of her bloomers. Perhaps my aunt knew her. Had she stopped to admire the flowering lilac, or tactfully attract my aunt's attention? Her quandary had about it something vaguely imploring, of a person hopefully expectant. If her presence in the picture gave it a moral, the word "losses" gave it an appropriate caption. Just losses, not specifying what they were.

My aunt lifted her head to call out, "Would you like to step in?" Over the years, over the decades, many people had. The very young had given way to the very old, defying all belief that they had ever been children. Perplexities of this sort might lead my aunt to place her face in her hands, as if weeping. What she hoped to contain was her laughter, not at all that of an elderly, religious woman. On my father's side all of my Protestant aunts shared a common ceremony to ease the pain of this world, uttering no word as they gathered their aprons to hurl them like tent flaps over their heads. My Aunt Winona laughed: one might think it the muffled mirth of a child. Her nephews and nieces, the offspring of God-fearing parents, had grown up to be thrice married or worse, and divorced, their belief limited to one remaining article of Faith—that *she* would understand. She did not understand, not for a moment, but their belief released the resources of her forgiveness, and gave proven sinners three to four times their share of her concern and love.

Perhaps the woman in the picture, poised like a worming robin, sensed the presence of strangers. She wheeled slowly, her dangling bag brushing the tops of the uncut grass. Her bearings taken, she went off in the direction from which she had come. The picture framed by the door, empty of its previous meaning, called to my attention the loose, dangerous boards of the porch. On the lower stoop one was curled like a ski tip. Over the years these boards had been mentioned, or were invisibly present, in much of my aunt's correspondence. One of her nephews always planned to do something about them. Recently, however—in the last twenty years—they have paid her only brief, flying visits, in which there was no time to be wasted repairing porches. Also, it was the porch itself now, not a few boards, that needed to be replaced. That would require removing the ambush of lilacs, replacing both the porch roof and one wall of the house. The floor in the bathroom tilted in a manner that delayed draining the tub. A late addition to the house, it had a self-opening door, and guests had to be warned.

On our arrival we had been given glasses of well water for refreshment. It was water but resembled broth in which life was emerging. About water she was eccentric. It was her opinion that water out of pipes lay at the root of many disorders, including some of her own. Well water, however, cleansed the system of its poisons. Water coursing through miles of pipes picked up poisons. This water came from the well of a friend, who brought it to her weekly, in gallon-size vinegar bottles. From there it was poured into mayonnaise jars and stored on the bottom shelf of the refrigerator. This shelf was cool but not cold: one might as well eat raw potatoes as pour ice-cold water on the stomach. After this water had sat for a spell, cooling, a sediment collected on the jar's bottom. Pouring the water from the jar into a glass stirred it up, so that the varieties of life could be studied. My wife had seen things swimming. I searched it for some sign of polliwogs.

The windows of the house were cluttered with plants that filtered the light like cataracts. Posses of flies had their own territories, and staged raiding parties. A fly swatter was used to break up these games if they got too rough. On the wall beside the couch, tucked into a loose strip of molding, were postcards from her far-flung friends. One from Perth, Australia, featured a baby kangaroo peering from its mother's pouch. There were numberless cards of kittens playing with balls of yarn, kittens stuffed into baskets, kittens asleep with puppies. Postcards from faraway places were not unusual, with so many of her friends being missionaries of the Adventist faith.

With her father and sisters—the sisters could be seen in a photo on the bric-a-brac shelf behind her—Aunt Winona had left the plains at the turn of the century to settle on a homestead near Boise, Idaho. Her father felt the plains of Nebraska were getting crowded, and moved his family of daughters westward. The two sons had already taken off on their own. Her father and mother were shown in a photo taken in the salon in Grand Island, Nebraska, in 1884. Her father is seated, and her mother stands at his side, her right hand resting on his left shoulder, more of a bride in appearance than the pioneer mother of seven children. The husband is holding the new child in the cradle of his arm. This child is my mother. She will die within a few days of my birth.

I was a young man of nineteen before I set eyes on my aunt and other members of my mother's family. I came west from Chicago, my locker covered with the stickers of Ivy League colleges I hoped to go to. I wore a blue serge suit and my pair of Paris garters. My grandfather was old but spry, a God-fearing man long prepared for God. I saw him in the flickering glow of kerosene lamps, a second-time child to his matronly daughters. Only my mother was missing: he searched my face to recoup that loss. I slept that night in a large bed with two uncles, who assured me that my lack of Adventist faith was not crucial. The love of my aunts would be more than enough to get me into Heaven, if that was my wish.

In the morning my Aunt Winona, the only one not to marry, stood in the sunlit kitchen and watched me eat. Her first love had been the Lord, the second her father, and in this world she had found no replacement. It was him she saw when she gazed at me. She gave to this farmhouse kitchen, the light flaming her hair, the time-stopped dazzle of Vermeer's paintings. She poured milk from a bowl, threaded a needle, picked up crumbs from the table with her tip-moistened finger. She was at once serene, vulnerable, and unshakable. The appalling facts of this world existed to be forgiven. In her presence I was subject to fevers of faith, to fits of stark belief. Like the grandfather, she saw me as a preacher in search of a flock.

In a recent letter she wrote:

> When your mother died my sister Violet, who was married, wanted to take you, but your father would not consent to it. He said, "He is all I have left of Grace." O dear boy, you were the center of so much suffering, so many losses you will never know, realize, or feel . . .

What is it I feel now, sitting here in the full knowledge of my loss? In my mind's eye I see her couch, now empty, the impression of her figure like that the wind leaves on tall grass.

No, in the flesh there was nothing much to her—she had reduced the terms by which we measure real gains and losses. "I always thought she needed me," her nephew wrote, "and now I find I'm the one who needs her." That's a miserable loss. I weigh mine each time I lift a glass of water and note its temperature, its color, and what it is that swims I can no longer see.

Slim Lighting Up, James Bama

It's Like Wyoming

WILLIAM STAFFORD

At sunset you have piled the empties and
come to the edge, where the wind kicks up
outside of town. A scatter of rain
rakes the desert. All this year's weather
whistles at once through the fence.

This land so wide, so gray, so still that
it carries you free—no one here need bother
except for their own breathing. You touch
a fencepost and the world steadies onward:
barbed wire, field, you, night.

About the Authors

Edward Abbey (1927–   ) Novelist and essayist, emphatically not a naturalist, Abbey prefers to be called a ranger. He has worked seasonally for the National Park Service and presently lives in Wolf Hole, Arizona. He is passionately concerned about the relationship between men and the land, as the selection from *Desert Solitaire* (1968) will show; his essay "The Second Rape of the West" in *The Journey Home* (1977) deserves the widest possible audience.

Maya Angelou (1928–   ) Born in the South, Ms. Angelou followed her mother west during the 1940s. After studying dance, she has been active in the theater, toured Africa and Europe for the State Department, produced a TV series on African traditions, and published two volumes of poetry. *I Know Why the Caged Bird Sings* (1970), the first volume of her autobiography, recounts her southern childhood and western coming of age, showing what one black American found in the Golden State.

Michael Arlen (1930–   ) Born in London, educated at Harvard, Arlen has contributed to many periodicals and won a Pulitzer Prize for *A Passage to Ararat* (1975), an autobiographical account of his search for family origins. As television critic for *The New Yorker*, he has written consistently thoughtful pieces about how the world is perceived electronically. The best of these have been collected in *The View from Highway 1* (1976).

Robert Boylan is a notable missing person, about whom the editor has been able to find nothing, beyond the fact that his poem "Wild West" was published in *The Saturday Review of Literature*, September 21, 1957.

Walter Van Tilburg Clark (1909–   ) A teacher and writer, Clark grew up in Reno, Nevada, and taught in public schools in New York. After the success of *The Ox-Bow Incident* (1940), recognized as a minor classic, he returned to the West, producing *The Watchful Gods and Other Stories* in 1950. His fiction treats conventional themes of the "Western" in unconventional ways and captures the stern magnificence and loveliness of the landscape.

About the Authors

Alistair Cooke (1908–   ) Born in England, after graduate school at Harvard, Cooke became a journalist for the B.B.C. and *Manchester Guardian* and took citizenship in 1941. Familiar on television, his 1972 series *America: A Personal History of the United States* earned many awards and was published in book form. An earlier collection of essays, *Talk About America* (1968), contained the account of one visit to California, "The New Californian."

Stephen Crane (1871–1900) Correspondent and novelist, Crane's struggle in New York to become a writer undermined his health, yet he produced fourteen volumes before his early death. After the success of his novel *The Red Badge of Courage* (1895), he was sent briefly to the Southwest as correspondent, and produced what many regard as a classic tale, "The Bride Comes to Yellow Sky." His realism was at odds with the prevalent melodramatic or romantic notions of the West.

Bernard De Voto (1889–1955) Historian and critic, De Voto was born in Ogden, Utah, and after studies at Harvard, remained at Cambridge as a teacher and writer. While occupant of "The Easy Chair" column of *Harper's Magazine* from 1935 to 1955, he stirred several lively controversies. An avid scholar of the American frontier, he journeyed extensively over the ground he wrote about, bringing to his histories *Year of Decision: 1846* (1943), *Across the Wide Missouri* (1947), and *Course of Empire* (1952), vividness and vitality rare in historical studies.

Joan Didion (1934–   ) Novelist and journalist, Didion was born in Sacramento, California, and lives in Los Angeles with her husband, writer John Gregory Dunne. Her nonfiction has appeared in several magazines, and a collection of essays, *Slouching Towards Bethlehem* (1961), brought the not-so-new techniques of New Journalism (which enable a reporter to become a direct part of his story and to employ fictional devices) to the golden shore. Her profile of John Wayne applies the techniques to a film legend who became a national institution.

J. Frank Dobie (1888–1964) A native Texan and professor at the University of Texas, Dobie is known principally as a folklorist and historian. His best known works, *Apache Gold and Yaqui Silver* (1939), *Longhorns* (1941), and *Mustangs* (1952), chronicle life on the Southwestern frontier. His essay, "The Conservatism of Charles M. Russell," was written to introduce a collection of Russell's paintings and is a tribute to the spirit of both men.

Loren Eiseley (1907–1977) Naturalist and poet, Eiseley was born in Nebraska and from his earliest years was "an intense observer of nature in all seasons." As University Professor of Anthropology and the History of Science at the Univer-

288

sity of Pennsylvania, his work was published in popular as well as learned journals. His best known writing, *The Immense Journey* (1957) and *The Unexpected Universe* (1969), finds marvels "in the flow of everyday events."

Bayliss John Fletcher (1859–1912) At the age of twenty, Fletcher rode up the Chisholm Trail, helping drive a herd of 2,500 longhorn cattle from Texas to Wyoming. His reminiscence *Up the Trail in '79* gives a lively account of the slogging daily adventure that stretched out over 1,200 miles and four months.

Allen Ginsberg (1926–) One of the founding fathers of the Beat Generation, Ginsberg achieved instant notoriety when his first volume, *Howl and Other Poems* (1956) became the center of an obscenity trial. Since then active in antiwar demonstrations and other protest movements, he has become an unofficial spokesman for the counterculture as well as a leading poet in the Whitman tradition of free swinging, bardic exuberance. For Ginsberg the poem becomes pure song and catalogue and formless, rhythmic incantation.

A. B. Guthrie, Jr. (1901–) Growing up in Montana, Guthrie developed from his father "a love for the West and for its history." He worked as a journalist and, following the success of *The Big Sky* (1947), certainly the best novel about the fur trade, became a freelance writer. He has produced a series of novels spanning western history and a short story collection, *The Big It and Other Stories* (1972).

W. Eugene Hollon (1913–) A professor of history at the University of Oklahoma, Hollon has contributed articles to *American Heritage* and *The American West* and served as president of the Western History Association. He is the author of eight books, among them *The Great American Desert* (1966) and *Frontier Violence* (1972).

Richard Hugo (1923–) Born in Seattle, Hugo, after military service and twelve years in the aviation industry, became a professor of English at the University of Montana. *The Lady in Kicking Horse Reservoir* (1973) is his best known collection of poems, and *What Thou Lovest Well, Remains American* (1975) was nominated for a National Book Award.

Lawson Fusao Inada (1938–) A third-generation Japanese-American, Inada was interned with his family during World War II and is currently on the faculty of Southern Oregon College. His poetry has appeared in many periodicals and anthologies and has been published in the volume *Before the War* (1971).

289

About the Authors

Robinson Jeffers (1887–1962) After early years of aimless study at several universities in the United States and Europe, Jeffers moved to Carmel, California, and on Point Sur erected with his own hands a house and tower of stone. There he wrote poetry celebrating the solitary and fierce beauty of the natural world in *Give Your Heart to the Hawks* (1933) and *Be Angry at the Sea* (1941). Noting the insignificance of that animal called man, in the end he named his austere vision Inhumanism and regarded civilization as "a transient sickness."

Oliver La Farge (1901–1963) Novelist and anthropologist, La Farge worked as an archaeologist in the Southwest and served as president of the American Association of Indian Affairs. One of the first Anglos to successfully portray Indian character with dignity, his novel about the Navaho, *Laughing Boy*, won the Pulitzer Prize in 1929. Much of his fiction dramatizes the erosion of traditional culture under the impact of white civilization.

Meriwether Lewis (1774–1809) and **William Clark** (1770–1838) Commissioned by Thomas Jefferson to explore the newly acquired Louisiana Territory, they led the expedition up the Missouri River, on to the Pacific and back to St. Louis between May, 1804, and August, 1806. As well as a record of epic adventure and endurance, their journals are filled with topographical and scientific observations and highly original spelling.

Jack London (1876–1916) Born in San Francisco, London grew up across the Bay in Oakland, left school at fourteen for work, went to sea, tramped across the United States, and prospected in the Klondike. From these experiences he became an energetic writer, turning out dozens of stories and novels like *The Call of the Wild* (1903) and *The Sea Wolf* (1904) which became hugely popular. London loved the idea of action and vigorous adventure, filling his stories with elemental struggles between people and natural forces in which only the fittest survive.

N. Scott Momaday (1934–   ) A Kiowa Indian who grew up on a reservation in the Southwest, Momaday is a professor of English at the University of California. He has written poems, a novel, and a remarkable chronicle of his people, *The Way to Rainy Mountain* (1969). By blending legend, oral history, and boyhood recollection, Momaday records the consciousness of an almost vanished culture.

Wright Morris (1910–   ) Known principally as a novelist for *Field of Vision* (1956) and *Ceremony at Lone Tree* (1973), Morris has also written criticism, taught the craft of fiction, and published photo essays, one of which, *God's Country and My People* (1968) deals eloquently with the prairie and his Nebraska origins. Now

290

living in America, he is a leading contender for the Most Neglected Writer in America Award.

John Muir (1838–1914) Largely self-taught, this Scottish-American naturalist grew up in a Wisconsin log cabin. Muir travelled extensively and settled in California, compelled by his love of mountains to become a leading advocate for a system of national parks. Founder of the Sierra Club and author of *The Mountains of California* (1894) and *The Yosemite* (1912), he began the fight against commercial exploitation of wilderness. On his first summer in the Sierra, helping herd sheep in what is now Yosemite Park, he kept a journal, "The Mono Trail."

Francis Parkman (1823–1893) An historian, Parkman, after studies at Harvard, followed his early interest in Indians to plan a "history of the American forest." In 1846, Parkman journeyed up the Oregon Trail as far as Fort Laramie, meeting along the way trappers, hunters, and emigrants, and living for a time among the Sioux. His account *The Oregon Trail* (1849), imbued "with the life and spirit of the times," contains what most western observers agree was the premier adventure of the plains—a buffalo hunt.

Katherine Anne Porter (1894–   ) Though she is hardly to be classed as a western writer, Porter was born in Texas and many of her best stories are placed in the Southwest. She has written criticism and the novel *Ship of Fools* (1962), but is known principally as a short story writer, her *Collected Stories* winning the Pulitzer Prize in 1966. A meticulous craftsman, her first story, "María Concepción," was rewritten "fifteen or sixteen times."

Theodore Roethke (1908–1963) Early experience in and around his father's greenhouse supplied the imagery of earth and flower and natural order that charges his poetry. Roethke's varied songs in *Words for the Wind* (1958) and *The Far Field* (1914) examine the struggle for existence and celebrate all that lives in the intensity of each moment. As poet in residence at the University of Washington, he exerted a great influence on other writers, particularly in the Pacific Northwest.

Sitting Bull (1831–1890) Leader of the Hunkpapa Sioux, renowned for the power of his oratory and medicine, Sitting Bull fought to protect the traditional hunting grounds and lands allotted by treaty. In 1876 after Little Big Horn, he fled to Canada but returned to the United States and later visited Washington and appeared in Buffalo Bill's Wild West Show. While being arrested to prevent the spread of the ghost dance religion among the Sioux, he was killed by Indian Agency police at Standing Rock Reservation.

291

About the Authors

Helena Huntington Smith. Magazine writer and historian, Smith was born and educated in the East. After a trip to Glacier National Park, she collaborated in two reminiscences of the rip-roaring West: *We Pointed them North: Recollections of a Cowpuncher* with E. C. Abbott, and *A Bride Goes West* with Nannie Tiffany Anderson. Her account of the classic confrontation between homesteading cowboys and the stockman's association in Johnson County, Wyoming, in 1890 is expanded into a full study in *The War on Powder River* (1966).

Gary Snyder (1930–) Born in San Francisco, Snyder worked as a seaman, logger, Forest Service lookout, and was active in the 1950s Beat movement. He has studied at a Zen monastery in Japan and hopes to establish a community of Western Buddhism in the California Sierra. Collections of his poetry, *The Back Country* (1967) and *Turtle Island* (1974) reflect his belief that "every landscape has its own demands, its own style, its own mythologies and colors."

William Stafford (1914–) Born in Kansas, Stafford presently teaches at Lewis and Clark College in Portland, Oregon. His collection, *Travelling Through the Dark* won the National Book Award for poetry in 1962, and *Allegiances* (1971) has received wide acclaim. Stafford has said he tries to make each poem "its own local event, not forced on the reader, but offered simply as what it is."

Wallace Stegner (1909–) Novelist and historian, Stegner has lived in many areas of the American West, taught writing at university level, and served as editor for *The American West* magazine. His novels *Big Rock Candy Mountain* (1943) and *Wolf Willow* (1962) deal with what happens to pioneer virtues "when the frontiers are gone and the opportunities all used up." His histories *Beyond the Hundredth Meridian* (1954) and *The Gathering of Zion* (1964) deal with the land and the settlement of the plateau province.

John Steinbeck (1902–1968) Born in Salinas, California, the scene of many of his stories, Steinbeck worked at many jobs before becoming a major writer, and from the beginning was sympathetic to the "oppressed, the misfits, and the distressed." Awarded the Nobel Prize in 1962, accepting he spoke of the writer's duty to "celebrate man's proven capacity for greatness of heart and spirit—for gallantry in defeat—for courage, compassion, and love." These qualities distinguish all his fiction, notably *The Grapes of Wrath* (1939) and the collection *The Long Valley*.

Elinore Pruitt Stewart. A widow with a young daughter, Stewart went to Wyoming in 1909. How she bettered her situation, filed on a homestead, and "proved up" on more than one hundred sixty acres is the story contained in *Letters* *of a Woman Homesteader.* Selected from correspondence with her former employer, the letters tell of life in the new land.

Adrien Stoutenberg (1916–) From a small farming community in Minnesota, Ms. Stoutenberg has moved west steadily. She has written children's books, collections of folk stories, and prize-winning poetry. Her "long interest in, and concern for, threatened wildlife and landscape" are reflected in *Heroes, Advise Us* (1964) and *Short History of the Fur Trade* (1969).

Mark Twain (1835–1910) As journalist, novelist, and humorist, Samuel Langhorne Clemens is a national institution, although riverboat pilot was the profession he most admired. During his western journey in the early 1860s, he worked as a miner, speculator, reporter for the *Territorial Enterprise* in Virginia City and *Call* in San Francisco, special correspondent for the Sacramento *Union*, and made his first appearance as a lecturer. His first published book, *The Celebrated Jumping Frog of Calaveras County and Other Sketches* (1867) offered a sample of Twain's characteristic humor, as seen in "A Page from a Californian Almanac." His personal narrative of six years spent in the mining camps and cities of the Far West, *Roughing It* (1871), combines elements of travelogue, tall tale, character sketch, autobiography, and adventure yarn.

Suggestions for Further Reading

Alert students will already have noted the absence of several truly great names and many fine works. Because novels should be read through and not in pieces, no chapters have been exerpted for this collection. Thus major novelists like Frank Norris, Willa Cather, and Ken Kesey, as well as accomplished craftsmen like Harvey Ferguson and Don Berry are regrettably missing. Because frequently collected, a number of outstanding short stories have been excluded, among them H. L. Davis' "Open Winter," Bret Harte's "The Outcasts of Poker Flat," Paul Horgan's "To the Mountains," William Saroyan's "The Pomegranate Trees," Mark Twain's "The Celebrated Jumping Frog of Calaveras County," and Willa Cather's superb "Neighbor Rosicky." These, however, can be easily located in most standard anthologies of American short fiction. Because so many first-rate histories have explored the westward movement with lively scholarship and appropriately energetic styles, only a fraction could be represented here. In particular, pieces by David Lavender, William Wellman, Walter Andrist, and Joseph Henry Jackson were eliminated with great reluctance, for their work is as stirring as the best fiction. Because the still unsettled and sometimes unsettling region continues to attract chroniclers as it makes history, shrewd observers like Neil Morgan and Tom Wolfe would have deserved inclusion, had space allowed. Finally, because the land has inspired poets and naturalists as well as photographers and artists, several volumes could not encompass their splendid visions, although the Sierra Club Format Series has made a noble effort to do just that. Therefore, the suggestions that follow lead toward further revelations. All deserve to be read, savored, prized.

SOME WESTERN NOVELS, INCLUDING A FEW "WESTERNS"

Abbey, Edward   *The Brave Cowboy; The Monkey Wrench Gang*

Baylor, Byrd   *Yes Is Better Than No*

Suggestions for Further Reading

Berger, Thomas	*Little Big Man*
Berry, Don	*Trask; Moontrap*
Binns, Archie	*The Land Is Bright*
Borland, Hal	*The Seventh Winter*
Brand, Max	*Destry Rides Again*
Brautigan, Richard	*Trout Fishing in America*
Cather, Willa	*O Pioneers; My Ántonia; Death Comes to the Archbishop*
Chandler, Raymond	*Farewell, My Lovely*
Clark, Walter V T	*The Ox-Bow Incident; Track of the Cat*
Corle, Edwin	*Coarse Gold*
Davis, H. L.	*Honey in the Horn*
Dobie, J. Frank	*Up the Trail from Texas*
Dunne, John Gregory	*True Confessions*
Eastlake, William	*The Bronc People*
Ferber, Edna	*Cimarron*
Fergusson, Harvey	*The Conquest of Don Pedro*
Fisher, Vardis	*Dark Bridwell*
Grey, Zane	*Riders of the Purple Sage*
Gold, Herbert	*The Great American Jackpot*
Guthrie, A. B.	*The Big Sky; The Way West*

296

Suggestions for Further Reading

Horgan, Paul	*A Distant Trumpet*
Hough, Emerson	*The Covered Wagon*
Humphrey, William	*The Ordways*
Jackson, Helen Hunt	*Ramona*
Kesey, Ken	*Sometimes a Great Notion; One Flew Over the Cuckoo's Nest*
Kerouac, Jack	*On the Road*
La Farge, Oliver	*Laughing Boy*
Lea, Tom	*The Primal Yoke*
LeMay, Alan	*The Searchers*
London, Jack	*The Call of the Wild; White Fang*
Manfred, Frederick	*Lord Grizzly*
McMurtry, Larry	*Horseman, Pass By*
McFadden, Cyra	*The Serial*
Morris, Wright	*Ceremony at Lone Tree; One Day*
Norris, Frank	*The Octopus*
Olsen, Tillie	*Yonondio*
Porter, Katherine Anne	*"Noon Wine"*
Portis, Charles	*True Grit*
Pynchon, Thomas	*The Crying of Lot 49*
Rhodes, Eugene Manlove	*"Paso Por Aqui"*

Suggestions for Further Reading

Richter, Conrad	*The Sea of Grass*
Rolvaag, Ole	*Giants in the Earth*
Sandoz, Mari	*Cheyenne Autumn*
Saroyan, William	*The Human Comedy; My Name is Aram*
Schaefer, Jack	*Shane*
Schulberg, Budd	*What Makes Sammy Run?*
Stegner, Wallace	*Wolfwillow; The Big Rock Candy Mountain*
Steinbeck, John	*The Pearl; The Grapes of Wrath*
Stewart, George	*Fire; Storm*
Taylor, Robert Lewis	*The Travels of Jamie McPheeters*
Waters, Frank	*The Man Who Killer the Deer*
Waugh, Evelyn	*The Loved One*
Welch, James	*Winter in the Blood*
West, Nathaniel	*The Day of the Locust*
Wister, Owen	*The Virginian*

SOME HISTORIES (NATURAL, CONTEMPORARY, BIOGRAPHICAL, OTHER)

Abbey, Edward	*The Journey Home; Desert Solitaire*
Adams, Andy	*The Log of a Cowboy*

Suggestions for Further Reading

Andrist, Walter	*The Long Death*
Austin, Mary	*Land of Little Rain*
Beagle, Peter	*The California Feeling*
Berry, Don	*A Majority of Scoundrels*
Black Elk	*Black Elk Speaks*
Brown, Dee	*Bury My Heart At Wounded Knee*
Cleland, John	*A Reckless Breed of Men*
Cunningham, Eugene	*Triggernometry*
Custer, George	*My Life on the Plains*
Dana, Richard Henry	*Two Years Before the Mast*
De Voto, Bernard	*Course of Empire; Across the Wide Missouri; Year of Decision: 1846; The Journals of Lewis and Clark*
Didion, Joan	*Slouching Towards Bethlehem*
Dobie, J. Frank	*The Longhorns; Coronado's Children*
Durham, Philip and Jones, Everett	*The Negro Cowboys*
Everson, William	*The Western*
Gard, Wayne	*Frontier Justice*
Greenway, John	*Folklore of the Great West*
Gregg, Josiah	*Commerce of the Prairies*
Grinnell, George	*The Fighting Cheyenne*

Suggestions for Further Reading

Haines, Francis — *The Nez Percé Indians*

Harris, Mark — *Ragged Dick, The Match Boy*

Hewitt, James — *Eye-witnesses to Wagon Trains West*

Hoagland, Edward — *Notes from the Century Before*

Hoig, Stan — *The Humor of the American Cowboy*

Holbrook, Stewart — *Holy Old Mackinaw*

Hollen, Eugene — *Frontier Violence*

Horgan, Paul — *The Heroic Triad*

Houston, Jean — *Return to Manzanar*

Irving, Washington — *Astoria*

Jackson, Joseph H. — *Anybody's Gold; Bad Company*

Josephy, Alvin, Jr. — *The Patriot Chiefs*

Kramer, James — *The Last Cowboy*

Kraus, George — *High Road to Promontory*

Kroeber, Theodora — *Ishii in Two Worlds*

Lavender, David — *Bent's Fort; Land of Giants*

Leckie, William — *The Buffalo Soldiers*

Lewis, Oscar — *The Big Four; Sketches of Early California*

McLuhan, T. C. — *Touch the Earth*

McPhee, John — *Coming into the Country*

Suggestions for Further Reading

Meek, Joe — *River of the West*

Momaday, N. Scott — *The Way to Rainy Mountain*

Morgan, Dale — *Jedediah Smith and the Opening of the West*

Morgan, Neil — *The California Syndrome*

Muir, John — *The Mountains of California*

Neider, Charles, Ed. — *The Great West*

Parkman, Francis — *The Oregon Trail*

Raphael, Ray — *An Everyday History of Somewhere; Edges*

Russell, C. M. — *Trails Plowed Under*

Russell, Osborne — *Journals of a Trapper*

Ruxton, George F. — *Life in the Far West*

Sandoz, Mari — *Sandhill Sundays; Old Jules*

Smith, Henry Nash — *Virgin Land*

Starr, Kevin — *Americans and the California Dream*

Stewart, George — *Ordeal By Hunger; The California Trail*

Stegner, Wallace — *Beyond the 100th Meridian; The Gathering of Zion*

Turner, Frederick Jackson — *The Frontier in American History*

Twain, Mark — *Roughing It*

Suggestions for Further Reading

Vestal, Stanley	*Sitting Bull, Champion of the Sioux*
Webb, Walter P.	*The Great Plains; The Texas Rangers*
Wellman, Paul	*A Dynasty of Western Outlaws; Glory, God, and Gold*
Wolfe, Tom	*The Electric Kool Aid Acid Test*
Zwinger, Anne	*Run, River, Run*
American Heritage, editors	*Great Adventures of the Old West*
Time-Life, editors	*The Old West Series*

SOME ART, SOME POETRY

Adams, Ansel	*Ansel Adams Images 1923–1874; These We Inherit: The Parklands of America*
Bama, James	*The Western Art of James Bama*
Bargell, Matthew	*Thomas Hart Benton*
Benét, Stephen Vincent	*Western Star*
Catlin, George	*North American Indians*
Curtis, Edward S.	*Portraits of North American Indian Life; In A Sacred Manner We Live*
Davidson, Harold	*Edward Borien, Cowboy Artist*
Dockstader, Frederick	*Indian Art In America*
Ewers, John	*Artists of the Old West*

302

Ferlinghetti, Laurence	*A Coney Island of the Mind*
Fife, Austin and Alta	*Ballads of the Great West*
Getlein, Frank	*The Lure of the Great West*
Ginsberg, Allen	*Howl and Other Poems*
Harper, J. Russell	*Paul Kane's Frontier*
Hass, Robert	*Field Guide*
Hassrick, Royal	*Western Painting Today*
Hassrick, Peter H.	*Frederic Remington*
Hendricks, Gordon	*Albert Bierstadt: Painter of the American West*
Horan, James D.	*The Life and Art of Charles Schreyvogal*
Hugo, Richard	*What Thou Lovest Well, Remains American; The Lady in Kicking Horse Reservoir*
Hyde, Philip	*Navaho Wildlands: As Long as the Rivers Shall Run*
Inada, Lawson	*Before the War: poems as they happened*
Jeffers, Robinson	*Give Your Heart to the Hawks; Not Man Apart: Photographs of the Big Sur Coast; Selected Poetry*
Kauffman, Richard	*The Gentle Wilderness: The Sierra Nevada*
Keithley, George	*The Donner Party*

Suggestions for Further Reading

Kopit, Arthur   *Indians*

Larson, Clinton &
Stafford, Wm.   *Modern Poetry of Western America*

Leydet, Francis   *Slickrock; Time and the River Flowing*

McCarthy, Frank   *The Western Paintings of Frank C. McCarthy*

McCracken, Harold   *Frederic Remington: Artist of the Old West*

Miles, Josephine   *Poems 1930–1960*

Muench, Joseph   *Anasazi: Ancient People of the Rock*

Neihardt, John   *A Cycle of the West*

O'Keeffe, Georgia   *Georgia O'Keeffe*

Peterson, Karen   *Plains Indian Art*

Porter, Eliot   *The Place No One Knows: Glen Canyon on the Colorado*

Reed, Walt   *John Clymer: An Artist's Rendezvous with the American West*

Renne, Frederick   *Charles M. Russell*

Rexroth, Kenneth   *The Collected Shorter Poems of Kenneth Rexroth*

Roethke, Theodore   *The Far Field; Collected Poems*

Ross, Marvin   *The West of Alfred Jacob Miller*

Rothenberg, Jerome   *Shaking the Pumpkin*

304

Suggestions for Further Reading

Russell, Charles M. — *The Western Art of Charles M. Russell*

Snidow, Gordon — *Gordon Snidow: Chronicler of the Contemporary West*

Snyder, Gary — *Turtle Island*

Spingarn, Laurence — *Poets West*

Stafford, William — *Allegiances; Traveling Through the Dark*

Stoutenberg, Adrian — *Short History of the Fur Trade*

von Schmidt, Harold — *Harold von Schmidt Draws and Paints the Old West*

Acknowledgments

(*continued from page iv*)

GARY SNYDER, "Black Mesa Mine #1," from Gary Snyder, *Turtle Island.* Copyright © 1972 by Gary Snyder. Reprinted by permission of New Directions.

WALTER VAN TILBURG CLARK, "Hook." Reprinted by permission of International Creative Management. Copyright © 1940, 1968 by Walter Van Tilburg Clark.

N. SCOTT MOMADAY, *The Way to Rainy Mountain* (Albuquerque: University of New Mexico Press, 1969), pp. 47–49. Reprinted by permission.

OLIVER LAFARGE, "All the Young Men." Reprinted by permission of the Estate of Oliver LaFarge. Copyright © 1935, 1962 by Oliver LaFarge.

KATHERINE ANNE PORTER, "María Concepción." Copyright, 1930, 1958, by Katherine Anne Porter. Reprinted from her volume *Flowering Judas and Other* Stories by permission of Harcourt Brace Jovanovich, Inc.

BERNARD DEVOTO, "Mountain Skills" from *Across the Wide Missouri* by Bernard DeVoto. Copyright 1947 by Houghton Mifflin Company, © renewed 1975 by Avis DeVoto and Joseph R. Porter. Reprinted by permission of Houghton Mifflin Company.

ADRIEN STOUTENBERG, "Trapper's Report" from *Short History of the Fur Trade* by Adrien Stoutenberg. Copyright © 1968 by Adrien Stoutenberg. Reprinted by permission of Houghton Mifflin Company.

A. B. GUTHRIE, JR. "Mountain Medicine" from *The Big It* by A. B. Guthrie, Jr. Copyright © 1960 by A. B. Guthrie, Jr. Reprinted by permission of Houghton Mifflin Company.

FRANCIS PARKMAN, "Buffalo Chase" from *Oregon Trail.* Copyright © 1931, 1957 Holt, Rinehart and Winston, Inc. Reprinted by permission of Holt, Rinehart and Winston, Inc.

WALLACE STEGNER, "This is the Place," from *The Gathering of Zion* by Wallace Stegner. Copyright © 1964 by Wallace Stegner. Used with permission of McGraw-Hill Book Company.

W. EUGENE HOLLON, "Not A Chinaman's Chance," from *Frontier Violence: Another Look* by W. Eugene Hollon. Copyright © 1974 by Oxford University Press, Inc. Reprinted by permission.

LOREN EISELEY, "Oregon Trail." Reprinted with the permission of Charles Scribner's Sons from *Notes from an Alchemist* by Loren Eiseley, copyright © 1972 Loren Eiseley.

BAYLIS JOHN FLETCHER, "Up the Trail," from *Up the Trail in '79,* by Baylis John Fletcher. Edited and with an introduction by Wayne Gard. New edition copyright 1968 by the University of Oklahoma Press. Reprinted by permission.

HELENA HUNTINGTON SMITH, "The Johnson County Cattle War." © 1961 by American Heritage Publishing Co., Inc. Reprinted by permission from *American Heritage* (April 1961).

ROBERT BOYLAN, "Wild West." © Saturday Review, 1957. All rights reserved. Reprinted by permission.

JOAN DIDION, "John Wayne: A Love Song," from *Slouching Towards Bethlehem* by Joan Didion, Copyright © 1965, 1968 by Joan Didion. Reprinted with the permission of Farrar, Straus Giroux, Inc.

JOHN STEINBECK, "The Leader of the People." From *The Long Valley* by John Steinbeck. Copyright 1938, renewed © 1966 by John Steinbeck. Reprinted by permission of The Viking Press.

MAYA ANGELOU, "Western Addition." From *I Know Why the Caged Bird Sings*, by Maya Angelou. Copyright © 1969 by Maya Angelou. Reprinted by permission of Random House, Inc.

Acknowledgments

ALISTAIR COOKE, "The New Californian." From *Talk About America*, by Alistair Cooke. Copyright © 1968 by Alistair Cooke. Reprinted by permission of Alfred A. Knopf, Inc.

ALLEN GINSBERG, "A Supermarket in California." Copyright © 1956, 1959 by Allen Ginsberg. Reprinted by permission of City Light Books.

THEODORE ROETHKE, "Night Journey," copyright 1940 by Theodore Roethke from *The Collected Poems of Theodore Roethke*. Reprinted by permission of Doubleday & Company, Inc.

FRANK J. DOBIE, "The Conservatism of Charles M. Russell." Reprinted by permission.

EDWARD ABBEY, "The Serpents of Paradise," from *Desert Solitaire* by Edward Abbey. Copyright © 1968 by Edward Abbey. Used with permission of McGraw-Hill Book Company.

LAWSON FUSAO INADA, "From Our Album." Reprinted by permission of William Morrow & Company from *Before the War* by Lawson Fusao Inada. Copyright © 1971 by Lawson Fusao Inada.

MICHAEL ARLEN, "White Man Still Speaks with Forked Tongue," from *The View From Highway 1* by Michael Arlen, Copyright © 1976, 1978 by Michael Arlen. First published in *The New Yorker*. Reprinted with permission of Farrar, Straus & Giroux, Inc.

RICHARD HUGO, "Plans for Altering the River" is reprinted from *What Thou Lovest Well, Remains American*, Poems by Richard Hugo, with the permission of W. W. Norton & Company, Inc. Copyright © 1975 by W. W. Norton & Company, Inc.

WRIGHT MORRIS, "Real Losses, Imaginary Gains" (pp. 1-6) from *Real Losses, Imaginary Gains* by Wright Morris. Originally appeared in *The New Yorker*. Copyright © 1973 by Wright Morris. By permission of Harper & Row, Publishers, Inc.

WILLIAM STAFFORD, "It's Like Wyoming," from *Going Places*, West Coast Poetry Review, 1974. Reprinted by permission of West Coast Poetry Review.

PICTURE CREDITS

Page 12: *Valley of the Yosemite*, Alfred Bierstadt. Courtesy of the Joslyn Art Museum, Omaha; Gift of Mrs. C. N. Dietz.

Page 17: *Cañon de Chelly—Navaho*, photo by D. T. Barry. Courtesy of the Pierpont Morgan Library.

Page 47: Jean-Claude LeJeune, STOCK/Boston.

Page 48: Courtesy of The National Archives.

Page 85: *Passage Through Stone Walls*, Karl Bodmer. Northern Natural Gas Co. Collection; Joslyn Art Museum, Omaha.

Page 90: Dime novel cover. Courtesy A. W. Janes.

Page 95: *Setting Traps for Beaver*, Alfred Jacob Miller. Northern Natural Gas Co. Collection; Joslyn Art Museum, Omaha.

Page 125: *North from Berthold Pass*. Courtesy of International Museum of Photography at George Eastman House.

Page 156: *Bob Rumsey's Place*, by James Bama. Photo by Jack Richard Studio. Courtesy of James Bama.

Page 166: Siringo's, *A Texas Cow Boy*, Courtesy, University of Illinois Library.

308

Acknowledgments

Page 200: *In Without Knocking*, Charles M. Russell. Courtesy Amon Carter Museum, Fort Worth, Texas.

Page 231: *Migrant Mother, Nipomo, California*. (1936), by Dorothea Lange. Photograph, 12½ x 9⅞. Collection, The Museum of Modern Art, New York. Purchase.

Page 250: *Powder Face*, Charles M. Russell. Courtesy Amon Carter Museum, Forth Worth, Texas.

Page 268: *Chief Joseph, Nez Percé* from Edward S. Curtis, *The North American Indian*, Vol. 8, facing p. 24. Courtesy of The New-York Historical Society, New York City.

Page 285: *Slim Lighting Up*, James Bama. Courtesy of James Bama.

Index

311

Index